WORLD'S GREATEST BEERS

250 Ales & Lagers from Pilsen to Portland

Selected by

PETE BROWN · CLAIRE BULLEN

JONNY GARRETT · JOHN HOLL · EMMA INCH

LOTTE PEPLOW · ROGER PROTZ · JOE STANGE

CAMRA BOOKS

Published by the Campaign for Real Ale Ltd

230 Hatfield Road, St Albans, Hertfordshire AL1 4LW

www.camra.org.uk/books

© Campaign for Real Ale Ltd. 2022
First published 2022

ISBN 978-1-85249-379-0

A CIP catalogue record for this book is available from the British Library

Printed in the UK by Cambrian Printers Ltd, part of The Pensord Group

Managing Editor: Alan Murphy
Design / typography: Dale Tomlinson
Picture research: Liz Vater
Sales & Marketing: Toby Langdon
Cover: Mulberry Advertising

PHOTO CREDITS

The publisher would like to thank all the breweries and others who kindly
granted permission for their photography to be used in this book.

Specific thanks go to: © OP1C, p212; © ashleycarterimages, p232; © Belgian
Beer Factory, p56; © Benoit/Flickr, p65; © Blackberry Farm Brewery, p113;
© clifflucasphoto, p18, 254; © Creature Comforts Brewing Co, p117; © Dogfish
Head Craft Brewery, p118; © Emily Ryan, p120; © Joe Stange, p250; © Laura
DuBro, p130; © Matthew Curtis, p143; © milo-profi.be, p226; © Robert Hughes,
p98, 127; © Samuel Adams, p134; © Sue Moen, p126; © Tim Bottchen, p135.
Also many thanks to **Beer Merchants** (beermerchants.com), p66, 71, 244, 260; **Beers
of Europe** (beersofeurope.co.uk), p246; **Beer Shop** (beershophq.uk), p248; **All Good
Beer** (allgoodbeer.co.uk), p243; **Hop Burns & Black** (hopburnsblack.co.uk), p249.

Contents

The authors 4–5

Introduction 6–10

PETE BROWN 11–42

CLAIRE BULLEN 43–74

JONNY GARRETT 75–106

JOHN HOLL 107–138

EMMA INCH 139–170

LOTTE PEPLOW 171–202

ROGER PROTZ 203–236

JOE STANGE 237–268

Index of beer styles 270–271

The authors

Pete Brown is a British writer, broadcaster and consultant specialising in food and drink, and how they help define us. He writes for newspapers and magazines around the world and is a regular contributor to radio and podcasts. He was named British Beer Writer of the Year in 2009, 2012, 2016 and 2021, has won three Fortnum & Mason Food and Drink Awards, been shortlisted twice for the Andre Simon Awards, and in 2020 was named an 'Industry Legend' at the Imbibe Hospitality Awards. He was recently accused of being the 31st most important person in the drinks industry.

Claire Bullen is the editor-in-chief of *Good Beer Hunting*, a James Beard Award-winning international beer publication. She is also a beer judge; a freelance drinks writer whose work has appeared in publications like *Imbibe, Pellicle, Glug*, and SIBA's *Independent Brewer Magazine*; and the author of *The Beer Lover's Table: Seasonal Recipes and Modern Beer Pairings*, an award-winning cookbook devoted to beer and food pairings.

Jonny Garrett is a multi-award-winning writer, photographer and broadcaster. He is co-founder of YouTube's Craft Beer Channel, a homebrewing, documentary and travel show with over 130,000 subscribers and 9 million views. He's also a journalist, podcaster and author of three books including the Fortnum & Mason Award-winning *A Year in Beer*. In 2019 the British Guild of Beer Writers named him Beer Writer of the Year.

John Holl has been covering the beer industry as a reporter and editor for nearly 20 years. Currently, he is the editor of *All About Beer* and a contributing editor for *Wine Enthusiast Magazine*. On-air he hosts the Drink Beer, Think Beer podcast, and co-hosts Steal This Beer. He is the author of several books including the recently published *The Craft Brewery Cookbook*.

Emma Inch is a multi-award-winning freelance writer and audio-maker, and former British Beer Writer of the Year. Having always loved both beer and writing, she brought the two together in one of the UK's first beer and brewing shows on FM radio. Since then, Emma has written about beer and pubs for a number of national and international publications. She also produces creative audio and podcasts for the drinks trade. Emma is the current Chair of the British Guild of Beer Writers.

Lotte Peplow is a Certified Cicerone, accredited Beer Sommelier, international beer judge and beer writer who conducts talks and tastings about American craft beer, organises events and is a keen beer and food pairing experimentalist. She's been involved with the Brewers Association, a trade association representing small and independent American craft brewers, for many years and in 2019 was awarded the title of Brewers Assocation American Craft Beer Ambassador for Europe.

Roger Protz is a campaigner and broadcaster and author of more than 25 books about beer and brewing. He was the editor of CAMRA's *Good Beer Guide* for over two decades and has received Lifetime Achievement Awards from the British Guild of Beer Writers and Society of Independent Brewers. Roger appears regularly in the media and in 2016 was the subject of a BBC 4 *Food Show* special. He gives frequent talks and beer tastings at events in the UK and has also lectured at the Smithsonian Institute and Beer Expo in Melbourne.

Joe Stange is managing editor of *Craft Beer & Brewing Magazine* and the *Brewing Industry Guide* in the United States, co-author of CAMRA's *Good Beer Guide Belgium*, and author of Cogan & Mater's *Around Brussels in 80 Beers*. He currently lives in Bangkok.

Introduction

PETE BROWN

What makes a beer one of the world's greatest?

Can a brewer wake up one day and say, 'I'm going to create one of the greatest beers the world has seen, that people will remember for decades?' Does it happen by accident? Either way, if you brew one, do you know when you taste it?

These are questions only a brewer can answer. And while many, if not all, of the contributors to this book have had a go at digging out a mash tun or adding hops to the boil, we've all decided that ultimately, we're better at drinking beer and writing about it than we are at brewing it.

Does that mean we're not the best qualified people to decide which beers are the world's greatest? Should we be asking brewers instead?

Well, no.

Great beers aren't just made of hops, barley, yeast and water. (Truly great beers aren't made from mango pulp or cake ingredients either, no matter how fascinating they are to the modern craft beer drinker.) Many brewers have access to the same ingredients. The difference between them is in skill, imagination and vision. When I think about the craft of brewing (in the true sense of what *craft* is, which is never even touched on in the endless debates around the definition of 'craft' beer) I'm always reminded of how my wife and I both make a basic pasta sauce using the same hob, the same pan, and the same ingredients from the same shop, and hers has a totally different taste and texture from mine. We chop onions slightly differently. We have different stirring actions, a different idea of what a 'gentle simmer' is, and a hundred other micro-differences. Both sauces are good. Neither is the greatest pasta sauce in the world. The world's best pasta sauce chef would make one better than ours, thanks partly to the way they chop, stir and simmer, often in ways that are so ingrained, they're no longer aware of them.

So, if brewers can't tell us what are the greatest beers in the world, we have to ask drinkers. The scope of beer styles is vast. A few rare brewers are adept at brewing across all styles, but most specialise in one tradition and maybe a handful of styles. Would you ask the guitarist in your favourite indie band who are the best classical pianists of all time? They might have an opinion, but it would be that of a listener, same as your own.

If we wanted to answer the question as objectively as possible, we might say we could decide the greatest beers in the world by doing a blind tasting with a panel of beer experts. In fact, many such competitions happen every year, and with one of two exceptions (featured in these pages) the results are always different.

Again, all of the contributors to this book have judged in beer awards. Some competitions ask you to favour how commercial the beer is, while others ask you to reward how closely the beer resembles a written description of the style it claims to be. We've all judged outstanding beers that were marked down because the consensus arrived at by a group of judges was that it wasn't 'to style'. Some competitions serve the beers too cold. Others in the wrong glasses. Sometimes you score beers individually and the results are added together. Other times you have to come to a collective decision as a group. In that situation, there are always some judges more dominant than others, and you get a wonky version of the jury in the movie *Twelve Angry Men*, with people being told their palates are wrong.

After all that, and probably because of all that, some of the best brewers in the world just aren't that bothered about entering these competitions. I once judged 30 Belgian Tripels, and asked myself what the point of it was, because none of them was Westmalle Tripel (you could tell, even blind tasting) and therefore none of them was the best Tripel.

So there's no perfectly rational, objective, foolproof way of determining the greatest beers in the world. What you're left with instead is opinion and belief.

Any list that forms the basis of a book covering 50, 300 or 1001 beers (or ciders, or pubs) to try before you die is usually compiled by one person. When you write such a book, you do so knowing that one day, someone is going to find you on social media or in real life and shout, 'Call yourself a beer expert? How can you possibly write this book and not even mention Old Scruttock's Horny Ballswinger!'

On behalf of all contributors, I'm going to make a confession: none of us have arrived at our lists of favourite beers by tasting all the beers in the world and then ranking them in order of preference. We haven't even tried.

There are 2,000 brewers in the UK alone, each producing an average of four to six regular beers, plus endless specials, seasonals and limited editions. Beer tickers and their modern equivalent, Untappd badge seekers, spend their lives trying to taste as many as possible and mainly just collect them, without trying to rank them. The most dedicated might tick 20,000 beers in a lifetime, and still not get close. So no, sorry, we've never tried Old Scruttock's Horny Ballswinger. I'm sure it's great though.

If you're going to enjoy a book like this one, you have to accept that it is a work of subjective opinion. All I can say in our defence is that, as people who spend our professional as well as personal lives tasting, evaluating and describing beer, our opinions are extremely well-informed.

That's not to say that, if you disagree with our opinions, we are right and you are wrong. Your palate is your own. We all have different numbers of tastebuds, and olfactory bulbs that work better or worse than other people's. It's possible to train your palate to a degree, and we've all done that. But beyond the tasting equipment we were born with, and genetic quirks that create oddities such as coriander tasting like soap for 30% of the population, your palate is shaped by your medical history, whether or not you smoke, allergies, and now, the lingering effects of COVID-19.

Beyond that, we interpret what our palates are telling us, not in the mouth but in the brain, mixed up with whatever other sensory information we are lucky enough to be able to receive. Why do we perceive a chilli's potency as 'hot' when it is cold to the touch? Why do we think dark beers are going to be more 'challenging' than pale beers? When I do my beer and music matching events, how do I make people think a beer tastes better when they're listening to Hendrix than it does when they're listening to Debussy?

If that's not complicated enough, whether or not you like a particular beer can be influenced by where and when you first tasted it and what you were doing, whether you got sick after drinking too much of it when you were a teenager, or who introduced you to it. If you're encountering it for the first time now, then the time of day, what you've had to eat recently, what the temperature is, whether or not the telly is on, and countless other factors all play their part. If you start thinking about it too much, as I obviously have, you can start to doubt if objective reality in flavour even exists. If a beer is drunk in a forest but there's no one there to tweet about it, does it contain hops?

With this book, the CAMRA Editor hit upon a novel way of tackling the issue. Instead of asking one beer writer to undertake the project, he asked eight. We were each invited to submit our 31 candidates for the world's greatest beers, all choosing them on whatever criteria we each saw fit. Naturally there were overlaps, and this is where it gets interesting.

Of the 250 beers in this book, more than 40 were chosen by more than one person. Perhaps that means these beers are the ones that truly belong here. One beer was chosen by five people, another by four. We had a meeting (in a pub, naturally) where our Editor had to wrangle a session of horse-trading. Several of us wanted to do Budvar, but Roger Protz has been visiting the brewery since before the rest of us were old enough to drink – obviously he had to get that (he also got to choose 33 beers to make a round 250). But if he was nabbing that one, it was only fair that I got Boon Oude Geuze, another one we both wanted to do. And so, in a very diplomatic, very English way (even though there are three Americans) we carved up the beers without any tears.

Looking at the original lists now, though, I'm surprised there wasn't greater overlap. How come only one of us chose Sierra Nevada Pale Ale or Samuel Adams Utopias? Part of this is politicking: Sierra Nevada Pale Ale is probably one of my top five beers in the world, but I assumed everyone else would choose it too and I don't do conflict well. Part of it is showing off: there's a tendency to choose beers you pray other people won't have heard of or tasted, so you can imagine you're cooler than the other writers. But I think more than all this, it demonstrates how our ideas of the world's greatest beers are formed by our different experiences.

The book is relatively weighted to the UK and North America because that's where our beer tastes were formed and it's where most of us continue to drink now. Out of the 250 beers here, I reckon I've drunk 160–171 of them. After struggling to get to 31 at one point, there are at least 50 that have made me go, 'Damn, why didn't I think of that?'

There are other beers where I think 'I wouldn't have chosen that,' but I look at who did and I think, 'There's a story there. That beer means something much more to that person than it does to me. I wonder why?' Sometimes age has something to do with it – and so we're back to one's individual history with a beer, when it was first encountered, the role it has played in a life, where it's been drunk and with whom. The joy of reading this book is the passion someone displays in making their case that a beer you maybe thought was good, but not legendary, is so important that you need to look at it again.

Finally, it's the ones that really don't overlap, the 20 or 30 that I've never heard of before seeing them here, that are the most intriguing. Call yourself a beer expert, Pete? How can you be a contributor to this book and not even know about Bierstadt Lagerhouse The Slow Pour Pils? Sometimes you can feel a bit jaded in this job (often coinciding with being hungover). Going through our lists, I'm indignant and excited again about catching up with beers I've somehow missed in my 20-year beer writing career.

I hope you feel the same way too. If you're new to beer, you can feel confident that this book is a gateway to beers and beer moments that will inspire and delight you for the rest of your life. If you've been around the beer festival block a few times, I hope there are enough of your favourites here to confirm that we share excellent taste, and a slightly higher number that will give you a good excuse to go beer hunting again. We have definitely missed out some of your all-time favourites. If I told you that was deliberate, so we can use your feedback to pitch for a sequel – *Yet More of the World's Greatest Beers* – would you believe me?

Cheers!

Pete Brown

I first started writing about beer in 2003. As an advertising executive who was partly responsible for Heineken and Stella Artois ads, it was the cultural and social aspects of beer that first engaged me. I thought existing beer writers took the beer itself too seriously. I wanted to shake it up and have more fun.

I was well into the research for my second book by the time the sheer beauty and variety of beer became apparent to me. I did my first ever beer evaluation training just before trips to Belgium and America. My newly sensitised palate was blown away by what I found there, and I started to take the beer itself pretty seriously too.

As I argued in the introduction to this book, I believe a list of the world's greatest beers to be entirely subjective, a product not just of breweries, but also of the time, place and context where they were encountered. In my selection, I've done my best to give you a good idea of what the beer tastes like (to my palate at any rate) and where it fits in the broader world of beer – why it's an important beer rather than just why I like it.

I've also tried to broaden my scope a bit. I'm conscious that we all lean into the classic brewing nations of Britain, Belgium, Germany, Czech Republic and – now – the United States. I know it wasn't strictly the remit for this book, but where I'm aware of great beers from countries you might not expect, I've made sure they're represented.

In all cases, I've attempted to tell a story. It may be about my personal experience, or it may be wider. But each of my world's greatest beers is great not just for the way it tastes, but also because of the moments and feelings it has inspired.

Acorn
Barnsley Bitter

3.8% Bitter

Barnsley, South Yorkshire

When does a single beer become a beer style?

It happened to Pilsner lager, and more recently to ESB – beers that were so ground-breaking, so popular, that they were copied by brewers around the world. Coming from Barnsley, I'm biased, but I'd argue that Barnsley Bitter is just about there too. You can't trademark the name of a town, and there are at least two Barnsley Bitters being brewed in Yorkshire today, both to a similar style, both excellent. There used to be more.

The original Barnsley Bitter was brewed at the Oakwell Brewery in Barnsley. First brewed in 1854, it was beloved across Yorkshire. In the 1960s Oakwell was taken over by John Smith's of Tadcaster, swiftly closed down, and Barnsley Bitter disappeared. Given how popular it had been, a cynic, or a Barnsley fan (that's a pretty big Venn diagram overlap) might suggest that the move was motivated by a desire to get rid of superior competition.

Various brewers subsequently recreated the beer, including, distressingly, one in Lancashire. In 2003 Acorn brewery was founded in Wombwell, just outside Barnsley, to take their turn. It's done better than any version since the original, winning shelves full of awards.

Brewed with the original yeast strain, it pours a light-chestnut colour and has notes of treacle and chocolate on the nose. These are joined on the palate by a mix of red berry fruits and very gentle hints of marzipan nuttiness and spice on the nose.

Barnsley Bitter is sessionable and light enough to demolish a miner's thirst and clear the coal dust from their throat. But especially on cask, it also has far more character than a straightforward Bitter, something thicker and more earthy. The treacle and caramel suggest that this is a beer that could teach Pastry Stouts a thing or two, if it didn't think they were too pretentious to bother with.

Asahi
Super Dry

5.2%   Golden Lager

Osaka, Japan

It almost feels subversive including a mainstream 'macro' lager in a book about the world's greatest beers. Surely all big beers are tasteless and boring?

Well, no. There must be some good ones out there. It's a brave person who suggests that every single one of the billions of people who drink mainstream lager does so because they have poor taste.

While 'world beers' are – at least to the beer trade itself – aspirational because they come from somewhere remote and exciting, beers often make more sense when you encounter them on their own turf. Asahi is my beer of choice in any Japanese restaurant, because you don't want to pair anything too heavy with tuna sashimi. But I really *got* this beer when I visited Tokyo. There, you realise that a lot more Japanese food than you might imagine is fried or grilled in rich sauces or marinades. At train stations like Ginza in the heart of the city, commuters eat 'under the guardrail', in the brick arches below the noisy railway viaducts. Small cafés known as *izakaya* consist of a bar counter, a barbecue grill, a beer fridge and a few tables. Barkers stand at the front of each one, hustling people in to fill any seat as soon as it becomes available.

This is where Asahi really comes into its own. It was designed specifically to go with food without getting in its way. Words like crisp, clean and refreshing are often used as euphemisms for a complete lack of character: that's not the case here. Yes, it's clean and delicate, but the gentle bitterness gives it structure and there are some faint citrus hop notes. When you're munching your way through skewers of chicken thigh, breast, hearts, feet (we passed on the gizzards) this beer is an essential companion to cut through the grease and have your palate bounding back for more.

Baladin
Xyauyù

14%   Wood-aged beer

Piozzo, Italy

One of the most delightful aspects of the craft beer revolution was when countries you wouldn't normally associate with beer brewing decided to join the party.

There's a line across the middle of Europe, and above that line grain grows better; below it, grapes. So traditionally, countries like Britain, Germany, Czech Republic and Belgium were noted for beer; France, Italy and Spain for wine. The global craft brewing boom was originally based on the classic beer styles of those more northern countries.

When Italy decided to join them, it came at beer from a wine perspective. For a brewer, if you want to sell a premium, intriguing beer, you're not persuading people to switch from a generic lager – you're probably having to get them to switch from a decent wine, in a food setting. This means Italy's craft brewers had to start with a completely different frame of reference. Compatibility with food and 750ml bottles for sharing weren't some eccentric extravagance: they were expected.

With a centre of gravity somewhere between wine and beer, Baladin have created some extraordinary (in both senses of the word) beers over the years, but nothing quite tops Xyauyù. According to the brewery, it began as a vision to turn 'one of the typical flaws of beers – oxidation – into a strength'. This led to the creation of a strong Barley Wine that soon evolved into various different expressions. It's been aged in rum barrels, Scottish single malt barrels and traditional Japanese barrels used to ferment soy sauce. But for me, nothing beats the one-off Kentucky 2016, aged with Italian tobacco leaves. As a non-smoker myself, it's a triumph of earthy, smoky notes playing off against nuts and chocolate. This one is hard to find now, but tasting any expression of Xyauyù is worth both the effort and the expense.

Bale Breaker
Top Cutter

6.8% IPA

Yakima, Washington

Sometimes, your relationship with one of the greatest beers in the world is totally defined by where you first met.

In 2016, after a decade of dreaming about the possibility, I finally got to visit Yakima Valley, Washington State. Yakima is 1,000ft above sea level. It should be arid, but ancient volcanoes created fertile soil, and the snowmelt from the mountains allowed the valley to be irrigated in 1927. Yakima now grows around 65% of America's harvest of apples and peaches, as well as most of its hops. This is where the fruity, citrusy hop notes that inspired the global craft beer revolution were born. Our group spent a day picking hops on a farm that grows more than the whole of Britain's hop harvest combined. The fields were dry and dusty, the sun relentless.

Bale Breaker Brewing, founded in 2013, sits on a smaller, family-owned farm nearby. The brewhouse and taproom are surrounded by fields of Cascade hops. The beers we had there were always going to taste life-changingly amazing, the hops so fresh and so abundant. Incredibly, stripped of all that context, the can I have at my desk now tastes almost as good.

It is, refreshingly for an IPA these days, crystal clear. On the nose are hints of the pines you pass through on the drive up to Yakima, a mixed bag of citrus fruit and just a bit of tropical papaya. That fact that none of these dominates the others makes it all the more complex and rewarding. On the palate you get juicy malt first, a hint of banoffee as it plays with the fruit, an assertive bitterness that's resiny and chewy rather than just abrasive, and as you swallow, that fruit gives a retronasal encore, brightening and refreshing, compelling you to take another sip.

Batham's
Best Bitter

4.3%   Bitter

Brierley Hill, West Midlands

When you tell people you're a beer writer, reactions vary. Some find the concept of such a profession ridiculous. Others think it's the coolest job in the world. For about the first ten years, whenever I told someone from the Midlands that I was a beer writer, their reaction was always the same.

'Have you tried Batham's?'

'No. Why does everyone keep asking me that?'

'Oh. Ah well. Never mind.'

To this day, I've never seen it outside a small patch of the West Midlands. And why would you go the West Midlands just to drink a beer?

Finally, one fan put me out of my misery. I got to know the late Charles Campion, former restaurant critic for the *Evening Standard* and, at the time, one of the judges on *Masterchef*. He lived in Warwickshire, and when he asked the inevitable question and received the usual answer, he said, 'Well, we're going to have to do something about that, dear boy.'

A few weeks later we were in the Bull and Bladder – everyone calls it that, even though the name above the door is the Vine Inn – home of Batham's Brewery.

Charles ordered two pints of Batham's Best. I'd been building up to this for years. It smelt like ... Bitter, the traditional earthy, spicy notes of Fuggles and Goldings hops on the nose. On the palate, it was a little too sweet for me, a bit watery

perhaps? I went to take another sip to make sure, and was surprised that my glass was already empty. Surely only seconds had passed, but Charles was tapping his empty pint glass impatiently, saying, 'Your round, dear boy.'

The quintessential session Bitter, Batham's is modest and unassuming, but somehow happens to be the most drinkable beer in the world.

Big Drop
Galactic Milk Stout

0.5% Stout

Ipswich, Suffolk

In the critical rehabilitation of low-/no-alcohol beers, this one for me proved to be a turning point.

Traditionally, there are two ways of creating alcohol-free beer: one, you could use a weak yeast that can't convert sugars into alcohol. Typically, this results in beers with the 'worty' taste you get in brewer's mash, lacking the complexity of a finished beer. Two, you could brew a full-strength beer, then take out the alcohol. This usually gives a vegetal, boiled taste that's deeply unpleasant. Compound this with the fact that most low-/no-alcohol beers were lagers – the style that has less room to hide off-flavours than any other beer style – and the results were never good enough to justify choosing instead of a soft drink.

The craft beer boom revolutionised the range of styles you could play with, while the technology of de-alcoholisation has advanced rapidly. In 2016, friends James Kindred and Rob Fink launched Big Drop – the world's first brewer to specialise in low-/no-alcohol beers. If their beers were no good, there were no full-strength equivalents to save the business.

My personal epiphany was drinking my first bottle of milk chocolate, coffee and vanilla-hinted velvetiness, getting to the end of it, and thinking, 'That was great, I'd like another one of those.' This is something you get with a great beer, but not a great soft drink – if you're thirsty, you drink it, and it's done its job. This was behaving like a beer instead – a very good beer.

My enthusiasm was confirmed the following year when Galactic won gold in its category at the World Beer Awards. What makes this remarkable is that, at the time, there was no alcohol-free category in the awards: to win, this 0.5% ABV beer beat every full-strength Milk Stout in the competition.

Case closed.

Bokke
Zomersaison 2017

6%   Gueuze/Saison blend

Hasselt, Belgium

In 2018 I helped make a special edition of BBC Radio 4's *Food Programme* where presenter Dan Saladino and I explored the world of Belgian beer. The narrative was that we had to find a new beer style that Belgian beer expert Tim Webb had not come across before.

Our first stop was Hasselt in Limburg, West Flanders. There we met Raf Souvereyns, a young blender of Gueuze beers who has been creating ripples across the entire beer world since he began exploring beer in 2013.

As soon as you meet him, you can tell that Raf is one of those artists who simply doesn't approach the world the same way most of us do. He can get as excited by a bumper harvest of elderflower or finding a rare empty wine barrel as he does about picking up some fresh wort from one of the world's greatest Lambic breweries. Each of these is equally likely to take the creative lead in one of his projects.

Raf Souvereyns doesn't create base beers, he uses them as building blocks. He blends interesting liquids, often finds interesting fruits or plants to add to them, and ferments and/or ages them in an interesting container. This takes months if not years. In the handful of bars around the world that sell Bokke beers, they're usually around the equivalent of £65 for a 750ml bottle.

When I had the chance to buy one, I went for the Zomersaison 2017, a blend of the renowned Fantôme Saison with one- and two-year-old Lambics aged in barrel that had been freshly emptied of kriek Lambic and peach Lambic. It had everything you want these styles to have, but in moderation and balance that only increased its complexity: funk, bright acidity and vivid fruit all playing out against a soft malt base with gentle carbonation.

Boon
Oude Geuze

7[%]   Lambic

Lembeek, Belgium

Lambic beer has been called many things, from 'the Champagne of beer' (by Michael Jackson, the man who invented modern beer writing) to 'some beer that you've just sicked back up' (by me, a very long time ago). These days, I'm more aligned with Jackson than my younger self.

Frank Boon retired recently. Before that, he was probably the best Lambic brewer and Gueuze blender in the world. Boon is the only brewery to have won an award ten years running at the Beer World Cup. It took the whole podium in its category at the Brussels Beer Challenge in 2018.

Boon bought the last brewery in the town of Lembeek in 1975. 'It was like a time machine,' he told me in 2019. 'There had been no investment since the Second World War.' Many Lambic brewers were trying to sell up – typically, when the old man running it died, the brewery would close. 'Every brewery in Brussels sold to Belle Vue, all except Cantillon – they were so small, there was nothing to sell!' remembers Frank.

He completed a moved to a new brewery by 1989. Everything here is done slowly, in a place that smells like an old cider barn, the smell of drink-soaked oak topped by an extra hint of balsamic.

Where other Lambic brewers fetishize the coolship where the beer is born, for Frank Boon, it's all about the barrels where it ages. His barrel room is vast, and as he shows us around, it's like he never wants to leave this room. It enhances the flavour of the beer. The aroma is sharp and fruity, with a touch of violet, spicy and earthy. It makes the mouth water. On the palate it's dry, earthy, some grainy malt, a touch of umami, a gentle acidity at the end.

Brooklyn
Black Ops

12.4%   Stout

Brooklyn, New York

One of the most common stories in brewing is the beer that was produced as a one-off, that proved so popular it forced its way into mainstream production. Black Ops is – supposedly – one of those beers.

Its name comes from the fact that when it was first brewed, if you asked anyone, it didn't officially exist. Brooklyn now brews huge quantities of beer and sells around the globe, but brewmaster Garrett Oliver is always looking to push the boundaries, and will occasionally wander off into the bowels of his brewery for some creative experimenting.

The last two times I visited Brooklyn, Garret would show me a few of his beers and then at the end, he would swear Black Ops didn't exist while pulling a bottle from under the table. People would materialise as if from the walls and gather round.

Black Ops may or may not have different variants, but the basic idea is that it's an Imperial Stout aged in bourbon barrels, bottled flat and refermented in the bottle with Champagne yeast. Garrett adores wine as well as beer, and that's evident here: the beer is rich and complex throughout, with notes of oak and bourbon on the nose, broadening out the typical character of chocolate and coffee that dominates this style of beer. On the palate, the bourbon character sinks into the dark chocolate, and is joined by vanilla and red berry fruit notes.

The mystique is still there. While writing this, I Googled Black Ops and a link to it on the Brooklyn website comes up. 'The rumors are true: Brooklyn Black Ops is real' leads the text with the link. But when I click through to Brooklyn's beer range, there is no sign of it. The bottle in my cellar is under armed guard.

Devil's Peak
King's Blockhouse

6% IPA

Cape Town, South Africa

There's a trend in technology that each new innovation is adopted faster than the one before it. It took three decades for microwaves to make it into 80% of our homes, compared to just nine years for smartphones to do the same.

You see a similar pattern with countries embracing the modern idea of craft beer. South African craft brewers, relatively late to the party, are catching up with the US and UK after just a decade.

When Devil's Peak started brewing in Cape Town in 2012, nine in ten beers drunk in South Africa were brewed by South African breweries (SAB), which was swallowed by Anheuser Busch in 2016. SAB brewed two lagers – Carling and Lion. Throw in a bit of Heineken and Amstel, and that was the beer choice open to most South Africans.

It's in dire circumstances like this that craft beer can have its most dramatic growth. Craft brewers struggled for a while to get anything from decent ingredients to viable distribution, but Devil's Peak lit a fuse and the scene has now exploded.

Brewer J C Steyn was a keen homebrewer and worked for a decade in the wine industry. He brought these skills together in the taproom and the effect was immediate: flagship beer King's Blockhouse is a solid IPA in the American tradition. There's no twist on the formula of juicy, fruity hops, aromas of mango and papaya, joined by piney notes on the palate and an assertive, bitter finish. But that's not the point. The point is that it's as good as many IPAs brewed in the United States. It didn't take long for King's Blockhouse to become the most awarded beer in South Africa, inspiring hundreds of others to set up craft breweries of their own.

Duration
Remember When The Pub

7.1% IPA

West Acre, Norfolk

Remember when we were in lockdown, and all the pubs were closed? Remember when you didn't leave the house and you started to have beers delivered to your door?

That's when Duration warned us that 'Living in the past impedes us moving forward,' but also suggested that 'with an IPA a little nostalgia ain't no bad thing.'

I remember when IPAs used to taste like this. Once, when you asked for an IPA, this is what you got. Then, in the mid-2010s, juicy, Hazy IPAs landed on our shores, based on a modification to the style that originated in New England. Soon, when you asked for an IPA, you got this kind of beer instead. I've never felt older than the time in my local craft beer pub when I said, 'Look, have you got an IPA – not a New England IPA, an IPA that's clear and has some bitterness and malt character to it rather than this one-dimensional fruitiness?'

'Oh, you mean an *old school* IPA!' replied the barman.

Old School? Beers in this style hadn't even been in the UK for a decade by that point. But craft beer years are like dog years, I guess.

On its website, Duration completes the question asked by this beer as 'Remember when the pub first had a Westie on?' Mate, I'm old enough to remember when 'Westie' was the nickname for an obscure Belgian Trappist ale, and an IPA didn't need to have 'West Coast' prefixed to it to indicate what kind of beer it was; when IPAs had a malty, bready, backbone like the one given here by the darker Munich and Vienna malts; when the fruity flavours were balanced, like they are here, by resin and pine and soft caramel; and when, like here, the assertive bitter finish dried your palate and left it buzzing for more.

Duvel Moortgat
Duvel

8.5%   Belgian Golden Ale

Puurs-Sint-Amands, Belgium

Duvel is regal in its haughty dominance of the most eclectic beer scene in the world.

If you're a beer aficionado, it's probably one of the first great beers you encountered. You were probably thrilled and slightly scared by its 8.5% alcoholic hit, and confounded that you couldn't taste it in a beer that always urged you to drink it quicker and more deeply than you knew was wise. Then, you probably got bored of it. Not only is it the one beer you can find in any café in Belgium, it's available in pretty much every supermarket in the UK. Where's the challenge? The thrill of discovery? Isn't the company basically a big macro brewer these days?

If you've never had Duvel before, you've missed a readily available treat. If you used to love Duvel but have left it behind, do yourself a favour and give it another visit.

First, be careful how you pour it: it's an aggressive beer from the off, its foam gives the appearance of charging out of the glass to get to you. All that foam whips up the aroma compounds into a frenzy – give it a careful sniff and swirl, and you get delicate notes of citrus and apple acidity with the promise of sweetness waiting on the palate.

When you take a sip, the sweetness delivers, fruity and delicately sugary, with gentle acidity and a balancing bitterness. It finishes dry, tingling and refreshing, a fully rounded beer that stands as a paragon of strong Belgian Golden Ale. This may not be a fashionable beer category at the moment – and the Duvel brand has variants that pander to trends such as hoppier beers or barrel ageing – but when you become bored or disillusioned with contemporary fads, Duvel will always be there, waiting for you.

East African Breweries
Tusker Malt

5% Pale Lager

Nairobi, Kenya

In Kenya, Tusker accounts for about nine in ten beers sold. It can seem more like a religion than a beer. Its advertising slogan *Bia yangu, Nchi yangu* translates as 'My beer, My country'. In some Nairobi bars, when the Tusker ads come on at half-time during an English Premiership game, people stand up and sing along with the patriotic jingle, fists slammed across their chests. Pretty much every tourist who has ever been to Kenya has bought a Tusker T-shirt from the sprawling Duty Free shops in Nairobi airport.

East African Breweries Limited (EABL) was formed in 1922. Just a year later, George Hurst, the company's founder, was killed in an elephant hunting accident. In his memory, his brother Charles renamed their beer Tusker.

When you're in Kenya, the main Tusker beer is ubiquitous in its dusty-brown 500ml bottles. It's not the best beer in the world, but it's the perfect beer after a long game drive, or to accompany a seafood platter in Mombasa beach restaurants. The locals are suspicious of drinking beer too cold, so you have to specify whether you want it refrigerated or at room temperature.

It's better than most of those holiday beers you later regret bringing home with you, but perhaps to prepare for that disappointment, in 1996 EABL launched Tusker Malt, originally as an export-only beer. Where the main Tusker beer contains some less expensive adjuncts, Malt is, as the name suggests, an all-malt beer. It enjoys a decent lagering period, and is drier and cleaner than its bigger brother, grainy and crisp on the palate with a touch of lemon from the hops, a little sweetness, but perfectly balanced.

EABL may now be owned by Diageo, but in beer terms, Tusker remains the pride of East Africa.

Früh
Kölsch

4.8%   Kölsch

Cologne, Germany

When is a lager not a lager? There are two answers to that question. One, when it's not 'lagered', when it hasn't been through the weeks- or even months-long cold conditioning process that gives this family of beers its name. And two, when it hasn't been brewed with a lager yeast, which favours these conditions more than a traditional ale yeast does and contributes to the dry, clean taste we expect from a lager.

Many British 'lagers' are nothing of the sort. Brewers often use malt and hops that are commonly associated with lager, but don't use a lager yeast and don't do lager conditioning, so technically what they're brewing is a Pale Ale. Even if you're not a purist, if you're after a lager you might be disappointed by the lack of crispness, and the presence of fruity, estery notes from the ale yeast.

Such brewers would be more honest if they branded these beers as 'Cologne-style ales'. The city of Cologne, or Köln, has a centuries-old brewing rivalry with neighbouring Düsseldorf. Both cities decided to stick with traditional top-fermenting ale yeasts when the newer, bottom-fermenting lager yeasts swept through and eventually became the standard for the vast majority of German brewing. To compete with bottom-fermenting lagers, Kölsch brewers began lagering their ales. The modern style of Kölsch dates back to 1918, and since 1997 a Protected Geographical Indication means that it can only be brewed within 50km of Cologne.

The Kölsch Konvention lays down some strict rules about how the style should be brewed, so there's not much variation between brands, but Früh Kölsch is the easiest one to find outside Cologne. A fresh, bready aroma with hints of lemon and peppery spice develops more fully on the palate with a light sweetness and a gently spicy finish. It's what any ale pretending to be a lager should taste like, but rarely does.

Fuller, Smith & Turner
ESB

5.9%   Bitter

London, England

Fullers ESB is a beer steeped in legend, much of which may or may not be true. Legend has it that more than one of the first wave of American craft brewers began their careers attempting to recreate this beer, failed, and accidentally created American IPAs instead.

One story that's definitely true is that ESB, which stands for Extra Special Bitter, was once simply the name of a beer from Fuller's. But it has been imitated so many times that it has become a style in its own right, and Fuller's recently gave up trying to protect this particular piece of intellectual copyright. Obviously, this is the beer that was used as the basis of the style description for ESB in the Beer World Cup. Beer evolves quickly: two years later, it was rejected in the same competition for not being to style.

What's so special about it? Well, I find that any attempt to describe it doesn't do it justice. We often describe beers as malty or hoppy. We don't talk enough about the interplay between the two, the totality of the ingredients in perfect balance. To talk about this beer in terms of malt or hops would be to miss the point of it. I could say it has hints of caramel, or it echoes red wine, or that it has a grassy note. But what, actually, is the point of that? To reduce a beer like this to its component parts right now would feel like the behaviour a psychopathic child who performs a live dissection on his pet rabbit to see how it works, and gets upset when it doesn't want to play with him anymore.

Sometimes, you just need to drink a beer and enjoy it, allow it to have a little bit of mystery – like all legends do.

Fungtn
Chaga

0.4%   Lager

London, England

This beer is a classic example of the lesson that, with one or two notable NSFW exceptions, you shouldn't knock something till you've tried it. I'll be honest: I was deeply sceptical of a non-alcoholic beer made out of mushrooms. I only heard about it because a newspaper asked me to write about it. Five months later, I'm still buying it on a regular basis.

Up to a point, the more you learn about Fungtn, the less appealing it sounds. The beer is the brainchild of Zoey Henderson, a consultant to the hospitality industry who was left with no work when that industry was hammered by Covid lockdowns. She has no history in beer, and doesn't brew – Fungtn beers are contract-brewed for her.

But when you look at this from her perspective, it starts to make more sense. What Zoey does know an awful lot about are the health benefits of functional mushrooms – different from both 'magic mushrooms' and edible mushrooms – which have been used by people in the Far East for centuries. She was looking for different ways to take them after mixing them with coffee for years, and realised that many of their flavours – bitter, nutty, chocolate and cocoa – were also found in beer.

There are three beers in all, and all are good. Chaga lager is the best, though. It's a Belgian-style dark lager, chocolate-coloured, with nuts and gentle woodiness on the nose. On the palate it's smooth, with hints of chestnut, chocolate and tobacco. It doesn't taste 'mushroomy'. It's a great beer by any measure. For a low-alcohol beer, it's outstanding.

Oh, and those health benefits? The Chaga mushroom is vitamin rich, and may lower cholesterol among other effects that aren't quite proven, but surely that'll be enough for my doctor to reverse their previous advice and tell me to drink more beer?

Guinness
Foreign Extra Stout

7.5% Stout

Lagos, Nigeria

'Export Stout' is a style that, similar to IPA, had a reputation for being a bit stronger than the domestic product, so it would taste better after a long sea journey. Guinness used to export a lot of it to Africa, where it became so popular the Irish brand opened a brewery in Nigeria in the 1950s.

In a move that was enlightened for the time, Guinness installed local workers and management as soon as they could, and Guinness Foreign Extra Stout (FES) became, as far as Africans were concerned, an African brand. According to the tour guides at the Guinness Storehouse in Dublin, African workers would arrive in the city and say 'Oh, cool, you stock African beer in Ireland!'

Exported back to Ireland and the UK, Nigerian FES became so popular, Guinness felt upstaged and decided to brew it in Dublin too. Corner shops in multicultural communities often stock both versions, their labels subtly different.

Officially they are the same beer, but they actually taste quite different. The Dublin version has loads of chocolate up front on the nose, then a bit of espresso and some liquid caramel lurking at the back. On the palate, the main theme is bitter chocolate, and an emerging vinous alcohol weight, with smoke and yet more chocolate on the finish. It really would make an indulgent alternative to red wine.

Meanwhile, the Nigerian version has hardly any chocolate at all on the nose – it's more molasses, tobacco and Demerara sugar. It's much drier on the palate, much more like sherry or Madeira than red wine, with a slight tartness on the finish.

If you think you know Guinness, but have never tried FES, think again. The brewery doesn't shout about it, but it is by far the best beer they make.

Kompel
L'or Noir

8.2% Belgian Tripel

Maasmechelen, Belgium

When we're judging in beer competitions, we each have different standards for what qualifies a beer for a particular grade or award. For me, if we're awarding bronze, silver or gold, bronze is a beer I would finish and perhaps order again. Silver is a beer I would use in a tutored tasting as a good example of the style. Gold is a beer that I have to learn the identity of, so I can go out and buy a case.

In 2021 we judged the World Beer Awards via Zoom, each bottle or can delivered to us wrapped in black paper to obscure its identity. Judging was filmed to ensure none of us were cheating. After judging, I poured most of the remaining beers away. Anything I had scored a gold or silver got a little stopper in the bottle and put back in the fridge for later.

On day one, the best beer I tasted was listed as a Tripel. I assumed it was Westmalle, because I hadn't tasted any other Tripel this good. It was light and spritzy, dry and wine-like, with a lightly sweet, gently acidic lemony fruitiness. I knew it was strong, but it hid its alcohol well. A clear gold from me.

Later, after forms were submitted and there was no way of it influencing anyone's score, I tore off the paper and found Kompel L'or Noir, a beer and brewery I'd never seen before. Kompel is a tribute to the coal miners of Limburg, a term of brotherhood applied to everyone underground. 'Black gold' may be a misleading name for a shining golden beer such as this, but being from a former coal mining community myself, I let that pass. The beer went on to win gold in the overall Tripel class in the awards. So I guess our different judging standards line up fine in the end.

Little Creatures
Pale Ale

5.2%   Pale Ale

Fremantle, Western Australia

When I first visited Australia in 2004, there were some hard and fast rules about how beer was served and drunk. In most parts of the country it had to be served in glasses smaller than a pint, because otherwise it would get warm too quickly. Beer was served as close to freezing as possible, from ice-encrusted fonts. More than once, I was asked, 'Is it true you British drink beer at blood-heat?'

The beer that slowly helped break this down was Little Creatures Pale Ale. Founded in 2000, the brewery had one singular purpose: to brew an American-style Pale Ale using hops from the American north-west, in Australia. Little Creatures Pale Ale was born in 2001, and instantly set the craft beer world alight.

It's actually somewhere between a British-style and an American-style Pale Ale, having initially been designed by British-born brewers who had a fascination with citrusy, resiny hops like Cascade and Chinook, the varieties that ignited craft beer's love of hops.

You don't hear these varieties talked about much these days, thanks to the seemingly insatiable desire for hop varieties that are ever fruitier and juicier, and a style of brewing that shuns bitterness. But Little Creatures has kept the faith. The beer hasn't stood still entirely: the latest version at the time of writing blends Cascade with home-grown Galaxy from Tasmania and East Kent Goldings from the UK. As the beer evolves gently, it always combines intriguing aromas including nectarine and burnt toffee among the usual citrus fruit, fruity sweetness and crunchy grain on the palate, with an unapologetic bitter finish.

While Little Creatures is no longer independently owned, it remains a guilty pleasure for older Australian craft beer fans who still remember it as the first beer they drank that wasn't so cold it numbed the senses.

Lost and Grounded
Apophenia

8.8%   Belgian-style Tripel

Bristol, England

Apophenia is a suitably poetic-sounding word to describe the human tendency to look for patterns in random information and spot them even when they're not really there. When you get philosophical while sipping strong Belgian ales late at night, the tendency to see the hidden music of the spheres is never far away, so Apophenia is also the perfect name for a Belgian-style Tripel.

Bristol-based Lost and Grounded was founded in 2016 by Alex Troncoso and his partner, Annie Clements. Together they have lived all around the world, with Alex brewing for both large corporates and small start-ups. They share a huge love and respect for traditional European beer styles, and in particular they speak with great fondness about the time they spent living and brewing in Belgium. Most of their core range beers cleave pretty closely to classic Belgian styles.

Commercially, it's probably a foolish idea to brew an 8.8% Tripel as part of your core range. It's even braver to brew a Tripel that's straight

down the line, that hasn't been subject to such inspirations as 'Hey, why don't we do our own take on Tripel and brew it with Irn Bru and cashew nuts and age it in old sherry barrels?' A Tripel is a beer of quiet strength and elegance. It could totally win in a fight with any other beer, but it's too classy to start one, and keeps itself to itself.

Apophenia starts with a base of Pilsner malt, meaning there's nowhere for anything to hide. The higher alcohol comes from the addition of glucose to boost the fermentable sugars. The alcohol weight is definitely there, but skilfully blended in with the addition of orange peel, coriander seeds, and an uncharacteristic seasoning of Cascade hops. The result is fruity but warming, a welcoming, indulgent feast of orange, banana and spice.

Mantle Brewery
Dis-mantle

5.8%   Amber Ale

Cardigan, Wales

Every August, I'm lucky enough to present my beer and music matching show at the Green Man Festival in Wales. Most music festivals in the UK are run by large promoters who make licensing deals with global brewers, so the beer selection is usually as dire as it is at most music venues. Green Man is different: the main beer tents stocks a range of over 60 Welsh cask ales and 30 Welsh ciders. Each year, I match a selection of these with the bands playing onstage, using a mix of intuition, humour, and neuro-science.

Over ten years of doing this, I've developed a detailed knowledge of Welsh cask ale. The overall quality of beers is excellent, but until recently the range of styles brewed was conservative: each brewer chose to send similar Pale Ales, Best Bitters, and the occasional Stout.

Dis-mantle continually comes to my rescue. I like to vary the beers because the bands are different each year, but with so much sameness, I've ended up using Dis-mantle more than any other beer.

The Mantle Brewery was founded in Cardigan, West Wales, in 2013. Their beers are as you would expect: Golden Ale, Pale Ale, Best Bitter and so on. And then there's Dis-mantle, which they describe as a 'deep amber ale,' but I can't really categorise it against any other beers directly. At 5.8%, it has a deep body and thickness to it, but at the same time it's crisp and refreshing. It combines vibrant, grassy, spicy hop aromas with the deep caramel of a Best Bitter and the chocolatey hints of a Porter or Stout. It's kind of like an ESB, but even deeper and maltier. It's unique. And because of this, it can pair with anything from modern folk to heavy metal.

Molson Coors
Worthington's White Shield

5.6% IPA

Burton-upon-Trent, Staffordshire

Steve Wellington began brewing at Bass in Burton-upon-Trent in 1964, and tried to retire three or four times before finally succeeding. One of these times, retired bliss was interrupted when he read that Worthington White Shield – a bottle-conditioned beer from one of Burton's ancient and now long-defunct great houses of brewing – was facing the axe. It had been contracted out and passed around various breweries, gradually losing its sense of purpose. By 2000, the King & Barnes brewery in Sussex was turning out just 1,000 barrels a year. When it was announced that King & Barnes was due to close, many assumed this would be the end of the road for a once-great beer.

Steve convinced Molson Coors to bring it back home. He began brewing it in the old Museum Brewery in the middle of the Burton Museum of Brewing's visitors' complex, and steadily restored it to its cult status.

White Shield isn't flashy, loud or sensational, but it has depth. Like a favourite album, book or film, it rewards repeated attention. Just when you think you know it, it reveals something you hadn't noticed before – a note of orange marmalade here, a hint of chocolate there. When you're lured away by novelty, you find your way back to it and it grounds you, like coming home after a long journey.

I recently found a bottle Steve gave me years ago, with a 'best before' date of October 1988. Apparently, a case of the stuff had been found under a desk in a disused part of the brewing complex. Thirty years after its lifespan supposedly ended, it poured bright and foamy, thanks to its bottle conditioning. Those vibrant orange marmalade notes were long gone, replaced by dried fruit and marzipan. It still nagged and urged you to take one more sip, to discover one more layer, even after it was finished.

Orkney
Dark Island Reserve

10% Wood-aged beer

Stromness, Orkney Islands

Orkney sounds like a great place to brew beer. The water is pure, and there's good barley growing not too far away. There are also two whisky distilleries on the island, should you want to get creative.

Today – in craft beer circles at least – whisky-barrel-aged beers are commonplace. They were quite extraordinary when Orkney brewmaster Norman Sinclair decided he wanted to create a beer that made a real statement about not just his brewery and skill, but beer itself, and where it was capable of going. He conceived Dark Island Reserve as a beer that would stun people's palates but also blow them away with the elegance of its visual design.

Initially brewed as a strong Scottish ale, it's then aged for three months in oak casks that used to contain Scottish single malt whisky, taking on greater complexity and alcoholic strength.

While a stylish 330ml bottle is more common today, the original launch was in a 750ml bottle with a swing top, ideal for a beer to be savoured over more than one occasion. Over the stopper there's a paper seal, each one of this small batch signed and numbered by the brewer.

Pop the bottle open, and the beer pours oily and almost black, with very little carbonation. It's one of those rare beers where you become so absorbed in giving it a good sniff that you can carry on returning to it, forgetting to take a drink. The first time you go in you might get vanilla, tobacco or liquorice accenting the deep, dark, toasted malt. Go back again and it might be smoke or whisky, then figs and dates. The complexity is astonishing. With so much on the nose, it's not surprising that this variety of flavours develops on the palate, along with coffee, wood and spiciness. An absolute showstopper.

Rochefort
Rochefort 10

11.3% Trappist Ale

Rochefort, Belgium

Some 800 years ago, monasteries generally brewed the best beer everywhere in Europe. In Belgium, they still do. While many abbeys and monasteries have disappeared, or lost their names and identities to commercial brewers, a handful of Trappist brewers remain. They earn the designation because monks are still involved at some level with the brewing, which happens inside the abbey walls. Driven by different motivations from the simple maximisation of profit, they have different priorities in the beers they brew.

'Trappist' or 'Abbey' are not beer styles within themselves. Rather, they give you a clue about the kinds of beers that the brewery will produce: strong and rich, warming and sweet styles like Dubbel and Tripel, and the huge beers known more recently as 'Quads,' particularly when they're copied outside Belgium.

Rochefort 10 is not a Barley Wine (if we have to, we can call it a Quad) but it is more wine-like than beer-like in many ways. It pours a very deep chestnut-brown, and is again one of those beers whose aroma keeps drawing you back as it keeps unpacking a feast of different treats. First there's caramel and toffee, and dark fruit and dried fruit, with hints of marzipan and maybe walnut. It's like a Christmas cake without being as sweet and cloying, tempered by port or sherry notes.

On the palate it's definitely boozy, thick and unctuous. The surprisingly energetic carbonation adds a definite note of cola to the mix. There's caramel and toffee again, more dark fruit and a hint of nutmeg joining the party. It's a perfect Christmas Day beer, which is quite appropriate: because when you think about who made it and where it comes from, if you believe in that kind of thing, this is God's beer.

SNAB
Maelstrøm

9.2%   Barley Wine

Purmerend, Netherlands

Maelstrøm is a beer I haven't had for ten years but still talk about whenever I get the chance. It's the best example I've ever experienced of how flavour can be completely subjective.

I first encountered it in Arendsnest, a beer bar in Amsterdam that, back then, stocked every single beer brewed in the Netherlands. No one bar could ever do that now. Even then, the beer list was a weighty tome.

Snab is a brewing collective in the north, and was an early pioneer of bringing American craft beer sensibilities to the country. Maelstrøm was described as an English-style Barley Wine brewed with American hops. By a Dutch brewery. In other words, unmissable.

I was in Arendsnest with Liz. I ordered a bottle between us, which came with two brandy balloon-style glasses. I poured the beer into the two glasses, and we both raised them to our noses. Immediately, Liz said, 'This smells like Parma Violets,' while I said, 'It smells like walking through a pine forest.'

Pine forests and Parma Violets smell nothing alike. But at the time, I'd recently done some beer judging training. I knew the beer contained bags of American hops, I knew what I was looking for, and spotted it. I was primed to get piney notes. Liz had done no training, but was blown away by the vivid aromas, and that's where free association took her.

You should try Maelstrøm, and see what you make of it. Some people get grapefruit and flowers; others apricot and vanilla. Some people call it a strong IPA, others a Belgian-style Quadrupel. Whatever it is, and however it really tastes, it's a strong, indulgent beer, a Dutch twist on an American twist on an old English style that stands as a testament to beer's transatlantic tennis match.

Spaten
Münchner Hell

5.2%   Helles

Munich, Germany

In the 19th century, Vienna's Anton Dreher and Munich's Gabriel Sedlmayr visited Burton Pale Ale brewers as part of an information-gathering research tour, and indulged in a bit of industrial espionage along the way, collecting samples of wort and fermenting beer in hollowed-out walking sticks. Returning to Munich, Sedlmayr's brewery, Spaten, introduced a new, paler beer style influenced by British Pale Ale called Märzen. In 1995 Spaten went paler still and developed a new beer which it registered as Helles Lagerbier. It was sent for market testing in Hamburg and was an instant hit. Helles was subsequently introduced to Bavaria in 1895, and quickly became the defining style of Bavaria's beer gardens and cellars. While Pilsner is more popular further north in Germany, today Helles is what you get in Bavaria if you ask for *'Ein bier, bitte'*.

I hadn't heard of Spaten until I first went to Oktoberfest in Munich in 2004. Spaten is one of the six big traditional brewers of Munich and has one of the football-stadium-sized marquees at Oktoberfest. On the first day we arrived it was the only one we could find a seat in. We ended up back in there every day of our trip.

Spaten's Helles is like the Oktoberfest tent itself: it's a big-hearted beer that wants to give you a hug as soon as it meets you. Light, grainy notes on the nose signal a fuller, breadier malty character on the palate, opening up with some faint citrus sweetness and a crisp, bitter finish.

This is a great example of how a classic German lager is supposed to taste. There's a gulf between a good Helles and what passes for commercial lager in the UK today. If you think all lager is the same, insipid fizz, challenge your prejudice with this.

Stone & Wood
Pacific Ale

4.4%   Pale Ale

Byron Bay, Australia

Many of the world's greatest beers are rooted in a sense of place. In the case of this one, it was specifically designed to be drunk not just in one country or region, but in one specific bar.

Know to locals as 'the Beachie,' the Beach Hotel in Byron Bay sits on the beach-front in a tropical paradise. Byron is home to surfers, dreamers and burnt-out hippies, and the Beachie is its slow-beating heart.

Weary of the big beer business, the three founders of Stone & Wood saw this bar as the spiritual home for their flagship beer. They wanted to capture the feeling of coming up from the sea, sand between your toes and salty water drying on your legs, and ordering a cold schooner from one of the ice-encased fonts on the bar. Pacific Ale was to be the perfect beer for anyone drinking here, and a taste of Byron that could be sampled anywhere in the world.

Being in paradise can make a writer more florid, and the tasting notes I made while sitting in the Beachie could only have been written there. Would I be pushing things too much if I said the beer was the colour of sunlight? Probably, but unpasteurised and unfiltered, its golden haze always evokes summer. On the nose there was the unmistakable passion fruit aroma of the precious Galaxy hop, which is only grown in Tasmania and is showcased in this beer. It's clean, fruity and fresh. In the mouth, it has a touch of resiny bitterness, but is smooth and creamy, the fruit blooming, quenching and generous, just like the place and the people who live and work in Byron.

I've enjoyed Pacific Ale many times in Britain. But it never tastes quite the same as a schooner in the Beachie.

Thornbridge
Jaipur

5.9 IPA

Bakewell, Derbyshire

Twenty years ago, there was a transatlantic divide in beer culture. Britain had cask ale. It was great, but it was all a bit samey, a tradition that had once almost disappeared and was now being closely guarded. In America, there was a burgeoning craft beer market that had originally been inspired by British cask ale, but was now evolving into something different. American hops were brighter and more vivid in their flavours, and American brewers were shoving more and more of them into their beers.

I first encountered American IPAs at a craft beer festival in Oregon. I came home raving about them to anyone who would listen. Carrying as many in my suitcase as I could, I shared them sparingly. One or two British brewers had just started using American hops, but not like the Americans were using them, and I hadn't yet discovered them.

About a year later, on a trip to Derbyshire, I spotted a beer in the bar from a brewery I hadn't seen before. I ordered Thornbridge Jaipur expecting it to be a typical pint of cask ale. When I raised it to my mouth, my senses were snatched from Derbyshire and whisked instantly back to Oregon. 'This is it!' I yelled. 'This is like those beers I was talking about!'

Thornbridge had taken American hops and somehow made them work in a British cask ale. Jaipur was – and remains – a perfect hybrid of American and British brewing influences. Grapefruit, lemon and tropical fruit aromas stand on the shoulders of digestive-biscuit Maris Otter malt, creating an iconic beer that has won more awards than it can count.

BrewDog is often cited as the brewer that brought American-style craft beer to Britain. Well, two years before he co-founded BrewDog, brewer Martin Dickie was at Thornbridge. Brewing Jaipur.

Verzet
Rebel Local

8% Belgian Blonde Ale

Anzegem, Belgium

Various beers I've selected here showcase that 'new and exciting' and 'old and dull' depend largely on where you are. The bready, citrus delights of a classis Helles are spurned by Germans who yearn to taste hoppy IPA. Many craft beer drinkers in the UK think cask ale is boring, while brewers in the rest of the world wish they could replicate its subtle mastery of balance and complexity. Meanwhile in Belgium – the world's great beer laboratory – Dubbels, Tripels, Lambics, Blonde Ales, Wheat Beers and all the other traditions that stun every novice beer fan are dismissed by younger drinkers as the beer your dad drank. All the cool kids are drinking hazy Pale Ales, just like everyone else in the world.

That's why I was so delighted to meet Koen, Alex and Jens, three young guys who founded Verzet in Anzegem, West Flanders in 2016. In the brewery's barrel-ageing room, each individual is named after a music legend, from Chuck Berry to Amy Winehouse. Like me, they feel the parallels between beer and music are perfect.

When they're out in a bar themselves, they adore the same juicy IPAs and Pale Ales as their contemporaries, but when it comes to brewing, they don't go near them. 'We're like musicians. We have our idols, but we don't want to be a covers band,' they say. 'We want to make our own music, our own beer, not something just because it's trendy.'

And so they make 'balanced beers with a sense of place,' starting with the West Flanders tradition before exploring further. Rebel Local is just that: a beer rooted in a local tradition of Golden Ales but does things to it that may upset purists. It's fruity, floral and spicy on the nose, with sweet papaya, citrus and grassiness on the palate. It's still Belgian, but it's seen something of the world.

The White Hag
Black Pig

4.2%   Stout

Sligo, Ireland

When The White Hag opened in 2013, it was the first brewery to open in Sligo, on Ireland's west coast, for 100 years. Ireland is known primarily for one beer style and one brand in that style – to many drinkers globally, Guinness *is* Irish beer, and *is* Stout.

The White Hag are keen to be combine innovation with their local terroir and traditions. They're particularly noted for a programme of sour beers using ingredients sourced locally on the Atlantic Way, and have also crowdfunded a rapidly developing barrel-ageing programme.

That's what keeps the craft beer kids excited. But this is an Irish brewery that is competing with a brewing behemoth that has historically crushed all competition. From the start, White Hag knew that if they wanted to survive, their core range needed to focus heavily on Stouts.

In local legend, the Black Pig was a giant beast that killed anything or anyone in its path (remind of you of any beer brands?). But in the story, a group of intrepid Sligo hunters eventually caught and slayed the beast, burying it in dirt and leaves until it formed a mound that can still be seen today.

The famous Guinness 'nitro' serve, that mixes nitrogen with carbon dioxide for that characteristic smooth body and thick, white head, was considered a bit naff until some American craft brewers adopted it, and then suddenly it was cool. It's employed here, to give a smooth, creamy feel to a Stout that combines deep, roasty aromas with a lush, caramel thread throughout. Perhaps after the long absence of brewing in the town of Sligo, the residents might want to borrow a certain old TV advertising slogan and declare that this is a beer that was worth waiting for.

Wye Valley
HPA

4%   Pale Ale

Stoke Lacy, Herefordshire

Beer's connection to a time and place has never been more profound for me than with Wye Valley HPA. When we think beyond the glass to the emotional side of what beer does, what beer can be, and what it can mean, this is one of the most important beers in my life.

My wife's family are based in Abergavenny, south Wales. In September the town comes alive for the annual food festival, one of the best in the UK, but at other times of year it can feel like heaven's waiting room. In the centre of town, the Angel Hotel stands as a beacon of familiarity. It's stylish, contemporary, has amazing food and serves good beers.

In 2009 Liz's dad passed away. When he was first taken into hospital we didn't think it was serious, but he went downhill rapidly. When the inevitable became clear, Liz and I spent all the visiting hours with him that we could. But we had to leave the hospital between 4pm and 6pm. Every day, for two weeks, by 4.15pm we'd be in the Angel, nursing a couple of pints of HPA.

It's very pale, almost too pale for a beer, but has a pronounced nose of lemon sherbet and a crisp, juicy fruit character with a light bitterness. It's light enough that we could have a couple of pints and return to the ward at 6pm without being the worse for wear. It's refreshing enough to clear your throat of hospital air. It became a beacon to us, the beer that anchored our couple of hours of respite. It helped us get through an awful time.

After the funeral, we had a wake for him in the Angel. In the weird way grief works, we laughed like drains for the whole afternoon as we toasted his life with pints of shining gold.

Claire Bullen

What makes a good beer? That answer has changed throughout my drinking life. When I was coming of age in the US, I gravitated to dark beers – Porters, Bocks, Quadrupels, and specifically to Schneider Aventinus, the beer that my father taught me to love shortly after I turned 21. Later, my tastes evolved. Influenced by the breweries I was encountering on the East Coast, I became a Hazy IPA fanatic, disinclined to drink anything that wasn't the colour or viscosity of mango juice. My preferences changed, and broadened, when I relocated to the UK and discovered the pleasures of traditional British styles like Bitters and Milds, while frequent trips to mainland Europe sharpened my love of German and Belgian styles.

Today, I drink more eclectically than ever. I find it hard to choose between a perfectly conditioned Best Bitter or a Witbier, a Czech Pilsner or a West Coast IPA, so you can imagine how challenging it was to select just 31 beers to include in my list of favourites. To make it as accessible and useful as possible, I avoided one-off and limited-edition beers in favour of core-range picks and recurrently brewed releases. I've also selected beers I was able to find and purchase here in the UK, with the hope that readers will be able to do so as well.

These choices reflect a wide breadth of styles (with, perhaps, a noticeable emphasis on lager). They are also deeply personal and speak to cherished memories: visits to subterranean lager cellars in the Czech Republic, or halcyon days spent in pubs in Lewes, Manchester, and London. This is by no means a conclusive or objective list of the best beers out there, but it is mine, and I hope it speaks to you, too.

Alvinne
Wild West

6% Flemish Fruit Sour Ale

Moen, Belgium

For a brewery that's headquartered in Belgium, Brouwerij Alvinne, founded in 2004, has a surprisingly Gallic sensibility. Take its house mixed culture, Morpheus, used to brew both clean and sour beers. A mix of two yeast strains as well as *Lactobacillus* (which is 'deactivated' when brewing non-sour beers), it was captured from the Auvergne region of central France in 2008 by Marc De Keukeleire, who handles yeast management for the brewery, before being selected, isolated and cultivated. Then there are the brewery's barrels, which number around 75. 'We consider the wood the barrel is made from to be an active ingredient in our beer,' Alvinne notes on its website. Many of those ex-wine barrels come with French pedigree, to the tune of Sauternes and Pomerol, Banyuls and Calvados.

I think it's fitting that Alvinne's culture is named after the Greek god of dreams. There is a slightly fantastical delight to beers like Wild West. The barrel-aged version of the brewery's Omega, a pale sour session beer, Wild West evolves from batch to batch, but it is always elegant, with oak-derived character and a rewarding complexity that benefits from long periods of cellar ageing.

Recently, I was lucky enough to try a fruited version of Wild West, which uses the same Omega base but ages it in foeders rather than barrels, and then leaves it to macerate with fresh cherries and raspberries. The result is a beer that pours a luminous coral, with a fluffy, pink head that soon melts away. Candied notes of red fruit pop on the nose, but they're undergirded by a potently sour base, whose touch of acetic acid lends the beer a real kick. The stuff of dreams? Most assuredly.

| **Claire Bullen**

Augustiner
Lagerbier Hell

5.2% Helles

Munich, Germany

How do you make one of the world's best lagers? In the case of Augustiner, the combination of centuries of tradition, access to prime Bavarian ingredients, a long secondary fermentation, and the refusal to mess with a good thing (or the strictures of the Reinheitsgebot) have all played their part in making its Lagerbier Hell an icon of German brewing.

Augustiner's roots go back to the 14th century, when it was founded as the on-site brewery of Munich's Augustinian Abbey. The 19th century saw the brewhouse industrialise, and while Augustiner wasn't the first Bavarian brewery to produce the luminous Helles lager style made possible by new technical innovations – that was Spaten, in 1894 – it remains one of only six Munich breweries to participate in the city's main Oktoberfest celebrations at Theresienwiese each year, and is the only one to exclusively tap its beers from wooden barrels on the festival grounds.

Whether you drink it straight from the barrel or poured crystalline from the bottle, Augustiner Lagerbier Hell is a masterclass in balance and poise. For all that this flagship beer can be an easy pleasure during social occasions, or a thirst-slaking refresher on sultry summer days, its seeming simplicity is belied by the nuance that's revealed on closer inspection. There is that suggestion of white flowers and citrus on the nose (courtesy of the local Hallertau hops), and the house-malted grain's supple sweetness, like warmed sugar just starting to turn to caramel at the bottom of a saucepan, though it is never sticky or saccharine. Instead, a bright, lemony acidity keeps things fresh, and lifts the beer's bready heft, before it finishes dry with a glancing bitterness – just enough to make the next sip essential. It's impossible to drink it without feeling that unmistakable swell of *Gemütlichkeit*.

Ayinger
Celebrator

6.7% Doppelbock

Aying, Germany

Every spring, Starkbierfest (Strong Beer Fest) comes to Munich. Unlike the annual Oktoberfest frenzy, the crowds at Starkbierfest are typically smaller, and primarily composed of locals. And unlike the golden Festbiers that are poured every autumn, here, one style dominates: Doppelbock.

Doppelbock – literally, double bock – is a malt-forward, brooding, and yes, strong beer. The style was historically brewed to be rich and hearty, a 'liquid bread' substitute meant to sustain monks during their Lenten fasts (or to supplement their vegetarian diets, depending on who you ask). As a holdover from that history, most Doppelbock names today still end in '-ator', after the first example of the style: Paulaner's 18th-century Salvator, or 'Saviour'. While monastic tradition is no longer its animating force, Doppelbock has instead become an annual springtime signifier, labels typically adorned with gambolling billy goats (and, in the case of Ayinger Celebrator, the addition of a plastic goat pendant that hangs like a charm from the bottleneck).

Ayinger, among Bavaria's cohort of classic, centuries-old breweries, makes one of the most emblematic and beloved examples of the style. Its Celebrator is a ravishing beer, a deep cocoa brown in the glass but ruby red when held up against the light. It is full-bodied, its warm yeast profile mingling with an initial creamy, coffee-like sweetness and notes of raisin and spiced fruits, before it descends into a subterranean, roasty profundity. True to style, hop aromatics are virtually undetectable on the nose, though the gentle, balancing bitterness prevents Celebrator from ever feeling sticky or cloying. It's almost too easy to pour a maß down your throat. Then there's the warm flush of its alcoholic strength, which makes it an ideal candidate for those early spring days that are still frosted with winter's unwelcome hangover.

Beak Brewery
Parade IPA

6%   IPA

Lewes, East Sussex

To say that Beak Brewery's setting is dramatic would be putting it mildly. The brewery – founded by journalist Danny Tapper in 2016 as a nomadic project, and which settled permanently in Lewes in 2020 – is overshadowed by a soaring chalk cliff. Sitting at one of the folding tables outside offers the ideal vantage to watch gulls circle and the rare peregrine falcon plunge after them; stay long enough and you can see the chalk turn roseate in the fading light.

Yet for all that grandeur, Beak has a friendly, even humble ethos, conveyed via its inviting, primary-coloured labels and vision of itself as a 'neighbourhood brewery'. It brews on a 15-barrel kit and has recently started a wild fermentation project inspired by the surrounding South Downs countryside.

How lucky for Beak's neighbours to live near such a brewery, one that indulges its creative yen with a continuous stream of one-off releases, but which balances that with a core range that favours exceptional hoppy styles. A highlight is Parade IPA: made with Citra, Mosaic, and Idaho 7 hops, and fermented with London Fog yeast, it is juicy with notes of melon, bubblegum, and mango, full-bodied with a touch of sweetness, but never unbalanced.

Though Parade began life as one of the first beers Tapper tinkered with in Beak's early days, he credits head brewer Robin Head-Fourman with refining its recipe. 'Some of the biggest changes include the addition of more protein-rich grains to beef up the mouthfeel, and the inclusion of Idaho 7, which really makes the hop profile sing with lovely pineapple-like flavours,' Tapper says. 'We think Parade perfectly represents the kind of Pales and IPAs we enjoy brewing and drinking here at Beak: thick and aromatic with lots of juicy acidity but with plenty of bitterness and a little minerality.'

Boxcar
Dark Mild

3.6% Dark Mild

London, England

Boxcar's founder and head brewer Sam Dickison thinks of Dark Mild nostalgically, and creating his own began as a sentimental project. 'It started with me having a memory of some Dark Milds on cask I had years before, so probably very dreamlike and not what they actually tasted like, and then I went to the Great British Beer Festival one year to exclusively drink Dark Milds,' Dickison says. 'That was the research. Every batch has been adjusted since I first brewed it in 2018 [...] It became the core range mainly through everyone telling us it should be core range. If people want Mild, we'll give them Mild.'

These days, more and more do. Dickinson was years ahead of the present Dark Mild revival, and his interest looks prescient in hindsight; it's only surprising it took so long for other modern brewers and drinkers to catch on. After all, Dark Mild has a real utility. It is a style for those who prize darker malts as well as sessionability, who seek flavourful beer that can be drunk by the pint without collateral damage. It is light on its feet, free of a Stout's burly roastiness or an American Porter's bombastic hopping. Instead, there is just that unfurled, velvet splendour of the malt, which hints at cocoa and cream.

Against the light, this Dark Mild's opacity is revealed to be a mirage, glimmers of garnet beaming through the glass. On the nose there is a subtle perfume of chocolate and vanilla, and while those elements carry through to the palate, it's never close to cloying. Instead, a tartness like crushed raspberries underlies the coffee and caramel of the malt, and its dry finish and moderate carbonation make it a candidate for gulping.

| **Claire Bullen**

Braybrooke
Keller Lager

4.8% Kellerbier

Market Harborough, Leicestershire

In some ways, Braybrooke Beer Co is a curious outlier, a lager-centric brewery that appears to have been neatly sawed out of Bavaria and deposited in a quiet tract of Leicestershire countryside. It imports its malt, its hops, and even its yeast from Germany, and is dogmatic about traditional processes – most of its beers are decocted, undergo a minimum 30-day secondary fermentation, and are unfined and unfiltered. And yet the brewery has also proven itself willing to experiment and explore, as evidenced by limited-edition beers like its Cold Brew Lager and New Zealand Pilsner. Its sleek labels and culinary focus – its sister business is London restaurant 10 Greek Street – evince its savviness, and distinct approach.

It is Keller Lager, the brewery's flagship, that embodies its more traditional side. The beer is modelled after Franconia's Kellerbier, or 'cellar beer'. Unfiltered, russet-hued, and traditionally served straight from the wooden casks they were aged in, these lagers are notably malt- and yeast-forward, with just enough hopping to balance out that richness. True to form, this beer – devised after its founders' visits to Bamberg – has notes of toffee and a complex, estery nose that, in a recent pour, reminded me of roses. And yet its pleasingly dry and spicy finish, courtesy of Tettnang hops, adds balance; far from a sticky caramel-bomb, Keller Lager is a versatile everyday beer, designed to go on dinner tables.

'I like the fact that although Keller Lager does use quite a lot of hops this is a beer that is all about the malt, and the balance between the Pilsner and Munich malts we get from Bamber Malzerei,' says co-founder Nick Trower. 'I feel like the importance of malt in the final flavour of a beer is gaining traction again after so many years of being overlooked in favour of hops.'

Cantillon
Fou'Foune

6% Fruit Lambic

Brussels, Belgium

Cantillon is a survivor. Founded over 100 years ago, it managed to hang on during the trials and tribulations of the 20th century – war, conflict, changing social mores and tastes, brewery consolidations – and is today the only traditional Lambic and Gueuze brewery and blendery that remains within Brussels' city limits. Despite the adept way it has navigated those fluxes, the brewery itself has changed little in decades; much of its older equipment is still on display, its beers still broadly made according to long-established precedent, the coolship in its attic like some high altar.

There have been some evolutions, though. In 1999 the brewery switched to using primarily organic ingredients; later, it replaced its older barrels. Around the same time, the first vintage of Fou'Foune – now Cantillon's third-most-popular fruit Lambic after its Kriek and Rosé de Gambrinus – was made with a large shipment of apricots gifted by a farmer whose nickname was Fou'Foune. More recently, current owner Jean Van Roy took over from his father, Jean-Pierre Van Roy, and the beers have continued to shapeshift under his stewardship and palate.

Fou'Foune is made just once per year, a blend of 18-20-month-old Lambics and those juicy, sweet-tart Bergeron apricots, the first beer to kick off the bottling season every August. Those apricots are added at a ratio of 300g per litre, and though the Lambic rests on the fruit for only five weeks – relatively short in the timescale of fruit Lambic – it is enough for the stone fruit to impart their musky and floral fragrance to this symphonic beer. When Fou'Foune is fresh, those apricots feel close at hand, still sunny and ripening in your glass. With time, they recede into the background, leaving the beer's puckering, living, resplendent complexity to shine.

| **Claire Bullen**

Chimay
Blue

9% Belgian Strong Dark Ale

Chimay, Belgium

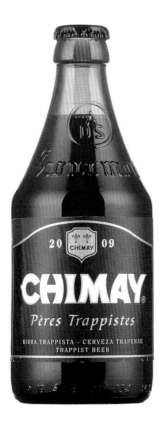

Chimay is one of just three Trappist breweries – alongside Rochefort and Orval – in Wallonia, Belgium's French-speaking region. Located at the Abbey of Notre Dame de Scourmont since 1862, the brewery was later modernised by Father Théodore (in collaboration with Belgian brewing scientist Jean De Clerck, who was called in to fix its persistent production problems and upgrade its set-up). Together, they isolated the yeast strain in 1948 that would come to define all of the brewery's future beers. And then they had a second stroke of genius: devising the beer that would become Chimay Bleue, or Chimay Blue.

Chimay Blue was first released in 1954 as a 'Spéciale Nöel' Christmas beer. It soon became one of the brewery's core releases, the strongest and darkest beer that it makes, and the candidate that's most suitable for ageing (the brewery recommends it be cellared for up to five years). Chimay Blue is also renamed Grand Réserve when it is sold in 750ml bottles and larger-format releases, making it a popular option around the holidays.

That's fair enough, as it's hard to think of a better winter warmer than this. It pours a slightly hazy dark brown that's revealed to be ruby in direct light, with a tight, light-brown head. The nose is redolent of toffee, dried fruit, and yeast-derived phenols and notes of sweet baking spices. A swirl of the glass reveals a sudden whiff of banana bread.

On the palate, those toffee notes deepen to burnished bronze. Disrupting the sweetness, however, is a reasonably high level of carbonation, which gives this beer a surprising lightness. Adding to the drinkability is a moderate but distinct bitter finish, which balances its spice-cake notes and makes taking another sip a welcome, even necessary, proposition.

Cvikov
Hvozd 11°

4.5%   Pale Lager

Cvikov, Czech Republic

Pivovar Cvikov – located near the Czech Republic's northern border with Germany, in the foothills of the Lusatian Mountains – has history running through its faucets, and not just because its story goes back to 1560. Its more recent past is defined by 20th-century upheaval, a brewery nationalised and then dismantled, the copper kettles hauled out for scrap and the buildings repurposed for a discotheque, a furniture bazaar, a vegetable warehouse.

It was only in 2013 that the site was purchased, renovated, and once again turned into a working brewery, complete with the traditional open fermenters and horizontal lagering tanks in their frozen cellars. And while it has an undeniable slickness now, Cvikov hasn't strayed from Bohemian tradition when it comes to its beers. (On a recent visit to the brewhouse, I noticed a small photograph tacked to a wooden beam: there was former Czech President Václav Havel in his youth, hauling a sack of malt over his shoulder.)

All of Cvikov's beers are exceptional, but the Hvozd 11° was the one I found myself returning to again and again. That drinkability is by design: though it is just 4.5% ABV, this golden, lightly hazy lager brims with Pilsner malt character, and tastes like a piece of toast slathered with a thick pat of butter and topped with a drizzle of honey. Underpinning that bounty is a fierce little rip of bitterness that follows each mouthful and lingers pleasantly on the tongue, an anchor for the sweetness and the secret weapon that makes this beer so moreish. Only it isn't courtesy of the expected Saaz hops – instead, it's thanks to the Premiant hop, a Czech cultivar first developed in 1996, and an example of the more modern aspects of the brewery's approach.

DEYA
Steady Rolling Man

5.2%   American Pale Ale

Cheltenham, Gloucestershire

'I am a steady rollin' man / And I roll both night and day,' sings blues legend Robert Johnson in his 1937 song, 'Steady Rollin' Man'. That pace was certainly true of the Cheltenham-based DEYA Brewing Company's early days. As founder Theo Freyne describes it, the business's beginning, when it was still a cuckoo brewery, was defined by hard graft, of brewing the same recipe over and over, soundtracked by blues songs, hoping to get closer with each batch to the ideal posed by the American Pale Ales that Freyne had tasted overseas.

For 18 months, Steady Rolling Man – which depicts a figure who resembles Johnson on its label, itself resembling the sleeve of an old blues record – was the only beer DEYA made, the recipe changing as it was able to access new hops and move to its current brick-and-mortar location. Today, it is the brewery's flagship, accounts for 50% of its production, and has become an undisputed modern classic. I'd argue it's the best American-style Pale Ale being made in the UK right now.

'I think it has a wide and crossover appeal which makes it very popular,' says Freyne. 'If you are a beer geek or someone just looking for a refreshing pint, it ticks the box.'

Made with a hop bill of Mosaic, Amarillo, Ekuanot, and El Dorado, Steady Rolling Man is perfectly pitched between juiciness and dankness, a citrus brightness and a subtly savoury bass note. It pours the colour of sun and is crowned with a jolly cap of foam; it manages to be both pillowy soft but exuberantly refreshing. 'Our house style is soft, hoppy beers,' says Freyne. 'We really look for clarity of flavour, drinkability, and expressing ingredients as best as possible.'

Donzoko
Big Foam

5%   Rustic Lager

Leith, Scotland

It took Reece Hugill – the founder of Donzoko Brewing Company, formerly based in Hartlepool and now headquartered in Leith, Edinburgh – several years to perfect the recipe of his Northern Helles, the brewery's flagship lager and a love letter to traditional Bavarian brewing. Big Foam, by contrast, was all about verve, experimentation, and deviating from classical perfection in favour of something altogether less-charted.

'As I became more confident as a brewer, brewing batch after batch of Helles, I developed my own tastes for slightly zingy, hopped-up lagers, unfiltered and a bit more rustic,' says Hugill. 'More loosely Franconia-style than Munich, but very much its own thing.'

Big Foam really is a singular lager, and not just because of its looks. (True to name, a careful pour will yield a glorious, snowy mountain of foam atop the glass, with long-lasting retention.) Big Foam's German inspiration aside, the beer also pays tribute to Hugill's home of north-east England. 'The area where I grew up, Teesside, is known for pouring cask beer with huge heads called "bankers." I used this as inspiration and tried to make the foamiest beer possible, with the most Donzoko character I could in it.'

That Donzoko character, as Hugill describes it, is zippy, acidified with a house lactic-acid culture and garlanded in 'tonnes of high-quality German hops direct from a single farm.' The malt bill is bready and rustic with spelt, and the body pleasingly full and hazy. Those elements give the beer its own flavour narrative: first there's lemon up front, and biscuity grain, followed by a bite of acidity giving way to a jubilant hop character that's abundant in soft peach and vinous notes. Each step is distinct, but the resulting impression is harmonious. Or, as Hugill puts it, there's 'a lot of taste under the hood.'

Duration
Bet the Farm

4.5%   Continental Pale Ale

King's Lynn, Norfolk

Duration Brewing's co-founders, Derek Bates and Miranda Hudson, knew they had to leave London to establish the 'progressive farm brewery' of their imaginings. They found its home in northern Norfolk, after locating a rural idyll: a ruined, Grade II-listed barn with its own water source and direct access to region's fields of barley and farms.

After a multi-year build-out, the brewery now feels fully of its place. The same could be said of its beers. Bates wanted to make beers that pushed boundaries and used unorthodox ingredients (past releases have included a purple carrot Saison, as well as an 'agricultural IPA' made with Norfolk honey and spelt malt) rather than exist within the strictures of 'IPA monoculture', as he puts it.

Bet the Farm feels emblematic of this approach. This 'Continental Pale Ale' is its own animal, alive and resistant to the strictures of style. It is co-pitched with various yeast strains, and there are playful esters on its nose that evoke Belgian Saisons. But the beer is also sharp as a blade, dry as a bone, with a vivid pepperiness, and a lingering bitter finish. That bracing character is both a contrast to and complemented by its soft citrus and floral notes, and makes Bet the Farm as thought-provoking as it is easy-drinking. (The brewery also makes a foeder-aged version of the beer, which deepens its mingled elegance and rusticity.)

'Here's this duality,' says Bates. 'Sniff, swirl, drink ... or just enjoy it as you like next to the grill, on the beach, at the pub. [And then] here's the same beer, aged over a year in foeder. [That's] how it reflects our ethos, just keeping tradition alive in both the conviviality of a day-to-day beer while also driving forth our interpretation of the more funky side of farmhouse brewing.'

Fantôme
Saison

8%   Saison

Soy, Belgium

Since its founding in 1988 by brewer Dany Prignon and his father, Brasserie Fantôme has always retained a baseline mystery. Much like the smiling ghost that adorns its labels, the brewery is at heart elusive, undefinable. Part of that is due to its remote location in the village of Soy, deep in the countryside of Belgium's Luxembourg province. Part of that is its refusal to stick to strict style limits, and the variability of its recipes. And part of that is attributable to Prignon himself, who is aloof about his methods and his ingredients (and who has claimed in past interviews that he's not even much of a beer drinker himself).

If Brasserie Fantôme has a mission statement, it is to celebrate its land, its place, and its community – Prignon was employed in local tourism services before founding the brewery. Visit the brewhouse and you'll see an idiosyncratic set-up, equipment old and patched (some of which was sourced from Brasserie d'Achouffe), schedules and approaches down to Prignon's rhythms. For all that Prignon and Fantôme seem to exist outside of the mainstream of the Belgian brewing scene, however, the brewery has earned cult-favourite status internationally. That's fed the legend of Fantôme, even while – as Prignon ages – there's some uncertainty about the brewery's future ownership and plans.

No batch of Fantôme's Saison is the same, but the bottle I have on hand is full of personality and quirk, evidence of Prignon's hand at work. Rich, toasty grain and an impression of fruity sweetness is followed by a generous quantity of farmyard funk. There's a subtle anise character that leads into a finishing, bitter astringency that dries out the mouth. In lieu of predictable, it is variable, distinct, and fully alive.

Fierce
Very Big Moose

12% Imperial Stout

Aberdeen, Scotland

I was not expecting a great deal the first time I was handed a glass of Fierce Brewing's Very Big Moose Stout. It was nothing against the brewery; it's just that boozy Pastry Stouts are rarely what I prefer to drink. I realised my mistake immediately, however, upon bringing the glass to my nose. Its aroma was abundant with vanilla – not the saccharine flavouring used in cheap ice cream, but real vanilla, as if I were holding cured vanilla pods in my hands, woody and musky and potent as perfume. Then there was the beer itself: black as oil, fathoms deep, and not at all the one-dimensional, sweet-tooth-baiting dessert beer I feared it might be.

Oil is fitting. Fierce Brewing hails from Aberdeen, and its co-founders Dave Grant and Dave McHardy were both employed in the city's oil and gas industry. Nurturing separate interests in homebrewing, and following a chance meeting, they decided to join forces and founded Fierce Brewing in 2015. Since then, Fierce has grown in leaps and bounds. Following two rounds of crowdfunding, locations in Edinburgh and Manchester, and now a sprawling new Aberdeen site, the brewery is living out its ambition.

With the theme of expansion in mind, Very Big Moose's brand family today includes a version aged in bourbon barrels, as well as editions dosed with coconut, tonka, maple, and more. But it's the original I find myself returning to, entranced as ever by that nose, the richness it promises, and its just-sweet-enough depths. 'We are all about full-on flavour,' says Grant. 'We called our brewery Fierce to reflect that, as we hate trying something that should be amazing, but fails to deliver. VBM is a perfect example of this: balanced, but full of flavour.'

Hof ten Dormaal
Zure Van Tildonk

6% Belgian Sour Ale

Tildonk, Belgium

Hof ten Dormaal is as much a farm as it is a brewery. Located amidst the lush, green countryside outside of Leuven, the business was taken over by the Janssens family in 2009, after father André – formerly an accountant – decided he needed a change of pace. His wife and two sons followed, and by 2011 they were brewing on site.

Hof ten Dormaal is unique among Belgian breweries in the depth of its relationship to its land. It doesn't just grow its own barley, but also wheat, spelt, rye, and oats. It doesn't only cultivate its own hops, but also harvests its wild yeast in open containers set among its fields. It doesn't just raise chicken, horses, and other farm animals (to whom it feeds its spent grain, in true closed-loop fashion), but also produces an array of exceptional beers, from Lambics macerated on its homegrown fruit and wine grapes to IPAs, Saisons, and beers made with its own fresh hops. Despite suffering a devastating fire in 2015, the brewery has since rebounded with an upgraded kit, seven fermentation vessels, a bottling line, a coolship, and an impressive collection of barrels.

Of all its releases, Zure van Tildonk – literally, 'Sour of Tildonk' – is my favourite. The wort is inoculated with local microflora in the coolship before maturing in oak barrels; the finished beer is a blend of six-month-old, 18-month-old, and three-year-old Lambics. That rustic, farmyard-like yeast character is evident on the nose, as well as on the palate, but this is not a simplistic funk bomb. Instead, that aspect gives way to a biscuity and toasty malt presence before finishing dry. It's a beer that full-throatedly sings of its place, and of all the humans and creatures, both great and small, that came together to make it.

J.W. Lees
Harvest Ale

11.5% Barley Wine

Manchester, England

Since 1986, J.W. Lees has brewed its Harvest Ale: a magnificent, mahogany-hued Barley Wine, made with the late summer's new hops and barley. In its early years, Harvest Ale was an experiment, a whimsical attempt to make a premium, high-strength beer that fitted a little unevenly among the rest of the brewery's output, including its cask Bitters and Pale Ales. But in recent years, as new generations of drinkers have discovered Harvest Ale, it's become a cult classic, a seasonal signifier, and a shapeshifter whose annual variations have made it an ideal candidate for vertical tastings.

For a beer that is notably changeable, Harvest Ale is surprisingly consistent in its production: each year it is made according to the same processes, the same handed-down recipe, and the same house yeast. The brewery attributes the variation among vintages to year-to-year fluctuations in the beer's raw materials; it also produces the occasional special edition aged in ex-spirit barrels.

While a single bottle of Harvest Ale is always a pleasure on its own, the beer really benefits from a comparative context, and so I recently tasted a 2015, a 2017, and a 2020 side by side. The 2015 was the most nuanced of the lot, woody and deep, with an oxidative note of sherry-soaked raisins and a hint of burnt toffee like the top of a flan. Despite being only two years younger, the 2017 was surprisingly less developed: it was sweetly brown-sugared, with notes of baking spice, but not overly complex. In the 2020, toasty notes of barley were more detectable on the palate, and there was an anise-like freshness. I could almost taste the beer's future nested within it, and all the ways it would evolve in the coming years.

The Kernel
Bière de Saison

4.4–5.4% *Various ABVs*   Saison

London, England

The Kernel is not a brewery that is interested in uniformity or replicability. In lieu of a static core range, The Kernel has, since its 2009 founding, varied its recipes from batch to batch. Yes, it consistently makes Pale Ales and IPAs, but every edition has a new hop bill, a distinct sensibility; they feel almost like vintages, changing with environmental conditions and the makers' whims. As the brewery has expanded to new styles and new formats, that mentality of mutability and exploration has persisted.

Bière de Saison is one example of this approach, less a constrained style than a broad category or family of beers. The brewery first began accumulating barrels in 2012 and released its first Bière de Saison in 2013. It has since amassed a collection of 70 ex-wine and -spirit barrels of varying sizes, as well as two 50-hl foeders.

'Each blend will be unique enough to in some ways be its own beer,' says founder Evin O'Riordain. 'Fruit will vary from farm to farm and harvest to harvest; we wilfully change certain parts of the beers' recipe (e.g., hops); some beers that are not brewed to be a Bière de Saison are also aged and fermented in wood that contained our Saisons and can end up becoming part of that family, like Foeder Beer and Foeder Lager.'

What unites (most of) The Kernel's Bières de Saison is the brewery's house mixed culture. Otherwise, past editions have featured differing single hop varieties, and many have also included fruits sourced from various local farms, from quinces to Bergeron apricots, damsons to crab apples. But my favourite is the sour cherry version, whose nose mingles jammy, floral opulence with a classic dose of farmyard rusticity, and whose Lambic-like tartness, and drying finish, dance alongside almandine cherry-stone notes.

Kutná Hora
Zlatá 12°

4.9%   Pale Lager

Kutná Hora, Czech Republic

The southern Bohemian town of Kutná Hora may be a UNESCO World Heritage Site – it was home to a thriving, medieval silver-mining industry, and is now known for its cathedrals and its ossuaries – but its local brewery wasn't always so protected. Instead, like so many others in the Czech Republic, it was nationalised in the 1950s; later, it was purchased by Heineken and then dismantled, the old brew kit torn out of its holdings and hauled away. It was only in 2016 that it was rebuilt, following a local outcry and various boycotts and campaigns.

If its recent guise is still shiny and new, however, Kutná Hora's approach to brewing is studied and time-tested, the result of handed-down recipes and a dedication to using all-Czech ingredients. As head brewer Jakub Hájek notes, the brewery works to do things properly when making its classic lagers: it double-decocts its beers, employs Moravian-grown malt and favours local hop varieties like Saaz and Sládek, profits from its water source, and leaves its beers to open-ferment, their krausens snowcapped and billowy.

All that work requires patience, no less because the beers spend some two months slumbering in the chilled horizontal lagering tanks in the cellars. But that time investment is worth it if lagers like Zlatá 12° are the result. The brewery's flagship, this Světlý Ležák is everything you'd wish for from the style: a bedrock of caramel-toned, bready malt, a whisper of diacetyl, and hop notes that add a herbal character and a floral touch, as well as a drying bitterness that counterbalances the malt. It's an elegant but abundant beer, one that was made for drinking in bounteous quantities. If you can have it straight from the tank in those ice-cold cellars, there are few better pints on earth.

Left Hand
Nitro Milk Stout

6%   Milk Stout

Longmont, Colorado

Long before there were Pastry Stouts dosed with caramel, made with brownies, and flavoured with nut brittle and gingerbread and toffee and vanilla, there was Left Hand Brewing's creamy, lightly sweet, and roasty Milk Stout.

The Colorado brewery launched the beer in 2001 as a seasonal draft offering, back when adding lactose to Stout was still a novelty for US drinkers. 'It was inspired by a trip to Africa by Dick Doore, one of our founders,' says Chris Lennert, Left Hand's COO. 'He tried Castle Milk Stout and loved it. When we introduced it in the US there were only two other breweries doing a Milk Stout.'

Later, the beer moved into 22-oz bombers, and then into six-packs. In 2011 Left Hand unveiled Nitro Milk Stout at the Great American Beer Festival, becoming the first craft brewery to sell a bottled nitrogenated beer sans plastic widget. After just a few short months, Nitro Milk Stout eclipsed the original Milk Stout, and is now the brewery's number-one seller. Today, it also comes in cans, and drinkers are instructed to upend and 'pour hard' into a glass to achieve those cascading billows of creamy foam. (Those cans also come inscribed with a telling plaudit: 'America's Favourite Stout'.)

Tasting Milk Stout in 2022 feels a bit like opening a time portal. It's admittedly hard to imagine a new craft brewery making a Stout its flagship these days, and I'm struck by how balanced, and even drying, it tastes. There's sweet cream at the front, the nitrogenated head smooth as silk, and notes of deep, burnished coffee and cocoa, all of which is followed by a tempering, roasty bitterness. For palates that have sweetened and slackened with all those dessert Stouts in the ensuing years, it feels like a welcome homecoming.

Marble
Manchester Bitter

4.2%   Best Bitter

Manchester, England

There are few more atmospheric places to drink in the world than the Marble Arch Inn in Manchester, on the edge of the Northern Quarter. With its famously sloping, mosaic floors, its vaulted ceilings and its pints of cask, the place is delightfully wonky, and perfectly snug when the skies open, as they so often do here. But while the Arch's looks are squarely out of the 19th century, and speak to an aspect of the city that is fading away with every new highrise that goes up, its status as Marble Brewery's birthplace has vested the pub with a present-tense vitality.

Much of Marble's output includes experimental twists on older formats – take its Earl Grey IPA, or its recent barrel-aged Stout, flavoured with pineapple, cacao, and açai – but its core-range stalwart Manchester Bitter sees the brewery at its most traditional. Inspired by Boddingtons – Manchester's 'fondly remembered original', as the can puts it – this Bitter is lightly hazy and notably golden, in contrast to the amber-hued Bitters you're likely to find down south. And whereas those beers often have the toffee and dried fruit notes to match their deeper shade, Manchester Bitter is brazenly, well, bitter, racy and acerbic, powered by its hop character.

Don't think Manchester Bitter too austere, though; it is not without its pleasures, its softer side. Alongside the malt's robust base, there is a very slight suggestion of sweetness, while the hop aromatics – courtesy of New World varieties like Cascade and Ekuanot – skate across lemon zest and towards white flowers. That fresh breeze gives the beer levity, enough to balance that anchoring bitterness.

A final recommendation: if you've already had it from a can, it's worth making a pilgrimage to the Arch to try Manchester Bitter on cask – sparkled, of course.

New Belgium Brewing
La Folie

7% Flanders-Style Sour Brown Ale

Fort Collins, Colorado

New Belgium's Foeder Forest makes a striking, even intimidating first impression. In the massive, cathedral-like space, dozens and dozens of towering oak foeders of various sizes and origins stand in marching order, like thick, squat tree trunks. (They are a favourite vessel of brewers who specialise in wild and mixed-fermentation beers, and are commonly used in winemaking.)

The Foeder Forest is unique among US breweries in terms of its scale and influence. That's no surprise, given it was first established by New Belgium's now-former brewmaster Peter Bouckaert, who previously built his career at Belgium's Rodenbach (itself in possession of a famous foeder collection). As the wood cellar director and blender Lauren Woods Limbach has described, each foeder is a unique character and has its own colony of microflora, its own flavours and traits that it imparts to the beers that rest within. Managing those many colonies, blending batches, and dialling in balance takes a savant's palate. La Folie, New Belgium's Flanders-style Sour Brown Ale, was birthed from this forest, from those expert palates, and from that vast terrain of oak. As the brewery notes, it is the product of America's oldest continuing sour culture.

While 'La Folie', means 'eccentric madness', this beer is really an example of masterful precision, and is best met in a contemplative frame. An initial impression of an almost molasses-like malt character is followed by warm, woody notes, and then a telltale funk. La Folie is a blend of one- and three-year-old base beers aged in various foeders, and it maintains a careful accord between that bready, sweet malt, those yeast-derived aromatics, and a persistent tartness. I like to think of it as a study in time and materiality, of bacteria and yeast's quiet, invisible work.

Pilsner Urquell
Pilsner Urquell

4.4%   Pale Lager

Pilsen, Czech Republic

Icon, legend, idol. Font of inspiration for brewers the world over, cherished by drinkers both Czech and international, and harbinger of a revolutionary new style of brewing. It's hard to overstate the enormity of Pilsner Urquell's influence, as well as its resulting

legacy. When it was brewed by Josef Groll in 1842 at the Citizen's Brewery of Plzeň, Pilsner Urquell became the world's first pale lager. Every other glass of golden, crisp, refreshing, foamy-headed lager you've had since then is its direct descendant – and given that some 95% of beer drunk globally is pale lager, it's not hyperbole to say that the beer's arrival amounted to no less than a sea change in brewing, one that has shown no sign of abating for 180 years.

Today, Pilsner Urquell is still brewed at its original brewery in Pilsen, using 100% Moravian malt, Saaz hops, and local water. It is triple-decocted, open-fermented, and aged in wooden lagering barrels. It is a marvel of time and history that still exists, joyously, in the present day.

If you can find it, the best way to savour this beer is in its tankovna form – unpasteurised, shipped fresh in copper tanks directly from Pilsen, and then poured from a 'side-pull' Lukr faucet. (You know your mug of Pilsner Urquell has been poured correctly when it looks like beer's Platonic ideal, bright and golden and topped with a generous inch – or several – of creamy foam.) Bring it to your nose to be greeted by its perfume of toasty, sweet malt, and just enough diacetyl so it smells almost uncannily like butterscotch. There is that cream and caramel on the palate, though the walloping bitterness of the Saaz hops cuts through all that like a blade, leaving behind only the urgent need to return for one more mouthful – and then another.

Põhjala
Öö

10.5% Imperial Baltic Porter

Tallinn, Estonia

Põhjala Brewery is an outlier in its native Estonia, the rare craft brewery in the wider Baltic region whose capacity has more than quadrupled since its founding, and which now fills out a 50-hl brewhouse. It has become an unignorable presence, the host of the annual Tallinn Craft Beer Weekend, and the brewery that put Estonia on the map for scores of international drinkers.

Põhjala was established by four local beer lovers – Peeter Keek, Tiit Paananen, Enn Parel, and Gren Noormets – in 2011. Its head brewer is the Scottish-born Chris Pilkington, who fell for Põhjala's mission when the founders made a visit to Scotland, and who joined in 2013. Initially situated in Tallinn's Nõmme district, just across from a forest, the brewery relocated to a sprawling new space in the Noblesser area (a former shipyard), directly overlooking the Baltic Sea. Nature is close at hand here, and in lines like its Forest Series, Põhjala makes creative use of Estonian ingredients – juniper berries and birch syrup, porcini mushrooms and rowan berries, lingonberries and heather tips.

If one thing has held steady since Põhjala's founding more than a decade ago, however, it's Öö: the brewery's Imperial Baltic Porter, and the first beer it ever produced. In Estonian, its name translates to 'night', and there is something deeply slumbrous about its inky depths and its 10.5% strength. On the nose there is a whisper of smoke, like a far-off bonfire whose scent carries on the cold night air, as well as a rich, chocolate profile. It is gorgeous and velveteen, full-bodied and viscous. There is still freshness, though: I detected a tart note of raspberry and redcurrant amidst the sweet roastiness, and if you hold the glass up to a flickering candle, you'll see a glowing, ruby transparency at its edges.

Queer Brewing
Flowers

4%   Witbier

London, England

As Queer Brewing's founder Lily Waite notes, it's not every day that a new brewery launches with a Witbier in its core range. Witbiers are mainly thought of as seasonals, she says, good for hot weather but not necessarily a style most drinkers innately reach for.

Why, then, did Queer Brewing make a core-range Witbier? Because of what Waite sees as the style's special ability to convert new beer drinkers, and appeal to a wide range of people and palates. '[W]e want to be able to present our beers to a broad spectrum of different people. Some of those people, inevitably, may not like beer – or what they see beer as, in a common, one-dimensional misconception of the flavours beer can offer – at all, and some may only like certain styles such as lager or pale ale,' Waite says on the Queer Brewing website. 'I believe that the low bitterness, bouquet of fruit, and light crispness present within Witbier can offer something different to those for whom beer isn't their favourite, or for whom beer hasn't yet presented the right combination of flavours.'

That emphasis on inclusion and accessibility is admirable, and it's true that Flowers is a deeply likeable, and drinkable, take on the style. Inspired in part by the seminal Allagash White, the hazy, sunny-hued beer has juicy tangerine on the nose, as well as yeasty notes of clove and foam banana, and a little green-pepper zing that becomes more prominent as it warms. Made with Saaz and Tettnang hops, and featuring the to-style additions of curaçao orange peel and coriander seeds, Flowers is soft, bright, herbal, and, yes, floral. It certainly would be an ideal choice for a balmy July day in the park, but, as Waite points out, it's also a beer to be enjoyed all year long.

Saint Mars of the Desert
Jack D'Or

6.5% *ABV varies*   Saison

Sheffield, South Yorkshire

It's the rare brewery that has its own patron saint, but Saint Mars of the Desert is far from typical. That 'small god' is Jack D'Or, a deity who happens to be an extravagantly moustachioed, golden grain of barley, and who gives his name to the brewery's flagship Saison.

The legend of Jack D'Or began years ago, when SMOD's co-founders, husband-and-wife team Dann Paquette and Martha Simpson-Holley, lived in Paquette's native Massachusetts, where they ran the nomadic brewery Pretty Things. The first batch was inspired by the Saisons of Wallonia. 'Martha and I love the "otherness" of these simple beers, and wanted to capture that in our own way,' says Paquette. But the couple had never given up on their dream of opening their own small brewery, and eventually they left the States behind and put down roots in Sheffield.

British drinkers are lucky that Jack D'Or has since pulled a Lazarus here (despite the fact that Paquette and Simpson-Holley held a mock funeral for him shortly before leaving Massachusetts in 2015), albeit in a slightly changed form. '[H]e's found his way back to us and his spirit is in our brand-new beer,' they write on their blog. 'This is not a replica of his former beer, but a modernization, a riff or maybe even the beginning of a grander series. We're happy to say that Jack D'Or yet lives.'

The most recent batch of Jack D'Or feels animal and alive, pouring the colour of deep honey with a rocky, off-white head of foam. The best Saisons have an edge of wildness, and here that quality is held in balance with a slightly sticky sweetness, and a resinous, bracing bitterness that sees every mouthful out with its drying finish. It's a special beer – one that might even verge on divine.

Sierra Nevada
Celebration

6.8% IPA

Chico, California

Since it debuted in 1981, Sierra Nevada's Celebration IPA has grown from a cult-favourite winter seasonal to an annual juggernaut. With its snug, red label bedecked with a snow-covered cabin, the beer, which lands on shelves every October, has become a welcome signifier that the holidays are on their way.

As is true of so many things that Sierra Nevada has done, Celebration was ahead of the curve when it first launched. Back then, in the early days of American craft beer, fresh-hop beers were a rarity – and one of the three now-ubiquitous hops that are used in the beer (Centennial in this case, alongside Cascade and Chinook) hadn't even been named yet.

Making a beer like this at scale is a race against time, and an act of devotion. The hops, sourced from the Pacific Northwest, must be picked when they are at peak ripeness, and then transported to the brewery to be used almost immediately, before they lose any of their vibrant flavours. In order to ensure their quality, Sierra Nevada's founder, Ken Grossman, maintains close relationships with his partner farmers, and visits the region to check on the hops' progress throughout the growing season.

Their vivid character is the first thing you notice upon pouring a can – that and the beer's amber complexion. There is the orange and grapefruit and pine that is Cascade's signature, while Centennial adds floral notes, and Chinook a bracing bitterness. A hearty dose of caramelised malt imparts sweetness and body, as well as a toffee profile that balances out the bitterness and feels somehow innately festive. It's a Christmas beer done like no one else – West Coast IPA is a seasonal rarity amidst the annual onslaught of Barley Wines and Belgian-inspired ales and barrel-aged Stouts – and even after more than 40 years of life it remains peerless.

St Bernardus
Abt 12

10.5% Quadrupel

Watou, Belgium

If Westvleteren 12 were a wine, it would be the most prized Burgundy, a Domaine de la Romanée-Conti. Made by the monks of Saint-Sixtus Abbey in rural Belgium, Westvleteren 12 is notoriously inaccessible; to get it, you need to drive to the abbey and pick up a case yourself (or trade with someone who has). I've seen it described as 'legendary', 'close-to-mythical', and 'the best beer in the world'. After finally getting my hands on a bottle, I did a blind tasting of the beer, alongside St Bernarndus 12 and Rochefort 10. You can imagine my surprise when in every metric – aroma, flavour, mouthfeel, finish – St Bernardus left Westy in the dust.

St Bernardus' story is in fact closely entwined with Westvleteren's. First established as a cheesemaking facility by monks who'd fled from France in the early 20th century, the brewery was taken over by Evariste Deconinck. Following the Second World War, Deconinck signed an agreement with Westvleteren's monks to brew their beers under licence, using Saint-Sixtus' house yeast. That agreement expired in 1992, and the brewery was rebranded as St Bernardus. (Despite its name, it's not a true Trappist brewery, as its production is not overseen by monks.) Today, St Bernardus Abt 12 is the brewery's flagship and best-selling release.

I'd argue the only reason St Bernardus isn't approached with the same fervour or reverence as its cousin is that it's easier to find. In truth, it's a masterpiece, an emblematic example of the Quadrupel style, and an ideal winter warmer. There's the Belgian yeast, its character like soft banana bread spiced with clove; there are the notes of raisin and date, cinnamon and brown sugar, and liquorice warmth; there is its tongue-coating mouthfeel. I'm happy to leave the hype-chasers to their white whales if it means more Abt 12 for me.

Tegernsee
Tegernseer Hell

4.8% Helles

Tegernsee, Germany

It's no surprise that one of Bavaria's best lagers comes from a brewery with centuries of pedigree. With a 'modern' incarnation that dates to 1675, and members of Germany's noble House of Wittelsbach as its owners, the Herzoglich Bayerisches Brauhaus Tegernsee (the Ducal Bavarian Brewery of Tegernsee) isn't exactly in thrall to contemporary trends. (Prior to its aristocratic ownership, the brewery was also affiliated with the Benedictine Tegernsee Abbey.)

Today, Tegernsee bears its Reinheitsgebot-dictated, tradition-beholden bona fides with pride, and nowhere is that more evident than in its flagship Helles. This crystal-clear, straw-coloured lager gleams when poured – fittingly, '*helles*' translates to 'bright' – and is made using the region's spring water, Bavarian hops, and locally malted grain.

And yet, this most classical of beers also stands apart. Compared with other regional examples of the style, it is abundantly, even jubilantly malty, with less of the lemony tartness and light hop character found in other bottles. It may sound counterintuitive to describe a lower-alcohol pale lager as 'rich', but the first gulp of Tegernseer Hell is overwhelmingly defined by notes of sweet cereal, golden toast, and a lasting, biscuity finish. But despite its trace bitterness, it is never cloying. I'd just as soon savour a glass as tear into a freshly made, still-warm bakery loaf. And while it wouldn't exactly be challenging to throw back a litre (or several) on a hot summer's day without a passing thought, Tegernseer Helles' bounty and beauty merit a slower, more contemplative approach.

Compared to Munich's 'big six' lager breweries, Tegernsee might still count as a lesser-known cult favourite. Still, it's good to see that in recent years, its reputation – and its popularity – have spread well beyond its ancestral homeland in the Alpine foothills of southern Bavaria.

Track
Sonoma

3.8% Pale Ale

Manchester, England

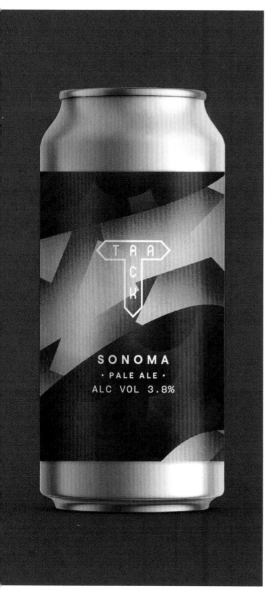

Sam Dyson founded Track Brewing Company in late 2014 in a tucked-away railway arch near Manchester's Piccadilly Station. Before that, he had worked at breweries like Camden Town to learn the ropes. And before that, he had embarked on a cross-country cycling trip across the United States, where he immersed himself in the country's brewing scene, and discovered the beers that would shape his palate (and later, his career).

After its founding, Track quickly distinguished itself for its American-inflected beers. Sonoma was only its second release: just 3.8% ABV, the beer promised a drinkability that session drinkers could appreciate alongside the kind of buoyant and abundant hop profile that craft beer fans prized. Together, that combination made it unstoppable. Sonoma is now Track's flagship, and accounts for the majority of its production.

'What I was trying to do was let the hops shine. I was less interested in the malt – sacrilege – but there was no crystal going anywhere near my beers,' Dyson commented on Track's *The Thirst Time* podcast. 'The reverse of what I was drinking when I was younger with my dad in the pub, and I'd have a half and he'd have a pint, of this sweet, malty, biscuity, raisiny type of beer. I was like, nope – out the door. I wanted something bright, zingy, hop-forward.'

There's something pleasantly old-school about Sonoma's hopping. C-hops, in this case Centennial and Citra, mingle with the dank earthiness of Mosaic, imparting notes of juicy citrus, and a whiff of tropicalia, alongside a pithy, marmalade bite. High, prickling carbonation furthers the sensation of bitter citrus, but ultimately this beer is a stone-cold refresher, just the kind of can you'd reach for after cycling thousands of miles across a continent. (That said, as local drinkers know, it's also excellent on cask, particularly when poured through a sparkler.)

Vinohradský
Vinohradská 11

4.5%   Pale Lager

Prague, Czech Republic

A beer like Vinohradská 11 feels like it carries the whole world in it.

Like a shining kernel, this lager holds the history of 19th, 20th, and 21st-century beer within its depths. The brewery that would eventually become Vinohradský Pivovar was founded in 1893 in the town of Vinohrady, several decades after Pilsner Urquell first unleashed the beer style that signalled a paradigm shift in brewing: golden, crisp, buoyant Pilsner.

Later decades brought change. Like other Czech breweries, its production was halted during the Second World War, and the business was later nationalised. Meanwhile, Prague spread and grew, and Vinohrady was gulped into its encroaching boundaries; today, it's a well-heeled easterly neighbourhood of the capital. Vinohradský Pivovar was only reborn in its contemporary form in 2014, and given a smart new makeover and more international outlook (including a range of American-inspired Pales and IPAs alongside its classic lagers).

The beer inside the minimal tall-boy can is a gorgeous synthesis of its constituent parts, all present in mutual dialogue. There is yeast: Vinohradská 11 is unfiltered, unpasteurised and lightly hazy, full in body and featuring a slight rusticity (diacetyl is present here, as in many Czech lagers, a to-style element that makes the beer feel as decadent as an oven-warm croissant). There are hops – noble Saaz and new-school Premiant – which bring a kicky but never puckering bitterness, and subtle suggestions of citrus and flowers. And most of all there is glorious malt, made from Czech and German barley, floor-malted and decocted, toasty and honeyed, this beer's big heart.

It feels impossible that a beer can contain these multitudes and yet also be so simply appealing, so easy and refreshing to drink. Toggle your attention off and you can drain a can almost unthinkingly; toggle it on and a universe emerges from the foam.

Weihenstephan
Hefeweissbier

5.4% Hefeweizen

Freising, Germany

Weihenstephan calls itself 'the world's oldest brewery', and it's true that its origins date back almost 1,000 years, to 1040 (though there is some argument about whether it has truly operated continuously since that time). Nevertheless, Weihenstephan distinguishes itself today for its association with the Brewing Science and Beverage Technology course at the Technical University of Munich; for the Weihenstephan yeast bank, home to one of the largest collections of brewing yeast in the world; and for its phenomenal, genre-defining wheat beer.

In lager-loving Bavaria, wheat beer – made with a proportion of at least 50% wheat – sometimes feels like a curious, top-fermenting outlier. That legacy is due in part to the Reinheitsgebot, which, as of 1516, prohibited wheat from being used in brewing, lest it cause food shortages. Later, local wheat beer production was dominated by Bavarian nobility until the 19th century, when it began to be brewed more widely once again (and gradually clawed back market share from dominant lagers). Nowadays, Hefeweizen is among Bavaria's most popular beer styles, universally recognisable in its tall, curved glasses, all golden-hued, hazy liquid, topped with a mountain of foam that resembles a scoop of ice cream.

Today, Weihenstephan makes one of the most acclaimed examples of the style. On the nose, there is a perfect harmony between the malt character – toasty, warm, honeyed – and that iconic Bavarian yeast profile. Yes, there are the banana esters; yes, there is bubblegum; yes, you can detect clove phenols, a slight pepperiness, as well as a sensation of vanilla-flecked cream. All of those aromatics carry through to the palate: the beer is sunny and citric but there is a real dessert-like richness to it, the suggestion of warm banana bread à la mode. The carbonation is sufficient to lift it and make drinking glass after glass an enticing summertime proposition.

Claire Bullen

Jonny Garrett

For me, there are two kinds of beer that could be labelled 'best in the world'. The first is one so delicious you just can't put it down, and keep going back to the bar for. The other is a unique beer that makes such a mark on the drinker's subconscious that their mind keeps going back to it, even if they never drink it again. Its influence goes beyond the moment, and becomes cultural.

Both are almost impossible to make. The former requires the singular pursuit of perfection, pint after pint. It means meticulous sourcing and attention to detail, as well as commitment to the concept. Many examples are deeply uncool, but they persist because enough people understand the joy of drinking something quietly better than everything else.

Making something culturally significant means busting through the barriers of expectation and tradition; it needs vision, imagination and daring. Many of these beers are maligned by purists and dismissed by beer snobs, and most are box tickers, bucket-listers. Even so, they change something about the industry that can't be undone.

Both such beers have one thing in common, though: they change the person that drinks it. Every one of the drinks I've chosen has changed the way I think about brewing, drinking culture or life. The fact there are so many of them, and that you'll have your own totally different list, is why beer is the greatest drink on earth.

The Alchemist
Focal Banger

7[%] IPA

Stowe, Vermont

I expect you'll be reading about a lot of Citra/Mosaic beers in the course of this book. In fact, most IPAs in the world at this point probably use these hops. But none of them will be like Focal Banger.

In many ways that should be a surprise. Not only because Focal Banger is one of the world's greatest beers, but because the brewer who made it started the New England IPA craze. John Kimmich is arguably the most influential brewer alive today, and his preference for combining mountains of American aroma hops with a fruity British yeast is seen as the origin of the NEIPA style. But few of those who ran with this idea do it in the same way.

Where Hazy IPAs are defined by their very low bitterness, Focal Banger is defined by how high it is. We're talking tongue-scrapingly, head-spinningly bitter; the kind of bitterness when you crave another sip just to wash it away. And let me tell you, it is exhilarating. That first sip is always raw and shocking. But as you get through the can it opens up, with pithy grapefruit and bitter orange clawing at your cheeks, refusing to go down easy. Underneath, smoother notes of peach and honey soothe and reassure you, fighting to rein it all in. Amazingly, it does start to resemble balance and drinkability. Like jumping into cold water, you become acclimatised, breathing in the hop oils and alpha acids as you gasp for air. By the end of the can you wonder how any other IPA can compare. This is your life now – the endless search for something as exciting and immersive as that first sip of Focal Banger.

Allagash
Allagash White

5.2%   Witbier

Portland, Maine

Making a Witbier your flagship is daring whenever and wherever your brewery is founded. In fact, aside from Hoegaarden, which had a glorious, hazy summer around 20 years ago, I think Allagash is the only one to have made it a viable business.

Allagash's head brewer, Jason Perkins, is acutely aware of that fact, and calls White 'the most innovative thing we've ever done'. If that doesn't sound like much of a statement, remember this brewery focuses on wild and spontaneous beers – and even ages beer in Roman-style amphoras.

The truth is Witbier is something of an oddity. It's a rich, smooth wheat beer spiked with dried orange peel and coriander, likely a vestige from a time before hops when all beers contained local spices and fruits. But what really makes it stand out is the yeast used. Not only does it help with the haze, it adds lemon yoghurt and banana notes to create this glorious, zesty, velvety, lemon meringue-like beer.

Now, I can't think of a more delicious sounding drink. But sadly, until NEIPA came along, hazy beer was the antithesis of what people wanted to drink – and its almost complete lack of hops means it is never going to be hitting the top of Untappd.

But if I were only allowed one beer to drink for the rest of my life, Allagash White might just get the nod. It is unfailingly delicious, whether you're drinking at the brewery, or the dingiest Boston dive you can imagine. It is a rare thing – a beer just as exciting and refreshing at the first sip as it is six pints deep. But don't take my word for it – just ask any New Englander. They've all been there.

Boon
Oude Geuze Black Label

6.4% Gueuze

Lembeek, Belgium

You could make an argument for pretty much any of Boon's beers to be included in a book about the world's best, but if there can only one, for me it should be Boon Black.

It was a special beer from the moment of its conception, marking a number of firsts for the brewery. It was released for Boon's 40th anniversary, and was also the first beer to be made entirely with wort from its current brewing site. In a nod to its old location, the label was based on the first ever Boon release. Most interestingly, though, it was made using the leftover Lambic from a collaboration with Mikkeller called Bone Dry. Both beers were a blend of one-, two- and three-year-old Lambic from barrels that had reached 100% fermentation – that is to say the wild yeasts and bacteria had eaten all the sugar in the beer, leaving it completely dry. That gave the beer a real Champagne quality, but some remarkable aromas and flavours on top. I remember notes of pineapple and mango, as well as citrus peel.

I say remember, because, unlike most Boon Geuzes, with later releases the brewery never tried to recreate the original blend's character. Instead, they simply took the concept of only using bone-dry Lambic to make it – as a result the second edition was more scrumpy like; the third had oak and vanilla notes that added body and sweetness; and the fourth was all green apple and Prosecco zing.

Making Lambic is a long, torturous process, but blending it into Gueuze is where the art is. Finding that sweet spot between dryness and body; teasing out beautiful aromas with the perfect amount of each age and barrel; and producing something so complex yet approachable is no mean feat. Neither is the fact that the top four Gueuzes I have ever tried all have Black on the label.

Burning Sky
Petite Saison

3.5%   Saison

Firle, East Sussex

It's probably historically nonsense, but the thing I enjoy most about drinking Petite Saison is the idea that this is how Saison might have once tasted.

The story goes that Saison is named after the 'saisonnaires' (seasonal workers) on farms in north-east France and Belgium, who would have slaked their thirst with it through their summer shifts. These Saisons would have been brewed after the previous year's harvest, using that season's grains, fruits and spices from the farm. The beer would then have been aged for six to nine months until summer came back around and the workers returned. During that time in oak the beer would have turned funky and a little sour from the wild yeasts, resulting in a rustic beer that really spoke of the local area.

While this history is hotly disputed in a corner of the internet that only the most hardened beer geeks visit, there aren't many alternative theories out there, and it has definitely influenced the formation of Petite Saison. It's made with a hearty mix of barley, wheat and spelt grains, which provide a Jacob's cracker-like base for the soft, yeast spice and lemony acidity that comes from the souring bacteria. The beer is then aged in oak barrels for months on end to gain a woody, wine-like dryness before being modestly dry-hopped to make that lemon peel note sing.

The result is something that feels rustic and wild, like drinking from a stream on a hike, and yet it's beautifully refined and consistent too. The fact that a brewery has decided to make such a difficult and slow-fermenting beer all year round is a source of endless wonder to me, and we're lucky to have breweries like Burning Sky who search for complexity and character even when the ABV drops below 3.5%.

Buxton
Axe Edge

6.8% IPA

Buxton, Derbyshire

Stood on either side of the bus entrance to Euston Station are two small, square Victorian buildings. They used to flank an 1870s Grecian arch that towered over Euston Road, with at least one of them being a post office. Chiselled into the brick and running right around both towers is an old list of Euston's destinations. Underneath Buxton, someone has graffitied 'Axe Edge'.

Quite why these two towers were spared when the arch was demolished in 1962 is unclear. After all – what could be done with two 24-square-foot towers? In true British fashion, they both became pubs – and for a few years around 2010 the Euston Tap boasted the best beer list in London.

The Axe Edge graffiti is a testament to that. Buxton Brewery were early adopters of modern US-style brewing in the UK and the Euston Tap was ahead of the times in stocking them so far away. The beer itself was – and remains – one of the best and most iconic West Coast IPAs in the country. It's been through multiple different versions, but has also remained true to its origins of being full-bodied, bitter and piney with plenty of malt depth to back it up.

On top of that, the brewery has, over the years, added elements of New England-style brewing by worrying less about the haze and more about getting those juicier, stone-fruit aromas that modern drinkers look for. The result is that one of the UK's classic IPAs is still relevant over a decade after it was first brewed, and more than worthy of being daubed on ancient walls where millions will see it.

Cloudwater
DIPA v3 (and its descendants)

9% DIPA

Manchester, England

It's difficult to put into words the impact that the Cloudwater DIPA series had on the UK craft beer scene, but through it you can track the entire revolution of New England brewing.

The first was a West Coaster, plain and simple. The second had this unlikely element of juiciness to it. V3 was the first IPA in the UK to use the fabled 'Vermont yeast' that was the genesis of hazy brewing, alongside a (for the time) hefty dose of Citra and Mosaic, lemony Centennial and zesty, oily Comet. The fourth was perhaps the first UK craft beer put in a 440ml can, now the industry norm. The series went on to introduce the idea of side-by-side comparisons of brews for drinkers and the promotion of hopping rates over IBUs – which led to the brewery pushing its dry hops as high as 30g per litre. And finally, there's the fact that the very concept of a numbered series blew apart the idea drinkers had that once a beer is brewed, the recipe remained the same. By the time the final DIPA – v13 – was released, New England beer was the dominant force in British craft brewing, and Cloudwater was the best-rated brewery in the country, whatever website you looked at.

Putting this beer in this book is a bit of a tease because it's not made anymore, so really this entry is about Cloudwater's endless cycle of new DIPAs – all of which are world class. It's also worth noting that DIPA v3 is very much a product of its time and likely wouldn't stand up to any of them. It is, however, the one that changed the whole brewing scene and those lucky enough to have tried it will always remember that revelatory moment.

Coniston
№9 Barley Wine

8.5%   Barley Wine

Coniston, Cumbria

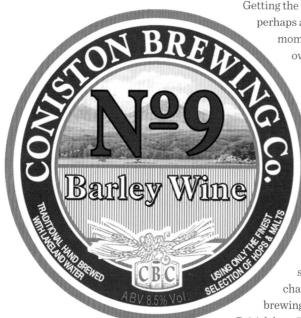

Sipping on a Coniston №9 by the fire at the Black Bull Inn in the Lake District should be on absolutely every beer lover's bucket list. Ideally, you'll also be damp and hungry after a bracing hike up the Old Man of Coniston, and working out which pie to order. Getting the Barley Wine before the pie is perhaps a little dangerous, but you need a moment just to drink this beer on its own. It is, for my money, the best Barley Wine in the world – and certainly the most drinkable.

When modern drinkers think about Barley Wine they expect booze, hop bitterness, liquorice and dark fruits. But this is the American way. A British Barley Wine sits at the end of the scale that starts with a Bitter, and goes through Best and ESB. That means the balance of caramel malt notes, spicy hop aromas and fruity yeast character that defines great British brewing. Number 9, more than any strong British beer I know, nails that. There's lots of Maris Otter-derived digestive biscuit, sweet toffee from the caramalt, floral honey from the big dose of Goldings, and banana and stone fruit from the yeast. Underneath are hints at the time the beer has spent in tank and in bottle – sticky orange, wafts of sherry and an oaky dryness. It's one of those beers best drunk in the right context, but so visceral that you could be on a sunny beach and still get transported back to autumn, Coniston, and that fire at the Black Bull Inn.

De Dolle Brouwers
Arabier

8[%] Strong Blond Ale

Esen, Belgium

Lowland brewers are notorious for being a little idiosyncratic, but the name De Dolle Brouwers – which literally means 'the mad brewers' – does no justice to the brewery's pure, unadulterated Belgian-ness.

Owner Kris Herteleer is usually found wearing his waistcoat fashioned from British bar towels and takes great pleasure in showing off the portraits he paints for the Order of the Butter Weighers. If that sounds like something from a storybook, it's nothing to what the brewery looks like: looming above the front yard is a giant, yellow cartoon yeast cell, complete with bow tie; and in the first floor brewhouse is a cobbled-together array of copper tanks, pipes and cogs that all pre-date World War Two. The beers he makes are just as unique and beautiful: there's the dark, fruity and slightly tart Oerbier; the honey, banana and brioche layered Easter beer, Boskeun; and, of course, the world-famous Stille Nacht, a Barley Wine-like beer that ages like Bordeaux. My favourite, however, is the inscrutable Arabier.

If you had to put it in a style guide, you'd call it a Strong Blond Ale, like Duvel and Delirium Tremens. But this beer is nothing like those – it's hazy as hell, with seemingly endless and irrepressible fluffy foam that climbs out the glass however carefully you pour. The aroma is a cacophony of banana, brioche, clove, nail polish, cedarwood, spring flowers and dewy grass. It riots around your palate – woody pine splintering through the banana bread malt notes and heady floral aroma. It is the very definition of bittersweet, coating your tongue with slick oil, only for the bitterness to dig its nails into the back of your throat. On the first sip it is a little too much, too all encompassing, but its aroma sucks you in for another sip, then dunks your head all the way under again. It is completely indefinable and utterly mad, but it is my favourite beer in the world.

Five Points
Railway Porter

4.8% Porter

London, England

Considering London is the home of Porter, it's hard to find any traces of it. Porter helped some of London's Victorian breweries become the biggest in the world – Truman's of Brick Lane and Barclay Perkins of Southwark both held that title at one time or another. It would have been drunk every day by the capital's hard-working street porters, and exported to India in far greater quantities than IPA ever was. And yet the word is rarely found in the old masonry of London's historic pubs, and nearly as rare on the bar.

Porter has gone from the world's most popular beer style to a bit of a curiosity, with the Guinness-like Irish Dry Stout taking any dark beer taps that could have been its home. But there is one brewery that has refused to let London's great Porter tradition disappear, and brews a truly sensational version of it just a few miles from Truman's old site.

Five Points Railway Porter is a beautiful, inky and brooding beer, with a latte-like creamy head. It smells of unsmoked tobacco, fruity coffee and rich, dark chocolate, foreshadowing flavours of black coffee, dates and lightly burnt toast. It's the perfect beer to enjoy on cask next to a roaring fire, but the occasion doesn't have to be so Dickensian. Its dry and drinkable nature means it's also brilliant in more modern settings like Five Point's taproom, with the pepperoni sourdough pizzas at the brewery's Pembury Tavern, or even by the bottle on a sunny day in London Fields.

It is, of course, a very different Porter to those that would have been drunk by the working classes in Victorian London, but it still feels like a wonderful link to the past – a taste of very different times, and perhaps better ones to come for the style.

Forest & Main
Solaire

4.5% Saison

Ambler, Pennsylvania

Outside the old townhouse that once contained Forest & Main brewery is an old cherry tree. In spring it bursts with white flowers, flushed pink as if they've had one too many beers. When the sun came out, the people of Ambler used to flock to drink wild fermented Saisons underneath it, probably unaware of its significance.

Although the brewery has moved to a more practical central brewpub (brewing in a townhouse has its complications), they still occasionally harvest the flowers to gather the yeasts and bacteria with which they ferment that year's Saisons – Saisons that I consider to be some of the best in the world.

Given the wild origins of these yeasts, and the uncontrolled way in which they are harvested, you'd expect the beers to be equally untamed – to be tart, funky and wild. And yet there is barely any of that expected 'mixed fermentation' character to them. Instead, they are lightly *Bretty*, bone dry and floral, which allows the malt tones of honey and straw to come through and even the soft hedgerow aromas of the often British hops that Forest & Main revere.

The brewery produces dozens of Saisons every year, using just a few base recipes then ageing them over fruit or hops, or in certain spirit barrels. Sometimes all three. Solaire is their flagship beer – the one from which all the others stem. The use of spelt adds a lemony freshness to a rich malt base, then the house yeast brings classic coriander, clove, banana, white pepper and rose. It is a curious beer, one that unfolds with each sip, aromas passing like perfume or flowers on a summer breeze. Even though the brewery has left the cherry tree behind, it's still there in every bottle they make.

Fyne Ales
Jarl

3.8%   Pale Ale

Argyll & Bute, Scotland

For such a small beer, there is a lot to love about Fyne Ales' Jarl. The northern tip of Loch Fyne is an unlikely place to find modern, American-inspired brewing, but that's exactly what the team have been doing since way back in 2010.

That said, Jarl is a deceptively simple cask ale – no one expects nuance and complexity in a beer that's mostly pale malt and all Citra hops. But Jarl is a lot more than the sum of its small parts. For a start, whether it is the hop selection, the hopping regime, or how the hops interplay with the other ingredients and processes (likely it's all three), it doesn't smell or taste like any other Citra beer I know. There's juicy grapefruit on the nose for sure, but there's also elderflower and lemon rind. On the finish there's a sting of nettles and the warmth of rubbed pine. That earthy bitterness cuts right through the sweet, honeyed malt and leaves you gasping for more, which leads me happily to another thing I love about Jarl – it's only 3.8%. Clearly this is a beer designed to be consumed in volume; the kind you order first and stick on for the rest of the night – which makes sense when you learn that the beer was released as a special for the brewery's annual beer festival but was so successful it has become their flagship.

For me, Jarl does something very few beers I've tried have managed: to deliver the intense waves of citrus unique to American hops without over-balancing a session strength brew. The entire US is trying to make a beer like this, and we've had it on cask in Scotland for over a decade now.

Goose Island
Bourbon County Stout

14%   Imperial Stout

Chicago, Illinois

When Bourbon County Stout was first brewed it was to mark a historic moment for Goose Island's original brewpub – its 1,000th brew. But this Imperial Stout ended up being more about its future – and indeed that of beer – than its past.

Ageing a beer in oak was nothing new in 1992. In fact, it was the norm right up to a few decades before. Even ageing beer in barrels that had contained something else boozy beforehand was common, especially in Belgium. What was new was the idea of extracting as much character and flavour from the barrel as possible.

Until head brewer Greg Hall had the idea after meeting the master distiller at Jim Beam, it hadn't really been done before on a commercial scale. Beer was one thing, whiskey was another. Could you really combine them? And what would you call it? Hall decided to find out, brewing the biggest, blackest Imperial Stout he could with his equipment, and ageing the resulting sticky tar in spent Jim Beam barrels. The result was a dark, brooding and liquorice-y beer that dripped with toasted oak, fudgy coconut, vanilla and bourbon-like heat. It divided brewers, drinkers and beer judges. It was kicked out of as many brewing competitions as it won. But as people came around to the idea of bourbon-aged beer, it started to gain cult status.

Its reputation certainly helped bring Goose Island to global attention, which would have aided its eventual sale to AB InBev. But while its core session beers have suffered by brewing at vast scale all over the US, Bourbon County Stout has remained inimitable. Thousands of imitators have followed in its wake, and many have been incredible beers in their own right, but the original is still more outrageous than all of them – a beer so visceral you can feel the heat of the toasting oak, the boozy ghost of the whiskey, and the sticky malt of the original wort.

Green Bench
Sunshine City

6.8%   IPA

St Petersburg, Florida

Brewing modern beer in a hot climate is no easy feat. Not only does it require the mother of all chillers to ferment the beer at 20°C and serve it around 6°C, but the beers have to suit the climate too. That explains why the state of Florida created the sour, heavily fruited Florida Weisse, but not why the state is also famous for its Pastry Stout.

Green Bench don't really go in for either of these styles, but they do make a lot of beer that's perfect for their location, just minutes from the beautiful, white-sand beaches of St Petersburg. Sunshine City, so called because St Pete gets the most sunshine of any city in the USA, is absolutely bursting with sub-tropical aromas. There's tangerine, pineapple and kiwi thanks to the double dry hop of Mosaic, Citra and Azacca, but this is no New England IPA. It's gently hazy, like the world through sunscreen-smeared sunglasses, and finishes with a heft whack of pithy, citrusy bitterness. As a result, it's incredibly refreshing, which leads us to the only problem with the beer: it's 6.8%.

That makes it far too alcoholic to session – a lesson I learned on the sunny terrace at the brewery, where I spent a fascinating afternoon once drinking with and talking to founder Khris Johnson about the brewery's name (taken from the now ripped-out green benches that made the city famous, but were out of bounds for people of colour like Khris). I love that his beers aren't only suitable for the climate, but that each and every one sold works to reclaim those words and take ownership of part of the city's identity.

Harvey's
Sussex Best Bitter

4%   Bitter

Lewes, East Sussex

When COVID closed Britain's pubs, cask brewers all over the country were staring down the barrel of financial ruin. With no cash coming in and bills to pay, it was a matter of hanging on for dear life. But Miles Jenner, owner and head brewer of Harvey's, wasn't sure whether hanging on would be enough.

His house yeast, which has been repitched from batch to batch since the fifties, has to be used regularly to survive. With brewing all but suspended, it was at risk of dying. If it did, it would likely take the brewery with it, such is its importance in the character of all his beers.

The Harvey's yeast enjoys almost mythical status in the world of brewers, such is its unmistakeable character but also its various forms. It manages to make a pretty clean and crisp little English IPA, while also adding *Bretted* notes to Harvey's Imperial Stout. It's most notable, however, in the brewery's flagship beer, Harvey's Best. To this oak-hued, caramalted Bitter it brings a heady mix of banana, fresh bread dough and green apple as well as a rich, oily body – perhaps because it leaves the beers a little sweeter than a Bitter really should be, strictly speaking. That's balanced out by a hefty dose of whole cone hops, all bought from the few remaining Kent and Sussex hop farms. These local varieties add earthy hedgerow fruits, fresh hay notes and plenty of refreshing bitterness. These rural aromas and flavours make Best feel almost like a mixed fermentation beer, but without the dryness, funk and acidity that comes with it. We're very, very lucky that the yeast that brings it all together survived.

Hook Norton
Old Hooky

4.6% Bitter

Hook Norton, Oxfordshire

There is nowhere in the world like Hook Norton Brewery. In fact, I'd describe the brewery as more of a time than a place – at a certain point up the winding, hedgerow-lined drive you're transported back to the Victorian era.

Hook Norton Brewery was designed by the prolific William Bradford, who had a hand in more than 70 breweries and maltings between 1879 and 1905. During that time he developed a signature style that cared as much for the beauty of the building as their practicality. Along with Harvey's in East Sussex, Hook Norton is perhaps the most beautiful. It is a tower brewery, with multiple, staggered floors that let gravity do the hard work of moving the water, while the outside is covered with wrought ironwork, triangular windows and gables. If you asked Quentin Blake to draw a brewery, I feel he'd come up with something like Hook Norton.

Well aware of the historic property they occupy, the brewers have stuck rigidly to tradition with their core, cask beers. Each one is open fermented with the brewery's ancient house yeast, and brewed using all British ingredients. Old Hooky is a dark-red, brooding Bitter with lots of raisin bread, molasses and date notes, brightened by apple and spice. I was born just a few miles from the brewery, and as a teen I drank plenty of it without giving a second's thought to the history and heritage in the glass. Old Hooky is now not just evocative of the fruits and spices, but of the shire horses that delivered it, the century-old copper that boiled, and the beautiful building that contained and inspired it.

The Kernel
Export Stout

7.5%   Stout

London, England

It's difficult to overstate the importance of Kernel as a brewery. Founder Evin O'Riordain's steady ship has helped launch a thousand others, while quietly and conscientiously making some of the best beers in the world. Pretty much every one of them could legitimately make this list, and the brewery makes so many different beers you could probably fill the whole book with them.

Their Damson Sour is one of the most gorgeous Wild Ales I know, the Citra Saison a thrilling clash of cultures, and their Table Beer has been a London cornershop miracle for as long as I have been into beer. But none of them quite deserve the reverence and book inches as the Export Stout.

Based on a 130-year-old Trumans Brewery recipe, it is an unctuous and adult beer that both pays homage to and makes a mockery of its historic origins. Brewed with the authentic brown malt that many modern Porter and Stout brewers now leave out, it combines more modern flavours of chocolate, coffee and toffee with leather and plums, and a smoky fug of tobacco. If you serve it chilled you'll get all the softer, sweeter notes, but let it warm and its complexity starts to seep out the glass and become the perfect after-dinner treat or cheese-board companion.

As if that isn't enough, the brewery recently started making fruited versions of the beer – adding tonnes of tart, tannic raspberries or richly sour damsons that brighten the beer while simultaneously making it deeper and more brooding.

Little Earth Project
It's Life, Jim

16.5% Barley Wine

Edwardstone, Suffolk

'Barley Wine is life', or so they say, and who are we to argue? This strong, malt-forward style has been part of British brewing for nearly two centuries now. Modern versions are usually well hopped and dark, oozing with caramel, toffee and liquorice notes; the perfect digestif or cheese accompaniment. Little Earth Project's version, however, has more in common with its origins.

Until the late 19th century, pretty much all beer would have had some kind of wild character – definitely some funky *Brett* and potentially some kind of souring bacteria. For this reason, beer was often either drunk very fresh to avoid such flavours, or aged for years to dry out and round off into a complex and stronger drink. Barley Wines of the 1800s fell into the latter group, being some of the strongest and longest-aged beers that a Victorian brewery would produce.

It's Life, Jim draws inspiration from these historical ales but takes it somewhere else entirely. Little Earth Project makes exclusively Wild Ale, fermenting the beers with cider yeast from the family cidery. Head brewer and founder Tom Norton also loves to use local and organic ingredients, and even grew some of the hops and malts that went into this beer. If all this sounds unusual, wait until you hear about the 26-hour boil and six months it spent in ex-whisky butts before being bottled. As a result, there is quite literally no other beer like his organic Barley Wine – nor has there ever been. It's sticky with caramel and raisins, but has a spike of oak and waves of acidity that present like cranberry or sour cherry. Life has never tasted so sweet, or sour.

Lost and Grounded
Keller Pils

4.8% Kellerbier

Bristol, England

It was only a few years ago that lagers were still looked down upon and dismissed by most drinkers in the craft beer scene. It was regarded as a bland, commercial product of giant factories, churned out as quickly as possible for the lowest possible cost.

Without a few vital people in the industry, it's likely that cliché would still be pervasive. There were a few raised eyebrows when Alex Troncoso opened the ambitously sized Lost and Grounded with his partner, Annie, in 2016. Essentially, the couple were starting again, fighting the same battles that early craft brewers did in persuading drinkers that beer didn't have to taste of virtually nothing, that there were all kinds of styles and flavours, that it shouldn't just be a cheap, throwaway product.

Alex and Annie have worked tirelessly in the brewhouse and outside it to champion lager brewing as an art form, and a tricky one at that. There are still relatively few great Pilsners made outside of Bavaria and Czech Republic, but Alex's Keller Pils certainly counts among them. It's also very unusual, combining the bitterness of a North German Pilsner with the fresh, doughy character of a Munich Kellerbier. It pours as pale as a barley field with a gentle morning haze. On the nose there's pepper, Jacob's crackers and hay – it's dry, almost arid. When you drink it, it's spiky: the carbonation and spicy hop bitterness biting at your tongue, before a bread and honey note washes over it. The finish is lemony and lightning fast, the very definition of the 'crisp' lager snap that us beer writers talk so much about. It's the definition of nuanced, and its subtleties still pass a lot of drinkers by, but only those who have always wondered why lager has become the most loved beer style on the planet.

Mahr's Bräu
aU

5.2% Kellerbier

Bamberg, Germany

I have drunk this amber Kellerbier on hundreds of occasions, but it took me most of them to realise that the 'a' isn't really part of the name of the beer. The beer is, really, called 'U' – and you order a 'U'. The brewery say it's designed to cut through the potential language barrier for any non-German drinker, but really, I think it's to save them having to come up with a name.

The 'U' itself stands for Ungespundet, which in English means 'unbunged', and in brewer speak means 'finished in an unpressurised container'. This means two things: one, it will be less carbonated because much of the CO_2 from the final fermentation escaped rather than being absorbed. But it also means the beer is more likely to be hazy, as the yeast can stay in suspension more easily. Unlike the Kellerbiers of Munich, which are bottled before the full clarification of the beer has finished, aU gets a full eight weeks of lagering, but still winds up being hazy enough to make some lager purists raise their eyebrows. The haze could also be enhanced by the ungodly amount of Hallertau Perle that gets tossed into the beer to layer honey and floral tea on top of its rich caramel and soft, sweet banana-tinged base beer.

Together these delicious flavours make aU sweet, full-bodied and moreish, feeling somehow nourishing, like a bowl of porridge the morning after a night out. Or at least that's what I tell myself every time I pour myself one.

Mikkeller
Beer Geek Brunch

10.9% Imperial Stout

Copehagen, Denmark

Beer Geek Brunch is the embodiment of so much that I love about beer. It was a mad idea – a big, bold coffee Imperial Stout – that was made in an utterly absurd way – adding hundreds of French press coffees to a fully fermented beer – with a completely unexpected result – it was rated the best beer in the world around 2007.

It was the imaginings of Mikkel Borg Bjergsø who had tried it on a homebrew scale but lacked the equipment and people power to scale it up for a commercial batch. For that he turned to Mike Murphy, who later became head brewer at Lervig, to make the boldest, richest beer of his career to date. Reading this story today you might think that Beer Geek Brunch was thick and sweet like most adjuncted Stouts, but even today it remains bone dry and roasty, with the aroma of a dingy Italian espresso bar – all smoke, leather and dark chocolate. On the palate it is bitter, berried and tannic, like slightly over-extracted cafetière coffee.

The beer is early proof of the validity of contract brewing, something still maligned by more traditional brewers. It gives creative and daring brewers the equipment, space and time to make something simply unviable on a smaller or less technological kit. Mikkeller became a think tank for new brewing ideas, which helped create a whole movement of experimental contract brewers in Scandinavia. Some of them – such as Omnipollo – have gone on to create even larger cultural ripples, but if you want to understand where it all began, it started on a long night in Denmark with a few hundred French presses and some very wired homebrewers.

Mills Brewing × Oliver's Cider
Foxbic

7–8.5%   Wild Ale

Berkeley, Gloucestershire

There is very little terroir in beer. This idea that a drink can be made of, and taste of, a particular region of the world is a powerful emotional tool in wine, and beer has long tried to use it. But with modern beer the idea has gotten harder and harder to sell.

Most exciting hops come from the American Pacific Northwest or even New Zealand; in the UK the malts are most likely to come from Norfolk or Suffolk, but they could also come from Germany or Czech Republic, or at least be inspired by them; and yeasts most likely come from a plethora of different factories depending on the strain and brand. So it's very rare to find a beer that uses local ingredients, let alone says something about its local environment enough to claim terroir. Foxbic, though, is the embodiment of Herefordshire – the place, the produce, the people.

It starts with British malt and wheat being turbid mashed to create lots of long-chain sugars that only the wildest of yeasts and bacteria can break down. It's then blended with fresh, razor-sharp Foxwhelp apple juice, harvested and pressed by none other than Tom Oliver of Oliver's cider, and transferred to oak barrels where the wild yeasts from the wort and apple skins start their steady work. Years later, Tom and Jonny and Gen Mills get together for a blending session, choosing quantities from each barrel to get the balance of funkiness, sweetness, acidity and character from the two original liquids. The terroir is already there, and their aim is just to create something delicious and unique. Every vintage is subtly different, but each one contains that signature tannin and bright acidity of the Foxwhelp, the farmyard funk and floral character of the spontaneous beer, and the earth and spice of the British hops. All of which come from, and speak of, this beautiful county on the Welsh borders.

Närke Kulturbryggeri
Kaggen Stormaktsporter

12%   Imperial Stout

Örebro, Sweden

I had pretty much given up on the idea of ever tasting Kaggen when it almost literally fell into my lap on a trip to Sweden. I was drinking at Omnipollo's Hatt with founder Henok Fentie when he proudly brought a bottle out. Its branding is so restrained I didn't actually realise what was being poured until I put it to my nose and finally experienced the aroma I had read about on hundreds of RateBeer reviews.

On Närke's website, presumably filtered through Google translate, it states that the brewery is 'both new and old at the same time,' and I can't think of a better way to describe their highly coveted smoked Porter, Kaggen.

On the one hand it is a deeply traditional beer. Historically, Porter had a smoky property, because it was created in response to a change in UK tax law that made using cheaper, smoky malts much more efficient. It would have then been well aged in oak to reduce that very smoky character, a process Kaggen also goes through. It's here, though, that the newness comes in. The beer was brewed to never fully ferment out, instead leaving lots of sweet maltiness and body. It was also further sweetened by the addition of heather honey, and finally aged not in neutral oak but in former whisky, rum and other spirit barrels, depending on the vintage. The result is a beer caught perfectly between two worlds – the 18th-century Stout Porter and the modern day (whisper it) Pastry Stout. In doing so it has become one of the most complex and sought-after beers in the world, although by a select few who *know*. Happily, you are now one of those people, and your search for the great Kaggen now begins.

Notch
The Standard

4.4%   Pilsner

Salem, Massachusetts

Czech Pilsner is perhaps the best-kept beer secret in the beer world. Almost unspoken of outside of a tiny subset of beer geeks, it is unceremoniously dumped in with the more Germanic-inspired world of pale lager brewing, where everything is cracker-dry and fizzy.

In reality, Czech lager couldn't be more different. By clinging on to the ancient practice of decoction, in which small portions of the mash are removed, boiled and placed back into the tun, Czech Pilsner has differentiated itself to anyone who takes the time to understand the nuance and

complexity underneath. Decoction adds a unique, caramelised and crusty bread sweetness that plays perfectly with the region's floral hops. The style's glory is in its bittersweetness, hitting every taste bud on the way down.

There are around 600 breweries in the Czech Republic, and pretty much every one of them will make a version that, at the time, you think is the best. But the standard is not made in the Czech Republic. It's not even made in Europe. It's made in Salem, on the outskirts of Boston, Massachusetts, by Notch Brewing. Founder Chris Lohring is a zealot for great lager, and has been banging its drum and brewing deeply unfashionable beer for over a decade. Thankfully, he makes the best Czech Pilsner outside of the Czech Republic itself, and he does it by being a slave to the traditions and beliefs of those brewers: double decoction, open fermentation, the correct malt and hop varieties. He's even tried to recreate the tar pitch that Pilsner Urquell historically used on its barrels back when it actually fermented in oak. This attention to detail, this passion and this knowledge leads to one of the best beers I have ever had the fortune to drink. Complex yet rudimental; sweet but bitter; rich but crushable; American but Czech.

Omnipollo × Dugges
Anagram

12%   Stout

Stockholm, Sweden

I can still taste that first sip. Given that it was six years ago, that's quite a lingering finish, but it's difficult to forget your first Omnipollo Pastry Stout. Whether you love it or hate it, everything changes in that moment because you think you've tasted the logical conclusion of beer – the very edge of how far it can be pushed.

Anagram is billed as a Blueberry Cheesecake Stout – a rich, thick, chocolatey Imperial Stout absolutely saturated in blueberry purée and milk sugar, to the point where it felt and tasted more like ice cream. Don't take that as a negative: it was decadent, sticky and immersive. I smiled from ear to ear as the texture conjured memories of making cream soda floats as a kid. The flavours reminded me of the cheapest, trashiest desserts I could think of: the kind you snuck seconds of at home while your parents were watching *Blind Date*. The kind that were stripped from supermarket shelves a few years ago in the name of nutrition and human decency. Anagram is the kind of beer that you can't not offer to everyone in the room, dangling it under their noses and going 'can you believe this is beer?' then reeling when they say they can't.

Because it definitely still is beer, whatever the snobs on Twitter may say. I've been to the brewery and drunk the delicious base Stouts before they received their customary doses of wild ingredients. I've seen the remarkable research co-founder Henok Fentie does in finding his adjuncts, even travelling all over the world to meet the coffee and cacao farmers. Just because you smile when you're drinking it, it doesn't mean you can't take it seriously.

Other Half
All Green Everything

10.5% IPA

Brooklyn, New York

When beer historians sit down to write the story of this era, a lot is bound to focus on Brooklyn's Other Half Brewing. Their cultural and technical impact on modern brewing is perhaps understated now, but with time it will become very clear.

If The Alchemist inspired the revolution and Treehouse started it, Other Half took it to the masses. As a beer geek in the mid 2010s they were the name you wanted to see on every festival line-up, the brewery you wanted your local to collaborate with.

More than perhaps any brewery in the world at the time, Other Half made brewing cool. Their urban setting, instantly iconic branding, and grasp of scarcity marketing (i.e., lack of supply to start) meant they had queues around the block from the very early days. There was even an article in *Punch* about how City financiers were bringing cans of Other Half hazies instead of Champagne to their glitzy house parties. Thankfully, this was all backed – or indeed created – by sensational, and at times groundbreaking, brewing. Their explorations with water chemistry helped create that pillowy mouthfeel NEIPAs are famous for, and they were generous in sharing their knowledge with other breweries.

It was this, and their prodigious use of hops, that set them apart and made it possible for them to make utterly absurd beers like All Green Everything, with Amarillo, Citra, Mosaic, and Motueka. The body is thick, juicy and sweet with just a hint of booziness to remind you this has gone through one hell of a fermentation. On top of that is layered sticky orange, grapefruit and pure Juicy Fruit chewing gum, with just a lick of lime from the Motueka. When the history books are written, it's beers like this that they'll find evidence of all over the internet, and wonder at how such a small brewery could make such a big impact.

Pressure Drop
Pale Fire

4.8%   Pale Ale

London, England

If you talk to the founders of Pressure Drop they'll tell you they got lucky, but I don't believe a word of it. For more than a decade now, Pale Fire has been one of the best American Pale Ales in the UK – which means it must also be one of the best in the world. That doesn't happen by accident.

Nor does the prophetic use of one of the hops that would go on to help define the aromas and flavours of modern craft brewing – Mosaic. As a result of using that hop as the star, Pale Fire – which was first brewed on a shed stove top in 2012 – pre-empted the obsession with juicy aromas that was about to start the New England IPA craze. Tangy grapefruit and fleshy orange aromas saturate a light, dry and slightly wheaty base that fizzes with zestiness.

In being both bright and juicy, Pale Fire has become one of the few pre-haze-craze American pales not to either go through a drastic recipe rewriting or rapid decline in popularity. Pale Fire is still as sharp and crisp as ever, retaining that pintable, same-again-please factor. It's difficult to know whether the brewery has enhanced that over the years or whether it's just in comparison to the thick, stone-fruit-led beers that now fill most taps. Either way it has stood the test of time so well that it's now older than most breweries in the UK, let alone beers. It was ahead of its time, and now is timeless.

Siren
Maiden

10–12% Barley Wine

Wokingham, Berkshire

When we talk about brewing we so rarely talk about blending. It's usually a source of surprise to drinkers that it actually happens all the time – to add complexity to Wild Ales, consistency between batches of the same IPA, and varied barrel character in Stouts and Barley Wines.

Perhaps blending is forgotten about because the action of it isn't very exciting – there's no big machinery, whirring pumps or giant bags of hops. But it does use the most important tool a brewer has – their palate. In the modern age of brewing, less and less is done by the senses, but blending has to be. What's more, it can get pretty complicated.

Siren Maiden, so called because it was the brewery's first ever brew, is about as complicated as it gets. Released once a year, it involves the blending of Barley Wine from several different spirit barrels with everything from bourbon and Scotch to tequila, rum and port. Often in blending the brewery is looking for a certain profile – for vanilla from the oak, lactic from the bacteria, funk from the yeast – but with Maiden the barrels decide the direction for themselves, and the brewers are left to look for the most exciting combination. That means every year is subtly different, with a rich, complex and boozy aroma that shifts subtly with each vintage while retaining the glorious brown toast, raisin and liquorice notes of the base Barley Wine. Siren has gone on to make world-class beer in every style, but this is still the beer I think defines them and what they're about: making bold and unique beer that is intoxicating in every way.

Tree House
Julius

6.8% IPA

Charlton, Massachusetts

My first pilgrimage to Tree House – perhaps the world's most famous Hazy IPA brewery – was back in 2016, when New England style brewing was on the cusp of going mainstream, and challenging everything we thought we knew about brewing hoppy beer. My travelling companions were unconvinced it was worth the detour as we trundled along a stony driveway, parked up in an unmarked gravel yard and headed towards a barn.

Inside the welcome was incredible. We were given a tour by a brewer, met the partners of the founders, and shown family photos of the day the barn was built. I was struck by how outsized the brewery's reputation was compared to its footprint. They didn't even have a licence to drink on site, so instead we cracked cans and shared them that night in our hotel room, decanting into plastic glasses from the bathroom. Even so, the beer dripped with orange juice, oily citrus peel and mango. Nowadays the combination of Citra and Mosaic is a little predicatable – but back then it was revelatory.

My second trip could not have been more different: the stony driveway was replaced with a kilometre-long, perfectly smooth road; the carpark was large enough for hundreds of cars, and there were shuttle buses taking drinkers from an overflow carpark by the highway; and instead of strolling in and meeting the family, we queued for three hours. The new building was at least ten times the size, with a huge brewhouse in the corner surrounded by floor-to-ceiling glass windows that opened out onto a forest.

We headed to the bar, where we could grab takeout pints and sit on benches outside, admiring the incredible journey the brewery and the Hazy IPA style had taken. The beer itself, however, was just the same. Juicy, citrusy and velvety but endlessly crushable. Julius is still the New England IPA I judge all others against.

Únětické
Pivo 12°

5% Pilsner

Prague, Czech Republic

Found just a short bus ride from Prague, from the outside Únětické looks more like a monastery than a brewery. Built in 1710 and hunched up against a hill, the taproom is a cosy, pillared cellar and the lagering caves go deep into the ground.

That instils a quiet to the whole building, a church-like hush that only makes the place feel more sacred. For those who know what's made here, this truly is a place of worship. Wherever you go you can smell the sweet malt and bready, doughy yeast that tops the open cylinders of fermenting beer. Save for some seasonals there are only two varieties – the dry, herbal and unholy delicious 10°, and the only lager I know that's better than it.

The brewery's 12° glows like the holy grail, alive with beautiful Moravian malt and floral hop oils. It's double decocted and saturated with local Saaz, before being open fermented and long matured. That gives it lots of brioche and spice aroma that carries right across your tongue, down your throat and into your belly – nourishing every inch that it touches.

It's best consumed in small measures so it remains ice cold and frothy. Even if you manage to get cans of it for home, keep the can in the fridge and pour half pints hard and fast. This is the way I consume it, this is the way the Czechs consume it, and it's probably the way God would consume it, too.

Utopian
Rainbock

7% Maibock

Crediton, Devon

As the person who literally wrote the book on seasonal brewing, any beer inspired by the time of year excites me. Our love of lager and IPA has dulled beer drinkers' sense of the seasons, and it's pretty much up to brewers to remind us how influential they can still be on what we brew and what we drink.

In Germany, the Maibock signals the start of beer garden season. Unlike the dark, brooding Doppelbocks that come in the months before them, Maibocks are pure gold, exploding with the colour of the early morning sun through the trees and bursting with sweet honey and floral aromas. While the style's history is disputed, it has come to be the beer that bridges the gap between spring and summer. The classics are pale like a Helles – indeed it is sometimes called a Helles Bock – but usually a good one or two percent stronger, and much hoppier to balance the sweetness and body that brings.

Utopian's Maibock would please even the pickiest German braumeister, but amazingly is brewed with all English ingredients. The Warminster Malt is double decocted to bring almost Caramac-like levels of sugary caramel, while the nettle sting from the British Boudicea hops stops it becoming cloying. I love how it almost seems to glow once its poured – brewed in the depths of winter and lagered for around 10 weeks, it is a literal promise of brighter things to come.

Verdant
Even Sharks Need Water

6.5% NEIPA

Penryn, Cornwall

Any happily married person will tell you that true love isn't loving despite, it's loving because. Those flaws that so infuriate are also the very thing that makes someone unique, special, unpredictable and brilliant.

This is how I think Verdant's brewers think about hops. The brewery is famous for its juicy IPAs – IPAs that manage to squeeze every last drop of citrus and sweetness from modern hops. But doing so means taking a little rough with the smooth, because hops aren't just juicy; they are wild flowers, and even the best varieties have their unique little quirks that set them apart. Verdant head brewer James Heffron knows this and embraces it. Most memorably, on the can of One More PSI, he celebrates the '80s gym sock' nature of Mosaic.

Most breweries try to suppress such character in their hops, balance them out with other flavours, or even avoid varieties entirely. One such variety treated with extreme caution is Galaxy. This Aussie hop is famous for presenting as harsh, grassy and tannic – masking all the glorious passion fruit and peach aromas that lie beneath. As a result, it's usually used in moderation – but not by Verdant. It makes up a third of the dry hop of their NEIPA, Even Sharks Need Water, and brings a lot of its wild, biting bitterness with it. It dries out this otherwise thick and Citra-led beer, and leaves you gasping for air like you really are fighting a shark. But once that bitterness fades you can taste that remarkable passion fruit stickiness and acidity, as well as citrus peel from the Citra and nectarine from Verdant's house yeast. It is as complex and refreshing as NEIPA gets.

John Holl

Every beer tells a story, and not just in the final product. From agriculture to technology, the ingenuity, ingredients, processes, inspiration and location that goes into every pint is something to consider and examine.

That's why, as a journalist, I enjoy covering the beer industry. It's not just about tasting notes – it's time in the fields and on bar stools talking with passionate people who enjoy what they do and are standing on the shoulders of generations before them to create something that is universally beloved but still manages to be a local product.

Books and lists like this can be polarizing but often lead to conversation. My personal favourites, the ones I enjoy drinking when I'm off the clock and out for fun or relaxing at home, are going to be different to yours, but we can still find common ground; beer that brings us together.

It was pretty easy to spot a pattern in my beers that follow. There are crisp lagers and complex IPAs that celebrate bitterness. The occasional boozy behemoth also pops up, and I seem to have a thing for Flanders Red.

Mostly, my contributions to this book are sessionable ales, low-ABV gems that are well-suited for several rounds without causing palate fatigue, but ultimately foster conversation with friends or help with a contemplative mood on solo days.

Beer is so much more than a liquid in the glass, and taking the time to explore those avenues leads to a richer drinking experience.

The Alchemist
Heady Topper

8%   Hazy Double IPA   100 IBUs

Stowe, Vermont

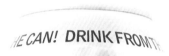

ALE
ALC. 8% BY VOL.
1 PINT

First brewed in 2003, Heady Topper is one of the originals in the New England-style IPA category, and two decades later remains the platinum standard that brewers and drinkers alike look to on how juicy haze should be done. It's the flagship brand from The Alchemist, the family-owned brewery in Vermont, which has demanded, in bold, black type, that it should be drunk from the can. Unpasteurized and unfiltered, brewer and owner John Kimmich has also encouraged that the beer be kept cold at all times.

With a limited distribution footprint and a reputation that even the best kind of press can't buy, it is sought after, traded for, and lusted over. Many first-time drinkers can instantly relate to the drawing on the label of a blushing, bearded man having a sip of beer (from a glass no less) and having a mind-blowing hop experience.

The hops are a blend that the brewery keeps close to their chest, but flow smoothly between pine and citrus, tropical fruits, berries and herbs. It works in tandem with a soft, crackery wheat malt bill, a slight mineral water profile, and a slightly fruity yeast ester. It is a four-way balance of ingredients so finely attuned that they could balance on the head of a pin.

What has made this beer such an enduring hit is not its scarcity – the brewery makes more than ever before, especially after moving into a new state-of-the-art facility six years ago – but how well constructed it is. Many brewers that have come after The Alchemist and have entered the hazy battlefield have perfected the art of the hype, charging big bucks for a Citra and Mosaic smoothie with an alluring label. Put Heady Topper up against any of those and the classic will emerge victorious.

Avery Brewing Co
Maharaja

10%   Double IPA   102 IBUs

Boulder, Colorado

Long before extreme became the norm in beer, there was Maharaja. An imperial India Pale Ale, it was an early adopter of over-the-top-hops and a kick of alcohol that served as an eye-opener to many a beer drinker in the United States of what aggressive, but nuanced hops could be in an ale.

With a name that translates from sanskrit to 'great king', this imperial ale has long been a leader in the space, even as more breweries have opened, and competition has become fiercer. It was first brewed in 2005, part of the 'dictator series' that also included The Czar, an Imperial Stout, and The Kaiser, a strong Oktoberfest, and quickly established itself as a then-seasonal to seek out when it was released, and to even stash away to allow to age over several years, slowly turning it into an American Barley Wine in the cellar.

As a fresh beer, however, in those early days it was vibrant with orange peel and grapefruit pith. Sweet berry aromas would peak through from time to time and then get pushed aside by pine tar, dried grass, and spruce needle aroma. It featured a caramel malt that was sweet and slightly nutty, and the fusel alcohol on the back end was unavoidable but completed the tasting experience.

As tastes and package preferences have evolved, so too has the Maharaja. Early on it was a seasonal or occasional offering, packaged in 22oz bottles, a format that is rarely seen today. The beer is now a year-round offering available in 12oz six-pack cans and the recipe has evolved. Dank is often a go-to word for the beer, and that is fair, but sniff past that layer and it becomes much more. Today it is dry hopped with Idaho7, Simcoe, and VicSecret, giving it a fruitier aroma of mango and candied grapefruit.

Beachwood Brewing
28 Haze Later

6.8%   Hazy IPA   45 IBUs

Long Beach, California

Beachwood Brewing has earned a reputation for creating well-adjusted West Coast IPAs that celebrate the clear, snappy bitterness of hops. Lessons learned over a decade of brewing and hop experimentation made them well-suited for creating and releasing a hazy, juicy New England-style IPA.

Using a proprietary yeast strain and the winning combination of Citra, Mosaic and Galaxy hops to the tune of 6lb per barrel, Beachwood, which has several locations in southern California, has had rousing success with this beer, which manages to use the hops in a way in which each variety can be expressed and not just blended and used as a blunt instrument.

In the glass, or straight from the can, this is a lively, murky concoction of hops and grain that plays up candy-like sweetness, a mélange of pineapple, tangerine, clementine, white peach and tropical fruitiness. A soft body with low carbonation and pleasing bitterness that does not appear until the glass is almost emptied.

It is that bitterness that helps to bridge the gap between the classic styles of IPA. Showcasing bitterness in a soft way can open the door to new or younger drinkers who have experienced IPAs that eschew bitterness.

So much of this is born from the mind of Julian Shrago, the co-founder and brewmaster of Beachwood. He's a thoughtful brewer, who takes big ideas and brings them down to a manageable level that are executed well. It's hard not to notice his thoughtful nature and his commitment to small brewers, traditional styles, and education, which is done through his pints.

The Hazy IPA has become a staple of brewery taps, and ubiquitous on shelves, but ones this like version, where great care and attention of ingredients, timing, and processes, as well as running vigorous trials before releasing a version to the public, show that the category is capable of maturation, nuance, and spot-on flavours.

This is an IPA that is a sign of a well-stocked fridge.

Bend Brewing Company
Fresh Trop

6.5% IPA

Bend, Oregon

Within weeks of the annual hop harvest a limited-availability beer begins popping up on draught lists: the fresh hop IPA. These ales are brewed with hops picked directly from the field and added to the kettle within hours of harvest. The result is typically fresh, vibrant, with a sticky wetness that is not as well replicated with processed cones.

In southern Oregon, Zach Beckwith, the head brewer of Bend Brewing Co, is on a mission of fresh hop exploration and education.

'They are truly the last seasonal beer and in my opinion can only really be brewed in the Pacific Northwest,' he says. 'It's building those direct relationships with the farmers that has helped to make fresh hop season a cultural holiday in the beer world of the Pacific Northwest.'

In recent years Beckwith has begun brewing a number of different fresh hopped beers over the course of harvest season, trying different hopping rates and times to see how newly picked hops are expressed in the glass.

He says the brewery has always used a modified hop back scenario (typically repurposing their mash tun and running the wort through the fresh hops before running it through the HEX) to great results.

'What you get is more akin to a typical beer where the hop flavour is imbued throughout, not just in the aroma. Think about the preservative quality of hops. When you're using 10 to 12lb per barrel of fresh hops, like we do, you're setting that beer up to stay "fresh" for a while,' he says. 'I've never been a fan of the "best before yesterday" messaging with hoppy beers. In our experience our IPAs typically peak in flavour three to five weeks from packaging. The beer needs time for the flavours to come together.'

Bierstadt Lagerhaus
The Slow Pour Pils

5.1% Pilsner

Denver, Colorado

In an age of instant gratification, waiting upwards of five minutes for a beer can seem like an eternity. Patience is rewarded at Denver's Bierstadt Lagerhaus in the form of a Slow Pour Pils, a hearty but delicate little number that comes in a stemmed Pilsner glass.

Pouring a proper glass takes not only time, but training. Bartenders are aiming the taps at the center of the glass to release carbonation and to start the building of a proper rocky head, aiming for two-thirds foam to one-third beer, says brewer and co-owner Ashleigh Carter. The beer is allowed to settle for a few moments before being filled to the line, and then after another short break is topped off to allow the foam to peak above the glass line. It often takes longer to pour the clear straw lager than drink it, so ordering in multiples is suggested.

While the Slow Pour Pils is the flagship of this brewery, founded in 2017, there are other lagers to explore, including core offerings, seasonals and collaborations.

Bierstadt Lagerhaus started off as a dream and is now the reality of Carter and Bill Eye, who saw potential in their warehouse and turned it into a temple of lager. No ales on tap, just lagers and Pilsners on the menu, brewed to tradition on a reclaimed German brewhouse and aged for weeks before serving.

Thanks to the slow pour, the carbonation in the Pilsner is softer, and the pale, crackery malt is more rounded. Noble hops add earthiness with a touch of spice to the palate, and it finishes with just a kiss of sweetness.

The brewery began canning during the pandemic, but still has a limited distribution footprint, so the best place to taste the beer is at the taproom. Just be ready to wait. Pro tip: order a half liter of Helles while the slow pour readies.

Blackberry Farm
Classic

6.3%   Farmhouse Ale   33 IBUs

Maryville, Tennessee

In rural eastern Tennessee, south of Knoxville, where open land and outdoor recreation is plentiful, is a destination hotel and resort, home to thoughtful dining experiences and uncompromising luxury. Blackberry Farm is known around the world via its reputation, magazine, and design studio. You might think that such a setting would play host to a winery or distillery, but the smart folks at the farm decided to install a brewery instead.

The brewery opened in 2011 and was initially serving just guests at the farm and some local specialty accounts. In 2015 a larger brewery was installed, and distribution grew throughout the United States. It's producing lagers and IPAs, but naturally, given its location and culinary influence, Saisons and Farmhouse Ales are the passion. Over the years Blackberry Farm Brewery has released speciality Saisons as collaborations or with different barrel treatments, but a constant has been a trustworthy Farmhouse Ale they simply call Classic.

The construction is just that. Farm water, classic two-row malt, noble hops that are slightly fruity and spicy, and a Belgian yeast strain that adds additional rustic fruitiness to the glass. While the can is not an uncommon vessel today, it can still be jarring to see this style in aluminum, and while the brewery does use glass for other beers, Classic in cans makes sense. It can be dressed up or down, a mid-afternoon firepit sipper straight to a roast dinner.

Saisons as a style, in my mind, can be a beer for toasting good times or occasions. A beer like Classic is the everyday occasion beer. Pulling a can from the six-pack in the refrigerator is for the occasion of it being a Tuesday evening, or a friend stopped by unexpectedly, or as a sipper while in the garden.

Boulevard Brewing Co
Tank 7

8.5% American Saison 38 IBUs

Kansas City, Missouri

This flagship beer of Boulevard Brewing is called an American Saison, and that is an accurate description for a vibrant, effervescent ale that has Belgian roots but leans a bit heavier into hopping, making it suited to a modern audience.

The hops are floral and citrus forward and add a pleasant bitterness to the strong ale which is named after the fermentation vessel used during beer trials. Boulevard was founded in 1989 by John McDonald and over the years – backed by some of the very best brewers, several of them from Belgium and schooled in the Belgian tradition – the brewery grew to be one of the largest in the Midwest, largely on the backs of Tank 7, which found a way to break through the bland lager barrier set up by larger producers. The brewery is now owned by Duvel Moortgat USA.

Yeast-derived peppery spice mixed with hop-focused grapefruit peel and citrus blossom have made this beer an ideal food companion. From spicy jambalaya to soft goat and cow milk cheeses, herb roasted chicken to lemon meringue, the beer is versatile alongside countless dishes. Robust carbonation scrubs the palate between bites.

Despite its stronger ABV and medium body, the ale drinks easy and can often trick the brain into thinking a second or third glass won't hurt too much, though all is revealed in the light of the following afternoon. Savouring this ale is best, taking time to let the citrusy hops and fruity Belgian yeast esters escape the glass and bouquet into the mind, allowing it to wander and appreciate the skill that brought together two brewing traditions into one stunning experience.

Carton Brewing
Boat

4.2%   Hazy Pale Ale   35 IBUs

Atlantic Highlands, New Jersey

The inclusion of Boat on this list might be a self-fulfilling prophecy by brewery co-founder Augie Carton. He talks about this beer a lot, some might say too much, on 'Steal This Beer', a podcast he's co-hosted with this author for the last seven years. Whenever it comes up, he'll call it 'the best beer in the world'.

Yes, it's marketing, but as the brewery's flagship, and not only an early adopter to hazy, hoppy beers but one with nuance in a sessionable package, it is indeed worthy of being on this list. It has familiar ingredients, including a malt base of floor-malted Pilsner and a touch of wheat, all combined with a robust blend of Cascade, Centennial, Columbus, Chinook, Citra, Amarillo, Galaxy and Nugget. It's fermented out with Kölsch yeast. The result is a snappy, citrus and white stone fruit ale that rides on the thin side of a medium body. This facilitates proper session drinking, nautical setting not required.

Like all creative brewers who have used ingredients in unexpected ways, the brewery at the top of the Jersey Shore gets a lot of attention for its creativity, whether it's using coffee in the place of hops in a bock, powdered cream cheese, or thieves oil, the key is to unlock flavours beyond the expected. This has included beers that push the boundaries of coffee, evoke memories of beloved dishes, pay homage to history through wood, or seek to better showcase hops.

But it's the core beers that pay the bills, and Boat, a staple at bars in the know and coolers along the beach, hits all of the flavours of a hazy Pale Ale while allowing each to intertwine and complement each other rather than coming off as blunt.

Chuckanut
Maibock

7% Maibock 25 IBUs

Burlington, Washington

Throughout the years, lagers of all kinds have flowed from the taps of Chuckanut, the brewery founded by Mari and Will Kemper in Washington State in 2008. The appreciation of lagers is evident, and the brewery has helped educate thirsty drinkers on the potential of the category, and train countless brewers who have worked the brew deck and in the cellars over the years.

There is a special time of year, however, usually towards the end of April, when the brewery releases its Maibock. It's a strong lager that ages for at least three months before serving, and the result is a rich, full-bodied beer experience

The Maibock is a rich, golden colour, deep and malty with flavours of grass and hay, raisin and dates, and a character that is mostly sweet on the finish before a pinch of pleasing hop bitterness.

Having spent much of its existence in a pub and warehouse in Bellingham, Washington, the brewery has since moved into a larger production facility to the south. The company also operates a taproom in Portland, Oregon.

The Maibock, long a fan favourite, has also won numerous awards, including a gold at the 2021 Great American Beer Festival. The brewery has also begun experimenting with ageing the beer for longer than three months, says Mari Kemper. Kegs are held for upwards of a year, to let the beer smooth out a bit and concentrate in flavours. These are often served side-by side with fresh pours to showcase the benefit of age.

Creature Comforts Brewing Co
Athena

4.5%   Berliner Weisse

Athens, Georgia

The Berliner Weisse has gone through an identity crisis in recent years. A simple, humble, low ABV German-style wheat ale that had been lovely to drink on its own, or with the occasional splash of raspberry or woodruff syrup, has become a base for all manner of high-impact fruiting and flavouring.

To find unadorned Berliner Weisse is actually a bit harder than one might think in the United States, especially in a packaged format. Creature Comforts delivers with Athena, a slightly tart ale derived from *Lactobacillus*. At times it imparts aromas of graham cracker, apple, vinous and citrus blossoms. It finishes semi-dry with a tongue-smacking quality that seeks out a quick follow-up sip.

Creature Comforts was founded by David Stein, Adam Beauchamp, and Chris Herron and has made a name for itself in the American south since launching in 2014. Through thoughtful beers that have mass appeal, the brewery has grown and gained fans who enjoy the balanced, easy-drinking beers the brewery produces. Sharp-eyed movie watchers also noticed that Athena was the preferred beer of Thor, played by Chris Hemsworth, in *Avengers: Endgame*. A brewery location is planned for California in partnership with Joe Russo, a co-director of the movie.

Athena is a splendid beer to have on warm spring afternoons or alongside garden salads. Light and refreshing with a tart character, it breaks out of the traditional warm session beers by bringing diversity to the glass.

It should be noted that Creature Comforts does, in fact, release a few varieties of Athena that are dosed with fruit flavourings under the Athena Paradiso label.

Dogfish Head
90 Minute IPA

9% Double IPA 90 IBUs

Milton, Delaware

The origin of this beer has become the stuff of legend, and told countless times by the brewery's co-founder Sam Calagione. Having watched a cooking documentary about a soup that was constantly peppered to achieve uniform and deep flavour, Calagione decided to do something similar with hops. He used an electronic football game table that buzzed and hummed to deliver hops to the kettle at a steady rate during the course of a 90-minute boil.

The result was a beer that helped reshape hoppy ales on the east coast, and to grow the brewery to its current size. It also helped inspire two others in the brewery's regular portfolio, the easier drinking (and lower ABV) 60 Minute IPA, and the imperial 120 minute IPA, which is more akin to an American Barley Wine. The brewery was also behind a Rastal glass collaboration several years ago to create a vessel – a ribbed, stemmed chalice – that was said to accentuate the attributes of a strong IPA.

90 Minute is chewy with hops, leaning into old-school flavours of pine and grapefruit for both aroma and flavour. A hearty malt bill brings forth flavours of dates and raisin, and dried fig. It routinely sits atop 'best of' and 'desert island' lists by brewing professionals and drinkers alike, and even in a world of Hazy IPA, still maintains strong sales and robust popularity. Amtrak, the US Rail Carrier, remains one of the largest purchasers of the beer, a strong tonic for weary commuters and excited travelers.

While it is crammed with hops and has unmistakable bitterness, there is a malt derived sweetness that never quite gives up and keeps the bite in check, inviting fresh swallows without palate fatigue settling in too quickly.

Ecliptic Brewing
Capella Porter

5.2%   Porter   39 IBUs

Portland, Oregon

Quick: name a Porter brewed in Oregon that from the first sip evokes a sense of deep brewing knowledge, balance of ingredients, and an easy-drinking nature that has earned it a spot as an American classic.

Faced with a rapid-fire question, the Black Butte Porter from Deschutes in Bend will likely escape the lips, but there is another Porter, the Capella Porter brewed by Ecliptic Brewing in Portland, that also fits the above bill.

This makes sense, of course, because the brewer behind Ecliptic is John Harris, the very same brewer who very early in his career put together the recipe for Black Butte. At his own place, which is the fusing of a hobby he has held since childhood – astronomy – and a passion career he's had since… well… for a long time, Harris is able to make the beers he wants, his way, without compromise.

Capella is smooth-bodied with semi-prickly carbonation, and a flavour that focuses on roasted malts to draw out some fun, slightly fruity esters. Whiffs of a herbal character mix with dark chocolate – this is a Porter that evolves as it warms – revealing a roasted depth to the ingredients that never teeters into bitter but manages to keep a liveliness going until the final sip.

In an age of IPA (a style the brewery makes and does so quite well) it's enjoyable to see a Porter as the flagship of a brewery and be so well received. Pair this beer with burgers or wings, sweets or charcuterie. It is versatile, and from the first sip helps you relax from the stresses of the day.

Good Word
Analog Life

3.6%   Dark Mild

Duluth, Georgia

A lot of breweries will talk about the desire to foster commonality, to bring people from all walks together, and to try and build a beer community. At this Georgia brewery those words are gospel, and the brewery is producing the beers that facilitate the goals.

Since launching in 2017, Todd DiMatteo and Ryan Skinner, two longtime friends and former employees of the Brick Store Pub, a bar dedicated to good craft beer and service, Good Word has become a bastion for low ABV beers (including an annual little beer festival) that look to traditional styles for inspiration.

Case in point is Analog Life, an English-style Dark Mild Ale. It's big on roasted malt character but without burnt undertones. The hops lean heavily into the subtle floral and low herbal aromas that give it a bit of a perfumy essence. With a fantastically low ABV, perfect for session drinking, it finishes dry and readies the tastebuds for the next sip.

Proper session drinks, that is ones with low ABV but with flavours that encourage multiple rounds of the same, are what help foster conversation among bar patrons. When the beer is easy and slips into the background so that thoughts and ideas can remain at the forefront of the brain, the brewer has done their job.

Dimpled mug after dimpled mug, Analog Life is a soft reminder that beer can be part of a fellowship but not at the constant centre.

Great Lakes Brewing Co
Edmund Fitzgerald Porter

6%   Porter   37 IBUs

Cleveland, Ohio

The Edmund Fitzgerald Porter is the gold standard of American-brewed Porters. Not only did it help put this Ohio brewery on the map, but more importantly it introduced the style to countless drinkers who had likely only largely experienced bland, light lagers.

The brewery was founded by brothers Pat and Dan Conway in 1988 and quickly began focusing on classic ale styles that were still largely missing from the American beer scene. The Porter is named after the famed freighter the SS *Edmund Fitzgerald*, which sank in a gale on the waters of Lake Superior in November of 1975. The story of the sinking, which claimed 29 souls, was later made into a song by Gordon Lightfoot.

The recipe for the beer still focuses on heritage hop varieties, including Cascade, Northern Brewer and Williamette, and a malt bill of 2-row, Crystal 77, Chocolate Malt and Roasted Barley. It's this simplicity of ingredients that is the great beauty of this Porter.

Roast-forward, with pleasing coffee and chocolate undertones and peppery, herbal, floral hop character, it has a slight chalky ash on the finish. A mid-strength ABV is also a feature, but it has enough heft to have that liquid bread mouthfeel. This is a Porter for the everyday, for any occasion, and feels solid on the soul. This lovely ale is a benchmark for the style, and is never out of fashion.

Heater Allen
Pils

5%   Pilsner   38 IBUs

McMinneville, Oregon

Thanks to is robust annual hop crop, it can be easy to think of Oregon as a land of Pale Ale and IPA, but there is a fondness for lagers that drinkers hold dear, and a demand that brewers deliver. Take, for example, Heater Allen, the brewery founded by 2007 by Rick Allen, a homebrewer who had a healthy respect for tradition and wanted to replicate and perfect many of the international lager styles that had captured his attention and imagination as a young drinker. If he was going to be a professional brewer, he wanted to make the beers he'd be most interested in drinking.

The beers are thoughtful and have a needle-like precision to detail, all the while remaining refreshing and endlessly quaffable. Rick's daughter, Lisa, now runs the brew house, even though that wasn't always the plan. While fascinated by fermentation and brewing science from a young age, Lisa first went into wine making. Fate, however, had other plans, and once she got into the family brewhouse to help out, she never left.

The Pilsner is the brewery's flagship, done in the Czech style. It combines pillowy softness and assertively crisp characters. There is no mistaking the patience, skill, and history that goes into the beer. In the can, it is easily identifiable with the script standing out against a yellow label, and this simplicity allows the beer to shine even brighter. On the palate there is a slightly toasted, bready character balanced by a spicy hop note. All of the ingredients are subtle and take some time to really show their true intentions.

When we talk about session beers, the kind that should be drunk in multiples over an afternoon, this is the lager we want.

Jack's Abby
Copper Legend

5.7%   Oktoberfest   22 IBUs

Framingham, Massachusetts

For a frustrating time in American beer history, autumn meant rows and rows of pumpkin pie-spiced ales, and little else, save for imported Oktoberfest lagers that worked in a pinch but often lacked the crispness desired following a long ocean voyage.

As craft breweries solely dedicated to lager production began to sprout up and grow, a cache of Oktoberfest lagers soon followed. Jack's Abby Craft Lagers was founded in 2011 in a Boston suburb by the Hendler brothers, who have spent the last decade working on and releasing a variety of lagers. Chief among the brewery's seasonals is Copper Legend, a Märzen that is available from August to October each year.

Sweet malt-forward with a spiciness from noble hops, the beauty of this beer is not only in how the traditional ingredients are well measured and work together in harmony, but the presentation as well. True to its name, it pours a vibrant, clear copper with a thick, white head that easily peaks above the rim of a ceramic stein.

Like all well-made Oktoberfests, this is best enjoyed over a few rounds, with friends and all of the normal fest bites, like pretzels and sausage, close at hand. As mugs empty the hops become a bit more pronounced with an earthy, leafy undertone, and the malt verges on lightly toasted nuts. Throughout it all it retains a crispness that never wavers.

It's the kind of Oktoberfest that makes you wish the season was celebrated all year round.

Lakefront
Pumpkin Lager

6.1%   Field Beer   10 IBUs

Milwaukee, Wisconsin

Pumpkin-flavoured beers are polarizing. Or should I say pumpkin pie-spiced-flavoured beers are polarizing: the over-the-top combination of baking spices that mix with the gourd and end up like a liquid slice in a glass. Often blonde ales, with fruity undertones, or Porters and Stouts with a bit of coffee or chocolate roast get the spice treatment as they add a bit of depth to the adjuncts.

Now here comes Lakefront Brewery, the stalwart operation that has been around since the late 1980s, with a lager that retains the characteristics of the style, but still smells like a Halloween candle. That's a good thing, especially for fans of big, bold flavours, and who spend the autumn months drinking pumpkin-flavoured coffee in the morning and ending the nights with pie-spiced Oreos.

This beer is unapologetic in its approach, but still has a beer soul. It's like having a slice of pie but in a glass. An overwhelming aroma of allspice, clove, ginger and cinnamon that is mellowed in the flavour and then wiped nearly clean in the finish, inviting another sip to revive the fall classic.

Pumpkin pie spice in beers has a long history going back even further than Lakefront's founding. Buffalo Bills, a California Brewery, is credited with the creation, and it helped build the style into a thriving category of beer. Nearly every brewery in the United States makes a pumpkin pie beer in the autumn, with many hitting stores and shelves as early as August and running through Thanksgiving.

Polarizing, yes. But when done correctly, like this beer, a pumpkin pie-spiced beer can be just the liquid treat without a trick.

The Lost Abbey
Red Poppy Ale

6.5%   Flanders Red Ale

San Marcos, California

For longer than most breweries have been operating in the United States, Tomme Arthur has been making beers in the Belgian tradition from various posts in Southern California. The Lost Abbey, the brewery he founded in 2006, is the workhorse that is a sanctuary of ingenuity and wood where ales and lagers made with a reverence for history and ingredients are fashioned.

Long-time fans of the brewery will have their own pick of Lost Abbey offerings that speak to their palate, but there is a special place for Red Poppy, the Flanders Red that is annually released in 375ml cage- and cork-topped bottles.

Starting off as a Brown Ale base, the beer is then aged in oak for a year before it's blended with lager. Cherries and poppy seeds are part of the equation, and it is the stone fruit that most benefits from the ambient yeast in the wood that increases the overall tartness. Still, it's never puckering, but lands on the palate with a call to action for the salvatory glands to kick into high gear, with whiffs here and there of balsamic and glimpses of vanilla.

With a manageable ABV, the brain can stay sharp through the whole glass, and taking a bit of time with a bottle pulled properly from the cellar, it becomes easier to notice a thread of nuttiness that runs through the whole experience.

There aren't a lot of occasions where someone will suggest popping open a bottle of Flanders Red, at least not in my experience. This doesn't have to be a special occasion beer, though: it's a Tuesday night get-out-of-the-rut beer, or the companion to a beef stew on a lazy Sunday at home.

New Glarus Brewing Co
Raspberry Tart

4% Fruit Beer

New Glarus, Wisconsin

New Glarus is one of the largest breweries in the United States and stands out as the unique business model for a company of its size: it only distributes within the borders of Wisconsin. That has pretty much made it the official beer of the state and a huge source of local pride, especially when long-established brands like Miller and Pabst have gone global with ownership or brewing elsewhere.

Deb and Daniel Carey founded the brewery, with Deb doing much of the business side of things and Daniel focusing on the beer. The flagship is Spotted Cow, a beer that has been described by the brewery as a cream ale or a farmhouse ale and sits in its own little space in the beer world. It's the best seller by a country mile and an easily crushable beer that can be dressed up or down depending on the occasion.

The real treat from the brewery, however, is the Raspberry Tart. It's a simple, low-ABV fruit beer made with local wheat, raspberries from Oregon and just enough Hallertau hops to give it a bit of leathery spice.

The brewery does lagers and Brown Ales, releases a well-respected Oktoberfest, and delights with its Kölsch, but it excels with fruit beers, and Raspberry Tart sits at the top of the basket.

The raspberry is ever present and has a jammy quality that suggests the fruit was picked at just the right time when it was sweet with some tang but had not started down the other side of freshness. It's not overly tart, and is only mildly assertive, which is perfect for the low ABV and smooth mouthfeel. It leaves a beautiful lacing on the glass, which you'll notice has emptied rather quickly.

Notch
Černé Pivo

4.5%   Black Lager

Salem, Massachusetts

Some of the finest afternoons I've had sitting at authentic biergarten tables was in Salem, Massachusetts, a town famous for witches. Chris Lohring set up his lager brewery in an old warehouse, hard against a canal in the bustling and cramped New England city, and has been turning out traditional lagers to great acclaim.

The brewery itself is perfect. Architecturally, the clean lines and sparse decor are inviting, and help to enhance the lager experience without visual bells and whistles getting in the way. A second location in a Boston suburb opened in 2021 with a similar feel. Anything that you order at the brewery is a smart decision, but there is something about the Schwarzbier that just stands out.

This black lager is the closest thing to what you'd get in Bavaria without having to leave New England. It's light and crisp with just a hint of coffee roast and an earthy hop bitterness. Where some brewers treat this style as just a Porter or Stout with lager yeast, Lohring and Notch's brewers stick with tradition.

As the mug – always enjoy this in a proper dimpled mug – empties it takes on a little bit of sweetness mixed with country bread malts and continues to be soft on the palate. Grassy hop bitterness is present but never overwhelming.

The low ABV makes this an ideal session beer for just about any occasion. It's smooth, refreshing, and thought provoking.

Parish Brewing Co
Ghost in the Machine

8%   Hazy Double IPA   100 IBUs

Broussard, Louisiana

This is one of the finest Hazy IPAs I've had in my day, and in addition to the flavours, I'm most tickled that it comes in a 12oz glass bottle. There's something so counterintuitive to serving the white-hot style of beer, one that helped usher in the aluminum era of craft beer, that it just elevates the whole juicy experience when tipping it out of a longneck.

While other breweries will create an elaborate cocktail of hops for their hazies, Parish is just focusing on one: Citra. And by being careful at the annual hop selection, they can find lots that pull out the flavours and aromas they desire.

Like all good things, it takes some time for this hazy, pineapple juice cocktail of a beer to truly reveal itself once poured into a glass (yes, pour it into a glass). It is bursting with tropical fruit notes, including mango and papaya, but layered with orange peel and tangerine flesh on an earthy wheat body.

The hop bitterness will grow as the glass empties, but it is such a slow process that the nature of the hops is never overshadowed, and we are reminded that there can, and should be, be a little bite in a juicy IPA.

That this comes out of Cajun country in Louisiana, far from the style's New England roots, just makes the beer a little bit better in the mind. Brewery owner and founder Andrew Godley and his team have created a bold yet nuanced hazy that does the hops proud.

Some might choose this as a nightcap, but it is perfectly suitable as a brunch beer if the rest of your day involves serious napping.

Revolution Brewing
Straight Jacket

13.1%   Barrel-aged Barleywine   31 IBUs

Chicago, Illinois

Sometimes a great beer can be a bad decision. There's always going to be a consequence for a double-digit ABV beer, especially one that's heavy on the sugars having rented out space inside a barrel that previously held bourbon.

Chicago is a city that appreciates barrel-ageing, and while attention might be paid to a bird-themed brewery, the real liquid art, in my opinion, is coming out of Revolution, a brewery that started as (and still operates) a brewpub and later moved into a large industrial space where not only IPAs are produced, but rows of stacked barrels of all stripes are cellaring strong beers of all types.

Straight Jacket is a bourbon-barrel-aged Barleywine that helped draw the attention of beverage thrill-seekers who have continued to follow the brewery deep into wood year after year. There are variations to the beers they put out, some with fruit, others with coffee, and maple syrup. Here, with Straight Jacket it's a traditional Barleywine base with the added benefit of booze-soaked wood, toffee and raisin, date, fig, a splash of cola, vanilla, and even the littlest bit of fudge.

It's not crazy or over the top, and it's even accessible to just about any drinker who wants it. No line waiting, no need for crazy cross-country trades: the brewery puts out a fair amount once a year, having dialed in the blending process. It has a following for good reason. There are even pages on social media where drinkers will chug a can and be applauded by fellow enthusiasts. I'm not advocating for that personally, but fun is fun.

With a little bit of bitterness and wood tannin on the finish, Straight Jacket never fully gives in to its boozy, sugary nature that would otherwise stunt the palate. The end is just the right amount of padding.

Rockwell Beer Co
Velour Tracksuit

7.7%   Hazy IPA   62 IBUs

St Louis, Missouri

One of the amusing byproducts of the recent beer Renaissance has been the naming of individual beers. Brewers have drawn from numerous wells, including obscure movie quotes, puns, locations, nicknames, and in the case of this Hazy IPA, leisure wear.

The name fits because this is a comfortable beer that feels stylish in your hand. It pours clearer than haze with aromas of berry that quickly escape after it splashes into the glass. Where many cut from the modern cloth will eschew bitterness, this ale brings it into the experience, but in a balanced way where the juicy character of dry hopping the hops is not lost.

The malt bill of 2-Row, Golden Naked Oats, Flaked Oats, Malted Oats, Carafoam and Acidulated gives it a medium body with baked bread, cracker and hearty cereal. Together it provides a great canvass for the Mosaic, Pahto, Simcoe and Strata hops, which brings warm melon, pineapple and stone fruit to the forefront. The pint ends with a delightful dankness.

This beer is a solid representation of the efforts that Rockwell, a relatively new brewery in the Midwest, is putting out. It's helmed by brewers who have cut their teeth in garages as homebrewers and then among stainless steel in professional breweries. Along the way they've learned a lot, but have maintained the mantra that beer should be 'fun, not fussy'.

Having launched in 2018, the brewery has established itself as a new generation leader in the well-established St Louis beer scene, and from regular offerings to seasonals like Velour Tracksuit, it is showing that it is both comfortable and stylish.

Rodenbach
Alexander

5.6%   Flanders

Roeslare, Belgium

Rodenbach is one of the world's most celebrated breweries, known for its complex sour ales and virtually unrivaled history. The beers have captured imaginations and led to brewing careers, and have been clinked in glasses for celebrations of all kinds going back to the 1820s. The Grand Cru is a delight and the Classic is just that, but for a long time Alexander, a beer named after one of the brewery's founding brothers, was the sought-after stuff of legend by brewers and serious beer connoisseurs alike.

It is based on the Grand Cru recipe, but has the blended addition of sour cherry juice before being aged in the brewery's famous and hulking oak foeders and only sporadically released; cellared bottles would be on the lists of some of the world's better beer cafés and bars, or pulled out at special occasions by those who would most appreciate it.

There is only a modest amount of cherry juice in the final bottle, and it adds a subtle tartness where skin and pit are perceived, but only slightly. Undertones of leather and sweet tobacco dance around and merge the blend of old and new beers that construct the base.

In 2016 the brewery brought the beer back into the marketplace with a widely distributed 750ml bottling (as well as draught) heralded as a chance for younger drinkers – who were eagerly snapping up sour ales from sour producers – a chance to try a classic from an early innovator in the category.

That led to regular production where now the beer is available in 11.2oz bottles in various markets. This is a beer that benefits from some home cellar time, allowing it to mellow a bit and smooth out any overly wooden edges.

Rothaus
Rothaus Pils Tannenzäpfle

5.1%   Pilsner   32 IBUs

Grafenhausen, Germany

As a brewery dating back to 1791, Badische Staatsbrauerei Rothaus has benefitted from a long, successful run to perfect its beers. It shows in the Tannenzäpfle, which translates to 'pinecone', which happen to be in abundance in the evergreen trees of the Black Forest, where this brewery is located.

The pinecones also appear on the beer's label, next to a woman named Biergit, holding in each hand a Willi Becher glass of perfectly poured Pilsner. The artwork is done in a geometric style that almost resembles 8-bit video games of yesteryear, and with bright colors and an inviting nature, the 33cl bottles stand out on shelves.

It's recently been imported to the United States where, in the hip neighborhoods of Brooklyn and throughout the New York metro area, it's captured attention and tastebuds. There's been a fondness for traditional beers, with long-established brands like Pabst or Narragansett finding new life through younger drinkers who long for simplicity (and a cool label).

Despite the near whimsical label, this is a serious beer brewed by serious brewers who wear the mantle of tradition with respect. When people talk of 'beer flavoured beer' this is what they mean: just the slightest touch of minerality in the water, traditional Pilsner malts that have a biscuity quality but never feel flabby or sweet, noble hops adding a touch of spice, and a little bit of country grass to the mix. Bitterness does not factor into the beer, but crispness and a refreshing, lively character is a hallmark.

Tradition and skill come with time, and the brewery, as it continues to export or bring drinkers to its home in southwestern Germany, is offering a masterclass in Pilsner with each glass poured.

Russian River
Pliny the Elder

8% West Coast Double IPA 100 IBUs

Santa Rosa, California

Even in this era of Hazy IPA, drinkers of all stripes still get a tingle of anticipation and excitement when three words are uttered: Pliny the Elder. The beloved, respected, and celebrated strong IPA from Russian River Brewing Co still delights after all these years and shows that bitterness need not be a bad word, but should be embraced.

Immediately recognizable by its hunter-green label with centred red circle, this beer is still only available in draft or 500ml bottle, although variations on the beer have been canned. A stronger version, Pliny the Younger, is released yearly.

As you'd expect, hops are centre stage and it is a jaunty combination of Amarillo, Centennial, Simcoe and CTZ (Columbus, Tomahawk, and Zeus) which all complement and bring something different to the mix. Poured vigorously into a glass, the clear, golden ale has a rocky head and immediately releases sweet, fruity hop aromas backed by cool pine. Citrus peel comes on with the first sip, with herbal, white stone fruit soon after. A patina of alcohol warmth washes over the palate at the finish.

The beer is a work in progress, says brewer and brewery co-founder Vinnie Cilurzo. He has worked to tweak and adjust the recipe over the years, playing into hop strengths, keeping up with equipment advances and respecting the local water source.

Big, full swallows is the way to enjoy this beer. Sips don't do the hops justice. Yes, the glass empties faster, but they make plenty so live a little. There is no place that this ale doesn't fit in. It's a celebration beer, a happy hour companion, a hair of the dog, or paired with a burger.

This IPA is a monument to modern beer.

Samuel Adams
Utopias

28%   Strong Ale   45 IBUs

Boston, Massachusetts

Every two years for the last 20 or so years, as the holidays near, the hype begins for this big, boozy, memorable beer that has become one of the most sought-after in the US, and has become known around the world.

Utopias is the assertive, 25%+ ABV beer released by the Boston Beer Company, served in ceramic, resealable bottles that resemble a classic copper brew kettle, and having a glass is an experience any serious beer adventurer should seek out.

The recipe varies with each iteration, sometimes leaning heavier into whisky barrels, other times port. Blends of previous vintages are mixed in and previous barrels reused. Still, have it once and there is no mistaking when it appears in your glass again. Aromas of toffee and rich, sweet soy are unmistakable hallmarks of this beer. With a consistency of light syrup, it will glaze the glass as sips resettle.

With a suggested retail price of US$240, full bottles will often be sold for double that price in stores, if you can find it, and sometimes for even more online. Empty bottles going back to 2002 often fetch a price comparable with today's modern four-pack. The brewery, which excels at marketing, has helped push this beer into the general consciousness thanks to news releases that claim the beer is 'illegal' in many US states due to its high alcohol content.

For unaccustomed drinkers who are more familiar with the brewery's year-round offerings like Samuel Adams Boston Lager or Summer Ale, Utopias can be bracing and nose turning. When taken as a special occasion drink, a slow sipper, and allowing time to tease out the various components, it becomes a memorable experience.

The 2021 version of the beer was aged on Blanton cherries and aged Sauternes oak wine casks, and it has undertones of rich maple and aged vanilla. If all goes according to tradition, a new version will be released in 2023.

Side Project Brewing
Grisette

4%   Grisette

Maplewood, Missouri

The Side Project Grisette is the other side of the coin for this well-known and respected brewery. For those who only know the Midwest brewery for its big, boozy Imperial Stouts and decadent Barleywines – the kind of beers that are traded for, argued over in online forums, and fetch a hefty price on the secondary market – a simple, 4% straw-coloured ale is unlikely to make waves.

But it should and certainly has for the fans of nuance who quickly snatch up bottles each time this beer is released. It varies with each iteration, spending time in different barrels or foeders before being sent to 750ml bottles for additional conditioning. Still, they all retain the same threads and soul.

The Grisette is a lovely all-day sipper that is lively with aromas of just-ripe strawberry and peach. It has Champagne-like carbonation and wakes up the taste buds and reveals a soft wheat character that is like lightly toasted country bread, followed by a slight earthy hop bite. On the finish is an oak character from the Missouri-harvested foeders used to age the beer.

Side Project is a brewery that takes wood seriously, putting most of their beers through barrels and similar vessels before their release. It's a skill that founders Cory and Karen King started as homebrewers and continued while he worked at nearby Perennial Brewing before opening Side Project in 2014.

The brewery has grown in reputation, with fans making the pilgrimage each year, or descending upon its invitational festival where big, bold beers are served in (hopefully) pleasant spring conditions. But amid the heft and high alcohol, spotting a bottle of Grisette is a welcome blessing and more than a palate cleanser.

King has been able to take a traditional Belgian-style ale and dress it up a bit, sharpen the lines without having the beer become harsh. The Grisette manages to be both traditional and modern in each sip, and while the bottle format might be built to share, it's a wonderful solo indulgence.

Verhaeghe
Duchesse de Bourgogne

6.2%   Flanders Red   11 IBUs

Vichte, Belgium

For more than a dozen years now the first beer I drink on Christmas Eve is Duchesse de Bourgogne. It started on a holiday when I had a few extra dollars in my pocket and wanted to expand my beer horizons past hops or lagers. The label, a portrait of Mary, the Duchess of Burgundy, is a familiar sight around the world and is the flagship offering from Brouwerij Verhaeghe in West Flanders, Belgium.

Flanders Red is not too common a style and can be difficult to make well. The base of rich roast malts and aged hops along with ambient yeast helps give the beer its distinctive taste. The final product is a blend of 18-month old and 8-month old double and spontaneously fermented ales that is aged in oak casks. There is also a cherry adjunct version of the beer available in some markets, but I suggest sticking with the original.

Poured into a chalice, this complex, tart ale has aromas and flavours of black cherry, toffee and balsamic vinegar. It is medium bodied and smooth, with a neat, little, dry finish that tickles the salvatory glands. It is artful and filled with so many layers that working through a four-pack will reveal new flavours or suggestions with each one.

Suitable whenever the mood strikes, this appeals to my inner Christmas nature. It can be paired with fruit cake and roasts, or just spending a little time with this beer in the quiet of the evening helps put the holiday into perspective, almost demanding that I slow down a bit and get lost in the twinkle of the lights on the tree. I always welcome the experience.

Weathered Souls Brewing Co
Black is Beautiful

8.8%   Imperial Stout

San Antonio, Texas

In the days after George Floyd was murdered by a police officer in Minneapolis, Minnesota, in May of 2020, Marcus Baskerville, the brewer at Weathered Souls Brewing Co in San Antonio, found himself talking with Jeffrey Stuffings, the founder of Jester King, a brewery in nearby Austin, Texas.

Baskerville wanted to brew a beer with proceeds going to social justice causes, and had planned that Black is Beautiful, an Imperial Stout, would be a brewery-only release. Stuffings encouraged him to share the recipe and the fundraising goals with the larger beer community, just as others had done for other causes, including wildfire relief and hospitality workers impacted by COVID-19.

Baskerville took the advice and within days dozens of breweries had signed up and brewed either the recipe provided by Weathered Souls, or variations of their own. Two years later and more than 1,200 breweries in 22 countries had brewed the beer.

The original is still regularly made by Weathered Souls and is distributed widely. It pours an inky black with a robust, rocky mocha head. It's ridiculously smooth on the mouthfeel with a ton of roast that never gets harsh and mimics espresso and dark chocolate fudge. A kiss of herbal hops adds bitterness to the finish. Throughout, the boozy qualities in the beer take on an almost port-like flavour and the first few sips bring a glow to the cheeks, but even as the glass empties the ale never feels too heavy. The goal of the beer is written along the side of the can: 'brewed to support justice and equality for people of color'.

Born from a preventable tragedy that reignited a movement, this beer continues to support important causes and remind drinkers that beer can be more than just beer: it can be a change agent for good.

Yazoo Brewing Company
Sue

9.1%   Rauchbier   44 IBUs

Madison, Tennessee

Geographically speaking, the southern United States was a tough nut to crack as the craft beer movement took hold in the country throughout the 1990s and early 2000s. Big lager was plentiful, affordable, and carried cultural significance.

In those early days many of the smaller breweries that opened did not compete in the lager space, but turned to hoppy or easy-drinking ales to capture attention, so it was a delight and a bold move when Yazoo released Sue, a big, smoky monster of a beer.

'We first kegged Sue in July 2009, after first getting a Tennessee distillery license to make it legally, since it was a "high-gravity beer",' says founder Linus Hall.

The rationale behind the beer, continues Hall, was that the south was fond of smoking meats, so a Rauchbier, made with applewood smoked malts, would resonate with drinkers. Turns out he was right, as the beer has become a regular offering from the brewery.

It's not quite a Porter or Stout, but sits comfortably in the dark ale territory. The smoke is not overwhelming, with bacon and campfire mixed in a skillful way. A fruity, sometimes herbal, hop character is present and offers a bit of sweetness to balance out the malts which verge on bitter.

As you would expect, this pairs perfectly with open-pit barbecue where savoury meats and spices are complimented by the beer's core components. A glass of this also goes well with another central Tennessee delicacy: Nashville Hot Chicken. The smoke and dark malts keep the extreme spice heat at bay, and the hefty alcohol content lowers inhibitions just enough to give you the courage to go for a higher heat level.

That this beer has remained popular and grown its fan base is a testament to smaller brewers that continue to change the perception of what beer can be, and find inroads to new customers.

Emma Inch

To earn its place in my list of great beers, each one had to be more than just a drink; it had to connect me to something.

Some beers I've chosen speak to me of cities, so vivid, so full of the chatter of strangers, that I can feel the stone beneath my feet as they guide me through their thoroughfares. Others draw me instead to a single patch of countryside, tucked between streams and hedges, where I can feel the pinch of a winter's night on my cheeks, or the hum of a late summer evening in the sweat on the back of my neck.

Other beers lead me to a moment in time. Like a resurrection of sorts, they colourise faded photographs, and allow me to feel on my own lips the same beer that my grandparents, my great-grandparents, or so many wonderful people who never imagined I could exist, felt on theirs.

And others connect me to a person. It could be the person I first shared the beer with, the one with whom I discovered the spaces in which to tuck each sip without disturbing the rhythm of our laughter-filled conversation. And, just sometimes, they connect me directly to the person who made them, the one with malt dust in their hair and the scent of hop oil still lingering on their hands.

Your list of great beers would no doubt look very different, but I hope you manage to find a few connections in mine.

S. Allsopp & Sons
Allsopp's India Pale Ale

5.6% (bottle); **5**% (cask)   IPA

London (currently brewed in Devon), England

Sometimes extinction doesn't last forever.

In the film Jurassic Park, the amber bulb that formed the head of John Hammond's cane contained the remains of a prehistoric mosquito. Using blood extracted from the insect's gut, Hammond was able to obtain DNA that allowed him to create a world of incredible creatures that hadn't walked the earth for 65 million years. Allsopp's Brewery wasn't dormant for quite so long, but the story of this wonderful beer contains just as much dedication and perseverance.

The Allsopp family began brewing beer in Burton-upon-Trent back in 1730. In 1822, pioneering brewer Samuel Allsopp brewed his first batch of India Pale Ale – in a teapot, according to legend – and by the 1830s this beer had made the brewery's name. It was bold, aspirational, and perfectly utilised the town's gypsum-laden water. However, a series of unsuccessful business decisions, an early dalliance with lager, and a sadly predictable wave of mergers and acquisitions meant that Allsopp's had vanished by the end of the 1950s.

Then, in 2021, along came a man with a mosquito trapped in amber. Jamie Allsopp is the seven-times great-grandson of Samuel Allsopp, and despite a career as a fund manager, always dreamed of resurrecting the family business. With the sole surviving copy of the brewing ledger and access to the original Allsopp's yeast, he set about gathering the scattered trademarks and faithfully recreating the original Burton IPA.

The resulting beer – itself a bright amber hue – has notes of dried fruit, candied peel and toffee, but the restrained sweetness and staunchly bitter aftertaste renders it exceptionally drinkable. This beer, brought back from extinction, gives us a glimpse into a fascinating past and, I hope, a highly successful future.

Emma Inch

Anspach & Hobday
The Porter

6.7% Porter

London, England

Having judged a number of homebrew competitions in my time, I know that beer cooked up on Heath Robinson-type contraptions in kitchens, bathrooms and garden sheds can sometimes taste much better than professionally brewed beers. Of course, not many of these homebrewed miracles ever escape the world of tea urns and airing cupboards, but Anspach & Hobday's The Porter is one that most definitely did.

Childhood friends Paul Anspach and John (Jack) Hobday began homebrewing in their London flat whilst studying at university. Inspired by the imported American, and early British, craft beer they were drinking, they began by making IPAs and pales, full of hops and bursting with bitterness. Then, on 1st November 2011, they brewed their first batch of The Porter which, according to Jack, turned out to be 'our first really good homebrew'.

In retrospect, it's hardly surprising that a Porter – a beer so enmeshed in the history of London, and so suited to the city's hard water – tasted so good. Coupled with Paul and Jack's determination to bring together tradition and modernity, it makes perfect sense that when the brewery launched commercially in a Bermondsey railway arch at the end of 2013, The Porter – now their flagship beer – was the first beer they brewed.

A blend of highly kilned and roasted malts coupled with American Cascade and British East Kent Goldings hops results in a firm coffee and chocolate bitterness, and a beer that sings of the city of its birth. The clean palate makes it perfect for pairing with the traditional and adopted food of London – pie and mash, jellied eels, curry, or street vendor falafels – or for drinking on its own, preferably within sight of the Thames.

Beak Brewery
Pencil India Porter

6% Porter

Lewes, East Sussex

If asked to name the location of the UK's deadliest avalanche, you could be forgiven for taking a guess at the mountains of Scotland, or perhaps even Wales. However, the British avalanche that claimed the most lives actually took place in the small market town of Lewes in rural East Sussex. On the edge of the town looms the chalk-white, sheer face of Cliffe Hill. In the winter of 1836 a storm whipped up snowdrifts and led to a massive overhang of deep snow on the edge of the hill. On 27th December that snow inevitably fell onto a row of workers' cottages on the street below. Seven people were rescued, but eight more sadly died.

It's in the shadow of this commanding cliff that, in 2020, food and drink writer Daniel Tapper chose to lay down the roots of the formerly nomadic Beak Brewery. Clearly not intimidated by the 100 metres of chalk face looming over it, or by its renowned brewing neighbours – the 230-year-old Harvey's Brewery is just a short walk away – Beak has rapidly become a critically acclaimed and much-loved brewery, producing a range of Pale Ales, IPAs, dark beers and mixed fermentation brews.

Inspired by dark beers produced by the likes of Bermondsey's Kernel Brewery, Pencil combines a Victorian malt grist – a blend of six amber, brown, chocolate, black and pale malts – with Columbus and Chinook hops. The resultant beer is confident and sure-footed, reminiscent of those produced by far more established breweries. It's as decadent as the chocolate you pop in your mouth before breakfast on Christmas morning, rich and boozy with layers of coffee and molasses, and a tight finish of uplifting woody bitterness.

Emma Inch

Burning Sky
Coolship (annual release)

6.5–6.8% (ABV varies)   Spontaneously fermented barrel-aged beer

Firle, East Sussex

At 217 metres, Firle Beacon is one of the highest points on the South Downs Way. If you're lucky enough to walk there, you can revel in spectacular 360-degree views that encompass both the indigo blue strip of the sea and the patchwork of green fields that clothe this part of East Sussex. The landscape is one of chalky ridges and grassy slopes. At your feet are buttercups and round-headed rampion, whilst overhead skylarks chatter against the blur of the sun. Look down and you'll see the tiny village of Firle, with its manor house, church, and brick and flint pub. And somewhere amongst those buildings the brewers at Burning Sky are not only motivated by their bucolic surroundings, but are capturing, blending, and bottling them into a very special beer.

Founder Mark Tranter knew he wanted to brew a beer of this kind – one inspired by the mixed and spontaneously fermented beers of Belgium – from the very start. Five years later his dream became reality.

As implied by its name, a coolship – a flat, open-topped vessel traditionally used for cooling hot wort – is used in the production of this beer. As the wort cools overnight it is

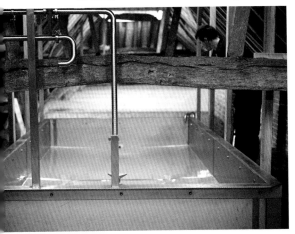

exposed to the air and becomes inoculated with wild yeasts unique to the brewery's surroundings.

'This beer is a total reflection of our landscape, the flora and fauna that surround us,' Mark explains. 'You could brew this beer exactly as we do elsewhere, and it would be completely different.'

After a lengthy fermentation in wooden barrels, the result is a funky, golden beer, with pleasant acidity and more than a whisper of oak. It's a beer that, like the chalk on your boots, tells a fine story of this remarkable place.

Burnt Mill
Pintle

4.3% Pale Ale

Badley, Suffolk

Brewing has always been women's work. From the earliest of times, since the very first civilisations, brewing was considered a domestic chore, and something over which women had dominion. Even the ancient goddesses and protectors of beer – Ninkasi, Hathor, Dea Latis – were all portrayed as female. It was only when beer began to be produced industrially and on a large scale that women were pushed out.

Nowadays, beer is often considered to be a 'man's drink', and women are grossly underrepresented within the industry. But thanks to Burnt Mill's head brewer, Sophie de Ronde, there is at least one day a year when women take over the brewing world. March 8th marks International Women's Collaboration Brew Day, a day when women come together to network, learn, and create a beer as a reminder of the important role women play in the world's favourite drink.

Sophie is a talented brewer and in 2019 she was awarded the prestigious title of British Guild of Beer Writers Brewer of the Year. However, a severe barley allergy means she is no longer able to drink the fruits of her labour. Luckily, years of experience, a powerful nose, and a great team around her means she's able to consistently produce great beers like Pintle.

Pintle was the very first beer brewed on Burnt Mill's brew kit back in May 2017, and was designed to be a core beer right from the very start. It pours as lively as sherbet, with a white, cottony head and citrus aroma. The added wheat, oats and flaked barley leaves it feeling soft in the mouth, whilst just the right level of bitterness, and a clean, dry finish, keeps you coming back for more.

Dark Star
Hophead

3.8%   Golden Ale

Partridge Green, West Sussex

Oftentimes, brewpubs, independent brewers, family brewers, and multinationals can feel like very disparate entities, with little in common. But some beers manage to join the dots between them all.

Dark Star Brewery began life in 1994, in the cellar of Brighton's Evening Star pub. Founder Rob Jones had already made his name at Pitfield Brewery where he brewed a beer – also called Dark Star after the song by The Grateful Dead – which won Champion Beer of Britain in 1987.

The pub cellar was tiny, and the brew kit was not much bigger than that of an enthusiastic homebrewer. Soon, Rob was joined in the brewery by one of the pub's regulars, a certain Mark Tranter who later went on to found Burning Sky Brewery. Together they brewed beer for the drinkers upstairs and formed what they called the 'Hophead Club', for which they created a series of beers, each showcasing a single hop.

The story goes that one of the pub's owners, Pete Halliday, brought some Cascade hops home from the US in his suitcase, and this single-hop brew quickly became the drinkers' favourite. This beer later became Hophead.

In 2001 Dark Star moved to Ansty in West Sussex, and in 2010 moved again, a few miles down the road to their current premises in Partridge Green. In February 2018 the brewery was acquired by family brewer Fuller's, which in turn was sold to multinational brewer Asahi less than a year later.

Throughout all of this, Hophead survived. The ultimate session beer, packed with elderflower aroma and a punch of grapefruit bitterness, this beer is best drunk on cask, in pints, ideally whilst propping up the bar at The Evening Star pub.

Elusive
Oregon Trail

5.8%   West Coast IPA

Finchampstead, Berkshire

In the mid-19th century Oregon Trail was an American wagon route that led gold prospectors and fur traders the 2,000 miles from Independence, Missouri, to Oregon's Willamette Valley. By the end of the 20th century Oregon Trail was a classic video game designed to teach children about the harsh reality of life on the wagon train. Now, in the 21st century, Elusive Brewing has managed to combine a journey to the West Coast with eight-bit-style branding in a beer that became a classic when it was barely a year old.

Elusive Brewing was founded in 2016 by Andy Parker, officially the 'nicest man in beer' (there was a Twitter poll to decide it so it must be true). Andy had been a homebrewer for a number of years, and in 2014 won first place in Craft Beer Co's National Homebrew Competition. The prize was £5,000 and the opportunity to brew his recipe at Dark Star Brewery. The winning beer – an American Red called Level Up – is now part of the Elusive core range.

Oregon Trail also has its roots in one of Andy's homebrew recipes – his first ever all-grain brew which was inspired by Green Flash's West Coast IPA. It was first brewed commercially in 2019 as a collaboration with Fareham's West Street Alehouse and is now the brewery's bestseller.

At a time when IPA has become synonymous with fruit, soft mouthfeel and lack of bitterness, this beer drags us straight back on that dusty wagon train to the hop fields of the West. It features barley sugar sweetness followed by a welcome punch of bitter marmalade, and is the only type of gold I'd be prepared to cross a continent for.

  Emma Inch

Five Points
Best

4.1% Best Bitter

London, England

For some, the so-called 'craft beer revolution' acted, at least in part, as a rejection of what they saw as 'twiggy' British beers. The influx of ales brewed with hugely aromatic hops from across the Atlantic, or novel ingredients such as marshmallows or passion fruit, caused certain drinkers to turn their backs on traditional English styles in favour of new trends. But there were many more of us who, whilst embracing new opportunities, never lost faith in the beers we'd grown up with, and who fervently hoped that at some point modern breweries would take those centuries of brewing heritage and make them their own.

Five Points began life in a railway arch in Hackney, East London, in 2013. According to director of brewing Greg Hobbs, he and fellow co-founder Ed Mason had wanted to brew a Best Bitter for some time but were unsure whether there would be a market for it amongst modern drinkers. Eventually, they bit the bullet and released Best at a Leeds craft beer festival.

'Launching Five Points Best at a fringe event during Hop City felt like a great idea [...] until the day before the event when it occurred to us that some of the world's best hop-forward brewers were going to be in town and we were launching a 4.1% Best Bitter hopped with Fuggle – almost the definition of a "boring brown bitter".'

Luckily, drinkers loved it, and Best is now firmly part of the core range. A biscuit bite of Maris Otter malt is perfectly balanced against the almost minty grassiness of Kentish Fuggles, and the final, bitter punch reminds you that sometimes tradition can embrace modernity and leave both the better for it.

Fuller, Smith & Turner
Golden Pride

8.5% Barley Wine

London, England

As football fans know, back in 1966 the English had good reason to celebrate. And in the same year that Geoff Hurst was blasting that winning goal into a Wembley net, just a few miles down the road in Chiswick, Fuller's Brewery was creating a beer it could take just as much pride in.

Golden Pride is a Barley Wine, made in the traditional parti-gyle method. This involves brewing more than one beer from a single batch of grain. Similar to reusing a teabag for two cups of tea – one strong and one weaker – the wort from the mash tun is split into two kettles. The first runnings are stronger and used to brew the Golden Pride, whilst the second runnings go to brew a beer with a lower ABV.

At 8.5%, this beer was originally served in nips – one-third of a pint bottles – but was later bottled in half pints. Former head brewer John Keeling, who worked at Fullers for 37 years, tells me he had colleagues who regularly drank a 'pint of blood', a punchy blend of a half pint of Chiswick Bitter mixed with a bottle of Golden Pride.

Golden Pride is brewed from the same base recipe as Fuller's Vintage Ale, but unlike that annual release, its hopping regime always consists of Target, Northdown Challenger and Golding. It has a boozy aroma and full-bodied, marmalade richness, offset by a warming mix of Christmas pudding, leather satchels, wooden benches, and the embers of a fireplace. And by a fireplace is exactly where this beer should be drunk, as the rain lashes against the windows and you momentarily forget that you still have a long walk home.

Fuller, Smith & Turner
London Porter

5.4% Porter

London, England

At one time Porter was as vital to the life of London as the mighty River Thames itself. The beer gained its name from those who drank it: the many thousands of porters who, in the 18th and 19th centuries, worked at the riverside and within the city, unloading, fetching, carrying, and generally keeping the business of London going.

However, by the mid-20th century London was a very different place and Porter had fallen out of favour. Fuller's Brewery had stopped making it, and it wasn't until 1996, when the brewery was looking for a follow-up to its celebrated 1845 Strong Ale, that the legendary Reg Drury – head brewer at the time – began to consider brewing London Porter. The beer he devised was a homage to past brews; a brand-new recipe, but based on a typical London-type Porter, combining pale, crystal, brown and chocolate malts with Fuggle hops for a traditional profile.

Former head brewer John Keeling worked alongside Reg Drury at the time and remembers the first brew: "we'd done it and put it in, put it into cask and it was flat. Reg said, "I can't understand why it's flat; the yeast count is correct; there's lots of sugar in it; I just think it's a matter of waiting." I've never seen Reg so worried. So we held it for four or five days on the floor and then we tested it and it made a load of condition [...] it was perfect. And it was a lovely drop of beer.'

And this award-winning Porter still is a lovely drop of beer. It's a satisfying gulp of creamy smoothness coupled with coffee and chocolate complexity and perhaps just a little smoky suggestion of the city of London itself.

Greene King
Strong Suffolk

6%   Old Ale

Bury St Edmunds, Suffolk

Wherever you are in the historic market town of Bury St Edmunds you can see the flag flying from the Westgate Brewery. The seven-storey, art deco brewhouse was built in 1938, but Greene King has been making beer on the site since 1799, and there is evidence in the Domesday Book that brewing in the town dates back much further than that. An understanding of the depth of brewing history here only adds to an appreciation of Strong Suffolk Ale.

This beer was probably first created in the 1920s. Blending of stored beers with younger running beers would once have been common amongst Britain's regional brewers, but, unusually, Greene King has not removed its oak vats and still continues the practice. Strong Suffolk is a blend of two beers: a unique 5.6% 'motherbrew' called BPA (Best Pale Ale) and the famous 12% 5X.

5X is brewed from pale and crystal malt, brewing sugar, cane sugar, English hops, and Greene King's own yeast strain. Once brewed, it's transferred to one of the brewery's three oak vats where it's stored for at least two years. The lids of the vats are covered in a layer of marl – a Suffolk word for the gravel found across the county. The weight of the marl apparently prevents the lids from lifting during secondary fermentation and limits the ingress of pests and wild yeasts.

Neither 5X nor BPA are available commercially, although Greene King often brings a firkin of the former to the Great British Beer Festival. The blend they create when they come together is deep mahogany with hints of garnet. Malty notes give way to dried fruit, marzipan and cherries, with a smooth, vinous quality and a complexity that speaks to its rich history.

Harvey's
Imperial Extra Double Stout

9%   Imperial Stout

Lewes, East Sussex

A few years ago I was lucky enough to be invited to a rare brew day of Harvey's Imperial Extra Double Stout. I arrived at the brewery – known locally as Lewes Cathedral – at 6.30am. It was a damp February morning but there was a note of Christmas-like excitement in the air. Head brewer and joint managing director Miles Jenner was waiting outside and led me into the warm copper and wood of the brewhouse.

Miles is a fifth-generation brewer whose father, Anthony, was head brewer at Harvey's before him. He was born at the brewery and his love and respect for what he calls 'the romance of brewing' is apparent in the story of this unique beer.

In the mid-19th century a Belgian merchant, Albert Le Coq, made his money importing strong Stout from London's Barclay Perkins Brewery, bottling it, and shipping it to the Baltic regions where it became very popular in the tsar's court. Some years later, Le Coq was invited to brew his beer inside the Russian Empire, and in 1912 brewing began in Tartu, in what is now Estonia. The brewery apparently still exists, but this strong Stout is no longer brewed. In 1998 an American importer was looking for a UK brewery to produce an authentic version of this beer. The Tartu Brewery agreed to provide the provenance and Harvey's took on the challenge.

The result is a truly remarkable beer that, according to Miles, 'is as your forebears would have drunk it in the eighteenth century'. It pours as thick as oil and serves up a mix of black cherry sweetness, vinous alcohol warmth, and a tart, savoury finish that perfectly showcases Miles' characteristic understated genius.

Harviestoun
Ola Dubh – 12 Year-Old Whisky Aged

10.5% (cask and keg); **8**% (bottles)   Barrel-Aged Stout

Alva, Clackmannanshire, Scotland

Sometimes a name tells you almost everything you need to know. Ola Dubh (pronounced 'ola-doo') is Gaelic for 'black oil', and the way this unique beer pours smoothly into a glass reveals a viscosity and unctuousness that fully justifies its appellation.

Harviestoun Brewery was founded in 1983, on a farm near Dollar in Clackmannanshire – Scotland's smallest county – by Ken Brooker, a former Ford Motors employee. Since 2004 it's been based in the small town of Alva, at the foot of the Ochil Hills. Its beers are brewed with naturally filtered local water and barley malted only four miles away in Alloa.

The inspiration for Ola Dubh came when the brewery's American importer asked if some of the beers could be aged in whisky casks for the US market. After trialling casks from a number of distilleries, in 2007 Harviestoun took the novel step of formally partnering with Highland Park Distillery in Orkney. It now provides the casks in which the full Ola Dubh range – the 12-, 14-, 16- and 18-year-old versions – is aged.

One of the brewery's existing beers, Old Engine Oil, a 6% Stout, is used as a base beer. Once fermented, it's transferred to the whisky casks where it matures for at least six months, picking up some of the flavour characteristics from the wood and the whisky formerly housed there. According to head brewer Amy Cockburn, 'The 12-year-old casks bring a lot of oaky character, a smokiness and bourbon aromas, and flavours that balance off nicely against the base beer's bittersweet chocolate, coffee and liquorice characters.'

The whisky certainly brings a welcome warmth to the chest, but it's coupled with a distinctive, bright, mountain-stream lightness that carries dark fruit, tobacco and cocoa nibs effortlessly across the palate.

Emma Inch

Hofmeister
Helles

5%   Helles

Brewed in Bavaria, Germany – brand HQ in Dorking, Surrey

Anyone who remembers, fondly or otherwise, the 3.2% faux-German lager marketed as Hofmeister in the 1980s and 1990s might be a little surprised to find it here, in a book celebrating the world's greatest beers. However much we may have enjoyed following the exploits of George the Bear, when the beer ceased production in 2003, I doubt too many tears were shed.

Almost 15 years later, however, two friends, Spencer Chambers and Richard Longhurst, felt there may still be some love out there for Hofmeister. After purchasing the brand from the then owners, Heineken, they travelled to Bavaria to find a brewery to brew an all-new Hofmeister, an authentic 5% German Helles. After an extensive search, they settled on Privatbrauerei Schweiger, which now slow brews Hofmeister in accordance with the Reinheitsgebot, the 16th-century Bavarian Purity Law.

The beer was relaunched in 2017, and within a year was named as the World's Best Lager in the International Wine & Spirits Competition (IWSC) Beer Awards. Numerous other awards have followed, and the beer has become a fixture on some of the smartest bars across the UK.

The new Hofmeister recipe includes malt and hops grown within a few miles of the brewery, and water drawn from an underground lake beneath the Ebersberger Forest, so pure it's also sold as mineral water. The result is a perfectly balanced Helles, rich with bready sweetness, offset by a bite of hop spice, and a bitterness that lingers. Served in a traditional stein, it's a bright gold, each facet of the glass working to reflect the sunniest of days.

But why revive a brand like Hofmeister?

'It made us smile,' Spencer explains. And you know what? It makes me smile, too.

Innis & Gunn
Vanishing Point

11% Barrel-Aged Imperial Stout

Edinburgh, Scotland

A few years ago, I paid a visit to Speyside Cooperage in Craigellachie alongside Dougal Sharp, master brewer and founder of Innis & Gunn. The cooperage produces, repairs, and recycles around 150,000 oak casks a year, and is where Dougal sources all the barrels he uses to age his beers.

Outside, pyramids of wooden casks loomed against the deep-blue Highland sky, whilst inside the odours of smoke and steam mixed with the sweat on the coopers' foreheads and the leather scent of their aprons. The noise of metal against metal was repetitive and jarring, and the rush of flame as each cask was charred was smarting hot. Dougal was in his element.

'Innis & Gunn was founded on barrel-ageing,' he tells me, 'And I am proud to have been a pioneer and innovator within the beer style.'

A second-generation brewer, Dougal founded the brewery in 2003. Vanishing Point, an annual release, was first brewed in 2016 and represents a long-term project in which each new iteration builds upon the last.

'The vanishing point is something far in the distance, something always slightly beyond reach; something that moves as you do,' Dougal explains. 'We thought this perfectly summed up our quest for continual improve-ment, to give the drinker the ultimate whisky-cask-matured beer experience, one which they can expect every year, but with each release hopefully surpassing their expectations.'

A classic Imperial Stout recipe, Vanishing Point is matured in single malt whisky casks, different for each release, for a period of 12 months. This serves to mellow the beer, but also to draw in flavour components from the barrels, including vanilla, oak and spirit, together with a complexity and depth that perfectly showcases the impact of barrel-ageing.

The Kernel
Imperial Brown Stout 1856

9.7%   Stout

London, England

When I first heard mention of the Durden Park Beer Circle, what immediately sprang to mind was a more alcohol-focused version of the Bloomsbury Set, a group of bohemian artists and thinkers who drifted between their London homes and a quirky pile in the country. I was, of course, mistaken.

The Durden Park Beer Circle is a group of homebrewers, formed in 1971, who meet in Perivale, a suburb in West London. Soon after it was founded, members of the group developed an interest in researching and recreating historical beers, and in 1976 published a book of recipes, scaled to homebrew volumes.

Kernel founder Evin O'Riordain met members of the Durden Park Beer Circle and tasted some of their historical brews when he was still a homebrewer. 'They blew my mind,' he tells me. 'To think that beer could taste like this was a revelation, and to think beers like this were being drunk 150 years ago was an eye-opener to a prejudiced mind.'

The Imperial Brown Stout is taken from the Durden Park brewing book and is based on an 1856 Barclay Perkins recipe of the same name. Modern brewing practices inevitably result in some differences, but essentially this beer provides a precious glimpse into the past.

'Part of the appeal of these historic recipes is that it brings a certain humility,' explains Evin, 'it reminds us that we are allowed our position because of the work done before by others that curated beer's place in the culture of this island.'

With each sip, roasted barley notes combine with a sprinkle of cinder toffee sweetness, and an almost dizzying depth, as savoury as Marmite and as bitter as tears. This is a beer for contemplation; a true thinker's drink.

Lacons
Audit Ale

8%   Barley Wine

Great Yarmouth, Norfolk

It may be a falcon that adorns the beer labels, but the story of Lacons Brewery is in many ways more akin to that of a phoenix. Established in Great Yarmouth, Norfolk, in 1760, the brewery successfully produced beer and managed pubs for more than two centuries. In 1965, in a story familiar to many other regional breweries of the time, brewing giant Whitbread bought Lacons, and in 1968 the brewery was closed.

It wasn't destined to remain that way, however, as some 45 years later the falcon rose from the ashes, thanks in large part to the hard work of Mick Carver who now heads up the brewery as managing director. Working alongside William Lacon, son of the last Lacon family member to work at the brewery, Mick managed to secure the rights, recipes, and even the original yeast – which had been stored at the National Yeast Bank – to enable him to revive Lacon's brewery.

Audit Ale brings with it its own tale of resurrection. Traditionally drunk at feasts held to celebrate the completion of annual audits – particularly those at the colleges of Oxford and Cambridge universities – audit ales were strong and special beers, brewed for sharing and celebration. For a while, Lacons provided the audit ale for some Oxbridge colleges, and in the late 1930s the ale was packaged in Champagne-style bottles and exported to New York where it was sold as a highly exclusive product.

This Audit Ale is a modern recreation of a recipe dating back to 1937. It's a copper-coloured Barley Wine with robust, dark fruit flavours and a gentle, orange marmalade bitterness. Deceptively easy to drink, it's a beer that drips with tradition and revels in its own revival.

   Emma Inch

Little Earth Project
Hedgerow Blend

4–6% *ABV varies*   Barrel-Aged Sour

Sudbury, Suffolk

There's a campsite just over the hedge from the timber barn where Little Earth Project founder Tom Norton brews his beer. I stayed there one muggy summer weekend and worked up a thirst by walking in the local area. Under the wide, blue Suffolk sky, I trekked through fields of wheat and barley, criss-crossed by verdant hedgerows. In a small copse a fellow camper spotted a badger, and during the dense humidity of one afternoon I watched a grass snake scutter across my path.

Little Earth Project is not Tom's first brewery. In 2008 he set up Mill Green on the same site brewing mostly cask ale for local pubs. But inspired by the likes of Jester King Brewery in the USA, in 2016 Tom decided to create a mixed fermentation brewery that reflected his own little piece of earth.

'Little Earth Project came about through a passion to build a brewery that was connected to nature, the changing seasons and our local environment,' Tom explains. 'A brewery of nature and the earth rather than of industrial processes.'

Hedgerow Blend perfectly embodies this endeavour and sprang from Tom's wish to create a beer that represented late summer in the Suffolk countryside. A golden sour beer is brewed with locally grown organic barley and hops, and water drawn from chalk 60 metres below the brewery. It's then aged in oak for months – or sometimes years – before two of the best barrels are chosen to be blended in a tank with fruit and wild hops foraged from the hedgerows in August and September.

The flavour varies year to year, but sharp plums, oak tannins, those abundant Suffolk hedgerows, and just a little bit of evening sunshine are always to the fore.

Oakham
Citra

4.2%(cask); **4.6**%(bottles)   Session IPA

Peterborough, Cambridgeshire

In the constant noise of the new, it's important to remember the originals.

Nowadays, Citra is one of the most commonly used hops in craft beer. Brewers, beer geeks, and even casual drinkers are familiar with its name, and with the fruity, floral notes it contributes to a beer. But we forget that just a few short decades ago it didn't even exist.

Oakham Ales' former brewing director John Bryan was one of the very first UK brewers to make annual hop-sourcing trips to the USA. During one such trip in 2009 he was introduced to a hop he'd never come across before. So impressed was he that he bought a third of what was available, and rather than waiting for it to be shipped across the Atlantic, he sent it back to the UK by air so he could brew with it as soon as possible.

On 20th November, the day after the 'air-mailed' hops arrived, the first batch of Oakham Ales Citra was brewed. With the rest of the UK consignment of this exciting new hop still making its way across the ocean, Oakham became Britain's very first commercial brewery to brew a beer entirely with Citra hops. So well received was the beer that it has been a permanent fixture since 2011, and the brewery's best-seller since 2016.

Brewed using Maris Otter malt and just a small amount of wheat, the beer is hopped six times during the brew. Consequently, each gulp leaves your mouth utterly saturated with bright lemon peel, drenched with a citrus tingle that reaches right to your tonsils and back again, and enough original bitterness to cut through at least some of that noise.

Polly's
Rosa

8.5% Double IPA

Mold, Flintshire, Wales

'What's in a name?' Juliet questioned from her balcony. Well, quite a lot if you happen to be one of the most acclaimed breweries in Wales.

Polly's Brew Co was started from the ashes of a short-lived cask brewery by Sean Wheldon in early 2018. The brewery was located in a farm building that had previously been home to Loka Island, a graphic design project run by Sean's twin brother, and before that, a stable for the now deceased family horse, Polly. Drawing together the history of the building, Sean called his new brewery Loka Polly, a name that sounded both modern and global, and clearly caught the attention of beer drinkers across the UK and beyond. In 2019 the Loka part was dropped following a challenge by a Scandanavian drinks brand of the same name, but the much-loved horse lives on in every colourful can.

Rosa was first brewed in April 2019, one of the original three beers launched as part of the brewery's Augment range. At the time, it was the biggest beer Polly's had produced, and one of the first above 8% ABV. It has the brewery's signature emphasis on freshness and fruit, and a list of hops – Citra, Ekuanot, Galaxy, Mosaic and Simcoe – to leave your mouth drenched.

'That which we call a rose, by any other word would smell as sweet,' Juliet continues. And this particular rose comes with a punch of mango-citrus aroma, and a taste so full it's like pushing six segments of blood orange into your mouth at once. But it doesn't simply fade to soft juice: a pucker of grapefruit bitterness and a gentle alcohol warmth carry this dramatic giant of a beer safely home.

Ramsgate
Gadds' Nº 3

5% Pale Ale

Broadstairs, Kent

Gadds' Nº 3 is a beer built around a true English hero. But the main protagonist in this tale isn't made of flesh and blood; she's made of leaves, bines and all-important cones.

Goldings hops originated in Kent and were named after the man who first developed them in the late 18th century. Although cultivated in other parts of the world, the ones grown in East Kent – the county of England closest to the European mainland – are considered something distinctly different, uniquely special. The area's location, between the rolling downs and the salty sea, creates a favourable microclimate in which they thrive, and in 2013 East Kent Goldings became the first hops to be granted Protected Designation of Origin Status.

Gadds' Brewery, now based in Broadstairs, was founded by Eddie and Lois Gadd in 2002 in the back of a Ramsgate pub. Eddie previously worked as brewer for the Firkin pub chain and had developed a passion for Kentish hops even before he moved to the county. According to Eddie, it's about 'balance and class. A good Golding is sweet as well as bitter, and the aroma of East Kent Golding, whilst subtle, is very classy.'

Gadds' Nº 3 was the very first beer Eddie brewed when he started his new brewery, and the recipe remains unchanged. According to him, he set out to create 'a beer for modern Kent', and he has certainly achieved that.

A supporting cast of Maris Otter malt champions the real star of the show, the East Kent Goldings hops, and in this classic Pale Ale they are allowed to soar. Golden and bitter, bright and effervescent, this beer is the perfect showcase for the soft, honeyed spice of this quintessential slice of England.

Emma Inch

Rooster's
Baby-Faced Assassin

6.1% IPA

Harrogate, North Yorkshire

Some beers give you no warning. They don't caution you to handle them with care or suggest that you sip them politely. They're silent, stealthy, and display no indication of the dangers they hold. Baby-Faced Assassin, however, has it's warning quite literally written across every pump clip. Whether you choose to heed it is another matter entirely.

Rooster's was founded by Sean Franklin in 1993. On his retirement in 2011, the brewery was sold to Ian Fozard and his sons, Oliver and Tom. At the beginning of that same year, Tom, now Rooster's commercial director, was working at Beer Ritz, a bottle shop in Leeds. It was there that he designed the homebrew recipe that was to become Baby-Faced Assassin.

'I'd been homebrewing for about a year and had managed to create and execute some reasonably good recipes, but I'd failed at creating an IPA that had real intensity to it when it came to aroma,' he explains.

Tom got hold of 500g of Citra hops – still new and not widely available to homebrewers – and pitched the whole lot into his new IPA. The result was much better than anticipated, and later in the year a limited run of 70 750ml bottles was brewed on Rooster's experimental brew kit. A couple of years later, Oliver (now head brewer) reworked the level of hopping to allow for commercial brewing on a large scale, and in 2014 it was added to the brewery's core range.

Each mouthful brings masses of tangerine marmalade aroma followed by brief caramel biscuit sweetness. Finally, grapefruit bitterness delivers a sucker punch to the tonsils. Urgently drinkable, this 6.1% beer can take you out at the knees pretty quickly: but you can't say it didn't warn you.

Siren
Broken Dream

6.5% Breakfast Stout

Finchampstead, Berkshire

People don't usually drink 6.5% coffee-infused cask-conditioned Stouts throughout heatwaves, but during the long, hot summer of 2018, all that changed. When Broken Dream was named as CAMRA's Champion Beer of Britain at the Great British Beer Festival, Siren felt the impact on sales almost immediately. 'People wanted a beer we had nothing of!', explains the brewery's founder, Darron Anley.

Darron set up Siren Craft Brew in 2013, following a career in IT security. Alongside his commercial acumen, he brought to the business a long-standing appreciation of good beer, a playful creativity, and an ongoing love affair with coffee. The latter has led to Siren becoming one of the UK's leading breweries in the field of beer and coffee, with growing expertise gleaned partly from an annual Project Barista initiative that sees the brewery pair up with different independent roasters to brew unique coffee beers. And at the heart of Siren's core range sits the Breakfast Stout, Broken Dream.

'Breakfast Stout is a style from the US that plays with everything you expect from breakfast, namely coffee, oats, chocolate and milk – and maybe a touch of bacon with the smoked malt,' explains Darron.

Broken Dream achieves this through a blend of Maris Otter, malted oats, roast barley and a mix of brown, aromatic, and smoked malts. Apollo hops bring aroma and bitterness, lactose adds a certain creaminess, and specialist coffee from the Minas Gerais region of Brazil contributes some luxurious cocoa notes.

The result is a liquorice-sweet, smoky-chocolate beer. It pours oil-black with an intense viscosity that fills the mouth, a treacle-toffee, cigar richness, and gentle warmth that invites you to drink this gem of a beer whatever the weather.

St Austell
Black Square

10–12.5% *ABV varies from year to year*   Barrel-Aged Imperial Stout

St Austell, Cornwall

I have a bottle of the 2020 vintage Black Square stashed away in my beer collection. Like all my aged or unique brews, I know I'll drink it one day; but that day will need to be very special indeed.

Black Square was first conceived by the much-loved Roger Ryman, former brewing director at St Austell Brewery. It was based on recipes for Stout brewed in England in the 18th and 19th centuries for export to Russia and the Baltic states. The first batch was brewed in Moscow in collaboration with New Riga Brewery, which Roger once told me gave it 'real Russian credentials!'

The beer was a big success for New Riga, and Roger decided to rebrew it back in Cornwall. It's now an annual release, produced on St Austell's small-batch brewery between Christmas and New Year. A grist including Maris Otter, roasted barley, and Demerara sugar meets a hop bill of Target, Challenger, Centennial and – Roger's favourite hop – Styrian Goldings, to produce a jet-black beer. Black Square is aged in bourbon barrels for 10 months, before being blended into just 4,000 bottles for release each December.

In 2019 Roger fulfilled a long-held ambition when Black Square was awarded a gold medal and trophy at the prestigious International Brewing Awards. He was rightly very proud of the singular beer he'd created. Sadly, in May 2020, Roger died, and that year's iteration of Black Square turned out to be his final brew.

Roger's legacy lives on, however, in this unique beer which is still brewed to the exact recipe in his honour. Strong and complex, with notes of vanilla oak and bitter chocolate, this is truly a beer to drink in remembrance and celebration of a remarkable man.

Tempest Brewing Co
All The Leaves Are Brown

11.2%   Barrel-Aged Imperial Brown Ale

Tweedbank, Scottish Borders

In my early teens, I had a cassette (remember them?) of The Mamas and The Papas greatest hits. For more than a year, I listened to it on headphones almost every night as I fell asleep, which is the reason why I can never read the name of this beer without bringing to mind the opening bars of *California Dreamin'*.

In many ways, an industrial estate in the Scottish Borders couldn't be further from the sun-drenched West Coast of the USA, but the beer brewed there certainly echoes some of the soaring melodies and pitch-perfect harmonies of that wonderful song.

Tempest Brewing undoubtedly brings many elements of the wider world into its beers. The brewery's founders, husband-and-wife team Gavin and Annika Meiklejohn, met in a brewpub in Canada whilst they were both travelling, and first started brewing in the garage of a house they shared in Christchurch, New Zealand. In 2010, having returned to Gavin's homeland, they set up Tempest in a disused dairy.

All The Leaves Are Brown was originally brewed in 2017 for the legendary Borefts Beer Festival, hosted by acclaimed Dutch brewery De Molen. Head brewer Douglas Rowe explains: 'It was around mid-September, so our idea was to brew something seasonal as we approached autumn. It also had to be imperial to please the Borefts drinkers.'

The result is a sticky, maple syrup-drenched, treacle toffee of a beer, to be drunk as a bonfire burns and dry branches crack underfoot. A woody bitterness mixed with bourbon sweetness comes from ageing in casks from Heaven Hill distillery in Kentucky, and the whole beer comes together with the same joyful intensity as listening to your favourite music through headphones.

Thornbridge
Necessary Evil

13% Barrel-Aged Stout

Bakewell, Derbyshire

Wherever we work, and whichever career we choose to pursue, there are always those parts of the job we're not particularly keen on. For me, it's the annual post-Christmas wrestling match I have with my online Self-Assessment Tax Return. For Rob Lovatt, it's brewing dark beers.

Rob is head brewer and production director at Thornbridge. He joined the Derbyshire-based brewery in 2010, five years after it was founded, following a successful brewing career in London at both Meantime and Camden Breweries.

Prior to Rob's arrival, Thornbridge had earned acclaim for creating dark beers such as St Petersburg, an Imperial Russian Stout, and Bracia, a jet-black beer brewed with Italian chestnut honey. However, under Rob's direction, a wonderful selection of Pale Ales, lagers and sours had developed, but Porters and Stouts had taken something of a back seat. Under pressure to add a dark beer to the portfolio, Rob did some research based on beers he'd enjoyed in the past.

'I went to Firestone Walker and tasted that Parabola that they do,' Rob tells me, 'I was kind of blown away with that. And it was the beer that inspired me to brew Necessary Evil.'

Rob uses a range of dark and roasted malts, along with Hallertau Magnum hops, and more than one yeast strain to produce a high-gravity beer. This is then fermented out, before being aged for a number of months in Kentucky bourbon barrels.

The name came from Rob himself, because for a pale beer lover like him, creating this beer originally felt like just one of those necessary evils. But even he now admits to enjoying this wonderfully complex, joyously smooth beer, with its notes of oak, vanilla, coffee, chocolate and lingering bourbon warmth.

Titanic
Plum Porter Grand Reserve

6.5% Porter

Stoke-on-Trent, Staffordshire

A pub near where I lived as a child apparently kept its Christmas decorations up all year round. Sadly, it wasn't due to any Wizzard-inspired wish to make it Christmas every day, or any love of festivities. The story went that a former landlady died one Christmas Eve and, out of respect, the dusty swathes of tinsel criss-crossing the ceiling, and the odd glistening bauble, had stayed exactly where they were ever since. On balmy summer's evenings the incongruence of those garlands was acutely felt. Some things are best enjoyed at Yuletide.

Titanic Brewery was founded in 1985 and was named in honour of Edward Smith, captain of the ill-fated vessel, who was born in the city. In 1988 the brewery was taken over by brothers Keith and David Bott, who remain at the helm to this day. This predominantly cask-focused brewery has a line-up of pale, amber and dark beers, the best known of which is the sublime 4.9% Plum Porter.

Given the widespread love for this beer, it's perhaps unsurprising the brewery developed it further, and the notion of a 6.5% 'Grand Reserve,' available only at Christmas, was born. From there, the addition of port seemed a natural step. 'The port is added at the end of fermentation,' explains Keith, '[and]something incredible happens during the maturation phase. The beer becomes more rounded, deeper in flavour, and warmer on the palate, much as you would recognise from drinking a good glass of port.'

The result is a festive punch of a beer; ruby-black with huge plum aroma and a dry fruit bitterness. It works best in a party hat with a plate of roast potatoes, but to be honest, if I could, I would drink it all year round.

UnBarred
Stoutzilla

10 %   Imperial Stout

Brighton, East Sussex

Victor Frankenstein may have created his monster in a laboratory, but this particular behemoth was born in a garden shed. UnBarred's founder and head brewer, Jordan Mower, started the brewery at home on a 100-litre brew kit back in 2014, and began picking up awards for his beer within the year. After a period of cuckoo brewing, the brewery laid down permanent roots by opening a brewhouse and taproom in central Brighton in the summer of 2019.

Stoutzilla is the only beer that has been produced by UnBarred every year since Jordan began brewing. First launched commercially in 2017, it was an instant cult classic, and has gradually grown from a meagre 8.3% to its current, perfect 10%. It's released in a limited edition run every winter in the lead-up to Christmas.

The can design and pumpclip feature a scratchboard image of Stoutzilla himself by artist Paul Jackson. In it, the monster is tearing up Brighton, smashing through the city's Regency-era Royal Pavilion, the tower of the i360 clutched tightly in his hand. The same image is carried over onto the 750ml bottles of Stoutzilla's big brother, an 11% barrel-aged version, first produced in 2021.

Stoutzilla's recipe combines roasted malts with cocoa nibs, Madagascan vanilla, Kentucky bourbon, and locally roasted, cold-steeped coffee. The result is a beer that perfectly captures the city of its birth: all the late nights and dirty weekends, non-conformists and creatives, the brash, the artistic, and the bizarre. It mixes last night's cigarillos with this morning's bright sunshine, pulling in the savoury sea spray, and the smooth sweetness of a stick of rock. As the brewery's strapline goes, this is a beer that is not only made in the city; Stoutzilla is unmistakably 'Made *of* Brighton'.

Utopian
Premium British Lager

4.7% Helles

Crediton, Devon

Conventional brewing wisdom dictates that a Helles-style lager should be made in Bavaria, or, at the very least, contain German malts and Hallertau hops. But Utopian Brewery, founded in early 2019, brings a different kind of wisdom to the brewhouse.

Head brewer Jeremy Swainson, twice shortlisted for the British Guild of Beer Writers Brewer of the Year award during the brewery's brief lifetime, was born in Canada but trained in Germany. Together with co-founder and managing director Richard Archer, he is committed to brewing a range of traditional European lager styles in the heart of rural Devon, from a somewhat less traditional mix of English ingredients.

'When the UK has such a rich history in malt, and over thirty varieties of hops, it seemed a bit crazy to me to be shipping ingredients from around the world, when we could buy home-produced, and significantly reduce the food miles in the beer,' explains Richard.

In tandem with the wish to brew more sustainably and support UK producers comes a commitment to making great beer accessible – both financially and in terms of flavour – and that's why this particular beer deserves a place in this book.

Premium British Lager is brewed with malts from Warminster maltings, and hopped with Fuggles, First Gold and East Kent Goldings. Traditional step mashing and long lagering produce a bright beer with a floral spice to rival its Bavarian cousins, tight bubbles of carbonation, and a biscuit snap of malt sweetness. It's crisp, clean, and at a time when it's not always that straightforward to declare pride in one's country, this is a true British hero of a pint that I would love to see on every bar.

Verdant
Pulp

8% Double IPA

Penryn, Cornwall

In a world in which hazy and juicy are words used to describe virtually every new IPA release, it's easy to forget that just a few years ago no one in the UK had even heard of a New England-style beer, let alone quaffed one with their pizza. For many, Verdant ushered in a new era of brewing, and it's all credit to their quality that they remain at the forefront of the style to this day.

Verdant was founded in 2014 by Adam Robertson, Richard White and James Heffron in Falmouth on the south coast of Cornwall. They were inspired by the hazy beers they saw coming out of breweries like Tree House and Trillium in Massachusetts, and recognized that no one was producing anything similar in the UK. The trio began by homebrewing in James's kitchen, but in the intervening years have progressed – via a shipping container and a tin warehouse – to a site with a taproom, a couple of miles away in Penryn.

Pulp was Verdant's first double IPA, and was initially brewed as a small-scale test batch in March 2016 using large amounts of hops late in the boil, in the whirlpool, and for dry hopping. 'The beer was mind-blowingly hoppy and was like drinking mangoes!' explains head brewer James.

That's not to say that Pulp is solely about the juice. The mouthfeel and murk certainly hold the massive stone fruit hit of New England IPAs, but the dry finish and distinct bitterness is much more reminiscent of the Golden State.

'Definitely a "mid-coast" DIPA,' says James, 'Elements of California married up with techniques from Vermont.'

Massively drinkable, with just a slight glow of alcohol warmth, this beer really is the best of both worlds.

Wild Beer Co
Modus Operandi

7%   Sour Red Barrel-Aged Beer

Shepton Mallet, Somerset

Something not many people know about me is that I'm a massive 'Inspector Morse' fan. As such, I'm very familiar with the phrase 'modus operandi'. In terms of murder, it means how someone operates, a signature methodology left at every crime scene. In terms of beer, it's pretty much the same; although no one dies, and the outcome is much more satisfying.

Brett Ellis and Andrew Cooper first considered setting up a brewery in 2011 whilst working together at Bristol Beer Factory. Brett was a chef from California, and Andrew was one of the first beer sommeliers. Inspired by food, and by barrel-aged, sour beers from Belgium and the US, they decided to create a brewery unlike any other in the UK at the time.

'Modus Operandi is our first born so is enormously important to us,' explains Andrew. 'I see it as the inspiration for all that we've done, and he [Brett] sees it as the beer we set out to discover how to make.'

Modus Operandi starts as a simple old ale which undergoes primary fermentation in foudre. It's then placed into bourbon and Burgundy red wine barrels, aged with *Brettanomyces*, and left to evolve. A couple of times a year, barrels are blended to create the finished beer. Some are more acidic, some have great depth, and others are 'X-factor barrels', barrels with a fault that adds a sprinkle of magic.

Each iteration is slightly different, but all possess mouth-drenching acidity that pinches your cheeks like when you're trying to hold back tears, coupled with cherry, dried fruit, chocolate and wood complexity.

It's a long way from a pint of ale in an Oxford boozer, but I have a feeling Morse would approve.

Lotte Peplow

Choosing 31 out of the 250 greatest beers
in the world has been both an honour and
a privilege and I'm indebted to CAMRA
for inviting me to participate. It was not
an easy task. There has never been a better
time to be a beer drinker and we are spoilt by
the plethora of amazing beers currently available.
My selection criteria was based on two main factors
– is the beer available in export markets and can I get my
hands on a sample to taste it? These factors prevented me
from including much-hyped beers that are very rare and
difficult to find overseas, although you'll have to forgive me
for including a handful of beers in my list that are sought-
after and/or barely make it outside their home state.

You may also be wondering why I have chosen all
American craft beers in a book that's about the greatest
beers in the world. I'm not trying to imply that only
American beers are great. They're simply what I know
best and where my heart lies. Throughout the beer journey
of my life, the majority of beers I've tasted are American
and I wanted to include beers that meant something to
me as well as classic interpretations of a style, or ones
that are famous in their own right. Such beers just happen
to be American. I hope you enjoy reading about my beer
choices as much as I've enjoyed writing about them.

3 Floyds
Zombie Dust

6.5%   Pale Ale   62 IBUs

Munster, Iowa

3 Floyds was created by three members of the same family – brothers Nick and Simon with father Mike – from humble beginnings in 1996 using a five-barrel wok-burner-fired brew kettle, a repurposed Swiss cheese fermenter and an old cola tank. Fast forward to the present day and they produce nearly 107,000 barrels a year and distribute to 18 US states

    Their aggressively hopped beers and apocalyptic cartoon packaging has drawn legions of fans from around the world. Despite brewing extreme beers, they adhere to the principles of

the German purity law stating that beer can only be made with four ingredients – malt, hops, water and yeast. The brewers of 3 Floyds find plenty of scope to brew 'not normal' extraordinary beers using sound brewing techniques, the highest quality ingredients and by pushing the innovation envelope. Brewing takes place to the strains of heavy metal and this influence, along with fantasy and sci-fi, is evident in their brand ethos.

    Their 'undead' Pale Ale was launched in 2010 using exclusively Citra hops, a relatively new hop at the time with a huge, fruity and bitter punch. 3 Floyds teamed up with comic artist Tim Seeley to create the fantasmagorical artwork which served to enhance the beer's popularity more by appealing to both beer and comic book geeks alike.

    So what's all the fuss about?

Zombie Dust is a lush, juicy, assertively hoppy Pale Ale with a full body and long, mouth-watering finish. Flavours of orange pith, nectarine, pink grapefruit and stone fruit mesh perfectly with the malt bill to give a supremely drinkable and moreish Pale Ale. This beer is a superb showcase of the Citra hop with great flavour and balance. Worth seeking out if you're ever on the east coast.

AleSmith Brewing Company
Speedway Stout

12%   Imperial Stout   70 IBUs

San Diego, California

Despite the motor-racing connotation, there is nothing fast about Speedway Stout. It should be savoured at a slow and leisurely pace as befits a beer of such depth and intensity. Almost black in colour, this Imperial Stout with locally roasted coffee is big, boozy and bold. Flavours of espresso coffee, dark chocolate, toffee and dried fruits mesh with licorice and umami to deliver a smooth, rich, multi-faceted Stout that offers a well-integrated but complex cohesion of flavours. The creamy mouthfeel and light carbonation make it deceptively easy to drink, even at 12% ABV.

The brewery, AleSmith, whose motto is hand-forged ales, was started in 1995 by a three-man team on a 15-barrel brew system crafting beers inspired by European classics. In 2002 BJCP Grand Master beer judge and homebrewer Peter Zien took ownership of the brewery and continued its upward trajectory. It was originally located in the Miramar area of San Diego, but in 2015 a larger, state-of-the-art brewery and tasting room was added. The brewery now uses a custom-made 85-barrel brew system, has won numerous awards at local, national and international competitions, and at 25,000 square feet, claims to have San Diego's largest tasting room. Beers are available in 28 American states and eight countries around the world.

If you fancy switching gears, AleSmith also produces a barrel-aged version of Speedway Stout and quarterly releases featuring creative new flavours that rev up the tasting experience, but alas, these beers are unavailable in the UK. Speedway Stout is consistently highly rated amongst consumer-generated beer websites and apps and is well worth tracking down.

Anderson Valley
Boont Amber Ale

5.8% Amber Ale   16 IBUs

Boonville, California

Classic beers are those that withstand the test of time and are as popular today as they were when first launched. One such classic is Boont Amber Ale, from one of the pioneering American craft breweries, Anderson Valley. It was first brewed in 1987 and remains the brewery's best-selling beer to this day. According to Anderson Valley, beer drinkers from near and far often say that Boont Amber Ale was their very first taste of American craft beer.

This is a beer where the malt does the talking. It pours a dense copper colour with a big hit of caramel, toffee, and a lightly toasted nutty malt aroma overlayed with floral, citrus orange and golden sultana notes from the noble hops. Taste-wise it is reminiscent of an English Bitter with a subtle caramel sweetness and a smooth, mellow mouthfeel. The four different whole cone hops, Columbus, Bravo, Northern Brewer and Mt Hood, take a back seat while the malts (Pale 2-row and Crystal) assert their presence front and centre giving a moreish, juicy-sweet finish with little residual bitterness. The balance between rich crystal malts and mellow noble hops gives a crisp, clean beer.

The beer's name, Boont, is derived from Boontling, a lost US language spoken by the local community when they didn't want others to know what they were saying. The brewery's mascot, a legendary Boonville bear with antlers called Barkley, adorns the front of the can and is a cross between a deer and a bear to make a ... beer! Anderson Valley claims to be the world's first solar-powered brewery and the site even has its own 18-hole golf course where players are allowed to enjoy an Anderson Valley beer as they play.

Athletic Brewing Co
Free Wave

0.5%   Hazy IPA   55 IBUs

Stratford, Connecticut

If I hadn't read the 'non-alcoholic' description on the can I would be 100% convinced award-winning Free Wave IPA is a tropical, hop-forward American IPA with an ABV of around 5–6%. But looks and smells can be deceiving. Pouring a hazy, burnished gold, the tantalisingly tropical aroma comprises huge wafts of juicy peach, papaya and pineapple combined with orange and orange zest that builds on the palate. So far so normal –

BUT this beer is only 0.5% ABV and 70 calories, with the appearance, aroma and flavours of an alcoholic version. It's hard to believe how a non-alcoholic beer can be so full of flavour without compromising mouthfeel or body! The combination of Amarillo, Citra and Mosaic hops deliver a not insignificant 55 IBUs in a mouth-watering and supremely refreshing beer that finishes with a gentle, pleasing bitterness.

Athletic uses a proprietary brewing process unique to the brewery which does not strip alcohol from the beer, instead it's fully fermented with 10–12 small changes to the traditional brewing process to ensure the final product has less than 0.5% ABV. I first encountered this beer blind-judging in an international beer competition in the UK. I instantly knew it would go far, and sure enough, Free Wave went on to win top honours.

Athletic Brewing Co was first started in 2017 by fitness fanatic Bill Shufelt, who gave up his safe and stable career in the finance industry to pursue his dream to make delicious, craft, non-alcoholic beers for the modern drinker to enjoy while still pursuing a healthy and active lifestyle. He was joined by craft brewer John Walker and together their goal is to set new standards for flavour in alcohol-free beers. If Free Wave is anything to go by, they are doing just that.

Belching Beaver
Viva La Beaver

7.5%   Stout   28 IBUs

San Diego, California

Back in 2012 Tom Vogel (current CEO), Dave Mobley and Troy Smith (current brewmaster) enjoyed playing poker, drinking homebrew and dreaming about opening a brewery. One day, they decided to quit their day jobs, empty their bank accounts, create Belching Beaver and have a 'damn good time' doing it. They started by brewing on a 15-barrel system and delivering beers themselves in a small van, but now operate multiple tasting rooms in and around San Diego and brew around 43,000 barrels a year.

Beginning with a Milk Stout made with lactose, they built their name on brewing Stouts with flavours. Many iterations followed and the awards started rolling in. One such iteration is Viva La Beaver Mexican chocolate peanut butter Stout, a chocolate lover's dream in liquid form.

Jet black in appearance with a compact, tan-coloured head, the beer's peanut, and chocolate aromas slap you in the face on first sniff. There's dark and milk chocolate, coffee, brown sugar, lashings of peanut and a warm, spicy, cinnamon note that will beguile and bewitch your olfactory senses. This beer is like drinking liquid velvet: it's thick, rich, indulgent and so, so smooth and creamy. The peanut and Ibarra Mexican chocolate assert themselves up front but a warming, spicy tickle from the cinnamon builds towards the finish, and the aftertaste is short and sweet with minimal bitterness. The 7.5% alcohol content is tempered by the powerful duo of peanut and chocolate giving malty but not roasty notes and huge appeal to anyone with a sweet tooth.

And, before you ask, the brewery's name just happened to come from a contact who was going to be a marketing partner in the company at one point. He had researched the name and created the logo and so, for want of anything else, it stuck!

Breakside
Wanderlust IPA

6.2%   IPA   64 IBUs

Portland, Oregon

When the reaction to cracking open a can of beer is 'Oh, wow!' anticipation builds and I know I'm in for a treat.

The can of beer eliciting such response is Wanderlust IPA, a bold showcase of five juicy hops (Amarillo, Cascade, Mosaic, Simcoe and Summit) from the Pacific Northwest, expressing themselves at their flavoursome best in this nuanced, balanced and well-crafted West coast IPA. Pouring a burnished gold colour, the intense aroma is instantly arresting. A tsunami of tropical/citrus notes ranging from succulent papaya, ripe melon and passion fruit to juicy nectarine, orange and grapefruit beguile and delight the senses while on the palate the 64 IBUs are held in check by a light, bready malt body. Taste-wise, it's smooth, rounded and luscious with an abundance of flavour as the raucous hops take centre stage, starting with bright, fruit notes and moving into dank, resin territory towards the end. The precise balance gives an irresistible aftertaste of bittersweet notes that compels the drinker to take another sip.

Try pairing this with carrot cake, orange mousse cake or any other fruity dessert. You'll be amazed at the harmonious interplay between juicy hops and fruity cake.

Breakside Brewery started life as a brewpub in 2010 but quickly gained recognition for its imaginative, experimental and flavoursome beers and a slew of awards followed. It now operates five different venues throughout Oregon, including a fully customised 1972 Winnebago kitted out with taps to keep the beer flowing. Breakside became employee owned in 2019, one of only a handful of employee-owned breweries in America, and now brews approximately 27,000 barrels a year.

It's no surprise that Wanderlust IPA is much decorated and, fortunately for those outside America, has recently become available in selected export markets. If you find it, try it – you won't be disappointed.

The Bruery
Black Tuesday

19.3%   Imperial Stout   40 IBUs

Placentia, California

I was lucky enough to taste Black Tuesday in the UK when friends brought back a bottle from a trip to the States. This rare and sought-after beer is a huge bourbon barrel-aged Imperial Stout with an ABV of 19.3%. It is only released once a year, on the last Tuesday in October, at the brewery or via direct-to-consumer delivery across nine states. First brewed in 2009, it forms the heart and soul of the brewery's barrel-ageing programme and staff at The Bruery celebrate its annual release by throwing a Black Tuesday party.

The Bruery was set up by Patrick Rue in 2008 in Placentia, California, and now produces 17,225 barrels a year. The head of production explains how Black Tuesday is made: 'Black Tuesday changes a bit from year to year. That's the beauty of vintaging. While we strive for a consistent product, the ability to make small changes to continually better the beer is part of the production process. Black Tuesday is a blend of barrel-aged Imperial Stout that usually uses about 200 physical barrels. Those barrels age anywhere from one to three years and are used to build complexity along with the multiple bourbon barrel types. Typically, we age in 4 Roses, Buffalo Trace, Heaven Hill as well as many specialty bourbon barrels. Occasionally we will even throw a Scotch barrel in for a bit of added complexity.'

Black Tuesday pours a dense black colour, with a bitter chocolate, figgy, roast coffee aroma with lashings of bourbon and a viscous, thick mouthfeel that's smooth and mellow. The perceived sweetness from the high alcohol helps to round out the body, but this decadent, dangerous beer does not drink like its ABV, so be warned. It will age well and become more seductive and nuanced with time.

Cigar City Brewing
Jai Alai

7.5%   IPA   65 IBUs

Tampa, Florida

Cigar City was founded in 2009 by Joey Redner, a Tampa native and fifth-generation Floridian who likes to bring the unique culture, history and cuisine of Tampa to an international audience through his beers. In the early days, Florida was an underserved craft beer scene with around 30–35 breweries, almost every one of which was a brewpub. But Redner knew there was a pent-up demand for craft beer and people out there who would support a local brewery. His timing was perfect as the craft beer revolution swept across America, and Redner's beers soon captured the hearts and minds of American craft beer geeks.

Jai Alai (pronounced 'hi-a-lie') American IPA is named after a fast and furious game native to the Basque region of Spain and played on a court called a 'fronton'. Tampa was once home to a bustling Jai Alai fronton itself, but, alas, all that remains is this beer which was named in tribute to the game.

While beer lovers in the UK and Europe may not be able to experience Jai Alai the game, at least we're able to enjoy the eponymous beer on this side of the Atlantic. And what a beer it is! Amber in colour and hopped with Amarillo, Simcoe, Cascade, Motueka, Centennial and CTZ, Jai Alai begins with a big, booming bouquet of sun-kissed Seville orange, tangerine and zesty orange rind. Dig a little deeper and a rich, caramel, biscuit malt profile gives a subtle counter-balance to the assertive bitterness. Full-bodied with a mouth-wateringly juicy mouthfeel awash with piney, resin notes, Jai Alai is bold but approachable, and with an ABV of 7.5% and 65 IBUs, will reward any hop-lover with its intense flavour and powerful aroma.

Denver Beer Co
Graham Cracker Porter

5.6%   Porter   15 IBUs

Denver, Colorado

To appreciate this beer one must first be familiar with graham crackers. Originating in America in the mid-19th century, they are a flat, hard, sweet biscuit made with a wholegrain wheat (graham) flour.

Denver Beer Co was founded by brewing maestros Charlie Berger and Patrick Crawford in 2011. Their aim was to use a variety of different recipes, keep their beers fresh and unique and never brew the same beer twice. Graham Cracker Porter was the third beer brewed at the original taproom in downtown Denver in 2011. However, the beer was so popular from day one that they had to continue brewing it and their stated aim failed at the first hurdle. The beer went on to win a slew of medals and cemented its place as one of the brewery's flagship beers.

Particularly popular during the winter months, this is a mild, easy-drinking Porter style with a twist. It takes inspiration from a s'more, a marshmallow, traditionally roasted over a campfire, topped and tailed with chocolate and sandwiched between two graham crackers to create a rich and indulgent treat. The beer uses chocolate and biscuit malts along with a touch of vanilla to produce the flavour and taste of graham crackers without using the actual biscuits in the recipe. The aroma is assertively chocolatey with coffee, brown sugar and subtle cinnamon/clove notes. It has a smooth, creamy mouthfeel and rich, full body that's well balanced with a finish that delivers subtle, bittersweet notes alongside the sweetness of the vanilla and biscuit malts. The brewery like to describe it as 'a campfire in a glass', but I like to describe it as 'chocolate marshmallow cake in a glass.'

Deschutes Brewery
Black Butte Porter

5.5% Porter 30 IBUs

Bend, Oregon

Deschutes Brewery was established by Gary Fish in 1988 as a brewpub in downtown Bend, Oregon, and named after the Deschutes river that flows through the town. In its first year the pub sold 310 barrels of beer: fast forward to today and 260,712 barrels was the last count, with a second pub in downtown Portland, a tasting room in Roanoke, Virginia, sales in 32 states and a growing international presence. Sustainably brewing beer with the lowest possible impact on the planet is ingrained in everything they do.

Back in 1988, Black Butte Porter was one of the three beers Deschutes first brewed and is named after the dark and imposing Black Butte in central Oregon. It was a bold move back then when lighter, golden style beers were all the rage, but Gary Fish and team spent many hours at festivals converting lighter beer drinkers, particularly women, into dark beer drinkers with samples of Black Butte Porter. It quickly grew in popularity and remains among the company's best sellers to this day. The beer was first bottled in 1994 and has remained largely unchanged since it was first launched.

Smooth and creamy, Black Butte Porter has a full-bodied, velvety mouthfeel with a coffee, chocolate, raisin and roasted character from a malt bill of 2-row, chocolate, wheat crystal and carapils. The beer is hopped with Cascade and Tettnang giving a subtle hop presence and a complex, bittersweet aftertaste long into the finish. Depth, complexity and balance are the hallmarks of this beer and at 5.5% ABV it is eminently sessionable and suitable for any drinking occasion at any time of the year. It also makes an ideal accompaniment to robust meat dishes, smoked meats, chocolate desserts or hard cheeses like cheddar or Gouda.

Firestone Walker
Double Barrel Parabola

15.5% Imperial Stout 48 IBUs

Paso Robles, California

Double Barrel Parabola is one big beast of a brew and the highest strength beer ever released by Firestone Walker. It's an extension of Parabola, the brewery's signature Imperial Stout first brewed in 2005, but in this case Double Barrel Parabola spends 12 months in premium bourbon barrels before being transferred to whisky barrels for an additional 12 months, giving two years of barrel-ageing in total.

Firestone Walker's barrel program manager, Eric Ponce, explains: 'This year's Parabola came out of Bourbon barrels after one year of maturation at 13.6% ABV. It was immediately transferred into 12-year-old Weller Wheated Whisky barrels for an additional year after which the ABV climbed even further to 15.5%. Still, it's such a smooth, almost dangerous beer. That additional barrel and extra time creates a beautiful, creamy mouthfeel with just a touch of mild oxidation which smooths out the high ABV character. There's also an added dimension of chocolate fudge and cereal grain-goodness.'

Pouring an ominous pitch black, Double Barrel Parabola has lashings of dried fruit, prune, chocolate and vanilla aromatics with incredible complexity of flavour and an oh, so luscious, smooth, rich mouthfeel. It drinks like liquid silk with a boozy warmth that lasts long into the finish, and perfectly exemplifies the extreme impact barrels can make on the character and flavour of a beer.

Firestone Walker was started by two brothers-in-law, Adam Firestone and David Walker, in 1996 in a second-hand brewhouse with converted wine-making equipment. They shared a passion for great beer, hard work and building stuff. It certainly paid off because today Firestone Walker is a top ten American craft brewing company producing approximately 528,000 barrels a year.

Double Barrel Parabola is the first of its kind and truly sensational. Future releases may differ depending on the spirits barrels used and maturation times.

Fremont
The Rusty Nail

12.3% Imperial Stout 40 IBUs

Seattle, Washington

For a big, booming aroma and powerful, punchy flavours look no further than Fremont's The Rusty Nail Bourbon Barrel-Aged Imperial Stout with Licorice and Cinnamon Bark. This is a beer to warm the cockles of your heart and share with your best friends and favourite family members.

First launched in 2016, The Rusty Nail began life as an Oatmeal Stout made with brewer's licorice, smoked barley, pale malt, Magnum and US Goldings hops, before being aged on cassia cinnamon chips. It then spends 15 months in 12-year old Kentucky bourbon barrels, after which it is released in limited edition, 660ml wax-capped bottles to eagerly awaiting beer lovers.

The aroma of this beer is truly sensational – a heady mix of chocolate, cinnamon, molasses, dried fruits and a whisper of licorice intermingles with a warming bourbon character. Dark and decadent, an intense sweet note hits the palate up front followed by a combination of cinnamon spice, brown sugar and a hint of toasted oak, giving a luscious, creamy mouthfeel and a long, memorable, bourbon-infused finish. The flavours become all the more intense as the beer warms up. At 12.3% The Rusty Nail is a beer to savour and enjoy with a piece of fruit cake or wedge of smoked gouda.

Fremont Brewing Co is a family-owned, award-winning craft brewery established in 2009 by founder Matt Lincecum with the aim of brewing small-batch artisan beers using local ingredients. As well as an extensive barrel programme, they also brew a wide range of beer styles ranging from perennial favourites like ales and IPAs to the Black Heron project (small batch experimental beers).

Washington state is home to the second largest hop growing region in the world, allowing Fremont's brewers to easily select high-quality hop varieties. With The Rusty Nail, Fremont have well and truly 'nailed' it!

Hoppin' Frog
Frogichlaus

13.5%   Double Doppelbock   30 IBUs

Akron, Ohio

Owner and Brewmaster of Hoppin' Frog Fred Karm has produced and designed 23 award-winning beers so it's fair to say he knows a thing or two about brewing. One such beer is Frogichlaus, a Swiss-style Celebration Lager, inspired by the beers of Switzerland and super-smooth lagers using the Zurich lager strain.

Karm explains: 'We wanted to create the character you'd get from a decoction mash so we used a tonne of great malts including 4% of German melanoidin malt to give an intense, rich, deep, satisfying flavour. It's the closest we can get to decoction mashing in our brewery.

'The beer contains 30 IBUs to balance it out and is hopped with two different additions of Hallertau Mittelfruh including a large one at the end of the boil to create a luscious character. It contains amber and clear Belgian candi sugar which is added right at the end of the brew to give intense flavour and character.'

According to Karm, it's hard to get a lager yeast to go above 8–10% ABV, but to get it to go to 13.5% is a little feat of scientific magic he learnt from brewers in the Netherlands, Norway and Denmark.

Frogichlaus comes in convenient 250ml/8oz cans and ABV varies from year to year. It was first brewed in 2018 and ages well. The 2020 version has notes of date, fig and caramel malt sweetness, with a thick, rich, full body and smooth, sweet finish. It's low in bitterness and has an unmistakable lager character despite its strength.

Hoppin' Frog was established in 2006 and is known for its high-alcohol beers. It has been rated one of the Top 100 brewers in the world by a beer rating website for 14 consecutive years.

Jester King
Atrial Rubicite

5.8% Wild Ale

Austin, Texas

I first sampled Atrial Rubicite at a beer and food pairing dinner in Denver, Colorado, on the eve of my first Great American Beer Festival in 2016, and the memory of it has stayed with me ever since. It was paired with a zeppole, a deep-fried Italian pastry filled with a rich, creamy, sweet centre and served with peach and raspberry preserves. Atrial Rubicite, with its intense, fresh raspberry elegance, provided the 'wow' factor and elevated the pairing into something very special.

A barrel-aged sour beer, Atrial Rubicite is refermented to dryness in oak barrels with raspberries from Washington and is brewed with Texas malt, well water, Goldings hops and native yeast from the Texas hill country. It is barrel-aged for a year prior to blending and refermentation. A huge hit of raspberries, 7lb per gallon, are added at this stage. It is unfiltered, unpasteurised and 100% naturally conditioned.

Atrial Rubicite was first brewed in 2013 and quickly shot into the Top Ten Wild Ales in the world among beer rating sites. A limited amount is released in 750ml bottles every year and is only available in limited quantities at the brewery. Last year bottles sold out in 15 minutes! You'll have to take my word for the fact that it's a truly incredible beer, and if you ever happen to visit Austin, Texas, it is well worth seeking out.

Beginning in 2010, Jester King is an authentic farmhouse brewery offering mixed culture and spontaneous fermentation beers as well as 'pure' culture from local yeast sources. They claim to incorporate the natural surroundings and local agriculture into their beers to make them uniquely tied to the place and the people.

Jolly Pumpkin
Bam Bière

4.5%   Farmhouse Ale   24 IBUs

Dexter, Michigan

When Ron Jeffries established Jolly Pumpkin Artisan Ales with his wife, Laurie, in 2004 it was one of the first sour, wood-aged breweries in the USA. Ron, who was something of a beer evangelist, took inspiration from Cantillon in Belgium and set about producing cask-conditioned sour ales using only natural bacteria and wild yeast from the oak barrels. In the early years, he would often get calls from bar managers complaining the beer was off, but nearly two decades later Jolly Pumpkin regularly wins awards for its beers, operates nine bars around its home state of Michigan, and exports to many international markets.

Jolly Pumpkin uses open fermentation vessels to allow wild yeast and bacteria naturally found in the air to inoculate the beer prior to ageing in oak barrels. Once inside the barrel the alchemy begins as wild yeasts work their magic to develop a depth and refinement of character. Beers can be wood-aged for any time between four weeks and two years or more. After oak maturation, beers are blended, re-yeasted with a little sugar and packaged/canned or kegged. Through the process of natural carbonation, yeast and sugar referment the beer in the vessel, giving additional layers of complexity to the finished product.

Bam Bière is a light, refreshing farmhouse style that spends two months in oak. It's brewed with oats and a small amount of flaked barley to give a rustic feel along with noble and American hops for a citrus note and then aged in oak to give a gentle tartness and little funk in the aroma. A golden, cloudy colour with aromas of lemon, lime, sherbert, oak and woodiness, Bam Bière is tart on the palate with a gentle spiciness and a crisp, refreshing, light bitterness.

Lickinghole Creek
Magnificent Pagan Beast

17.5% **Barrel-Aged Mega Ale** 110 IBUs

Goochland, Virginia

If ever there was a beer that lived up to its name, this would be it. Magnificent Pagan Beast from Lickinghole Creek Craft Brewery (LCCB) is truly magnificent. Calling itself a bourbon barrel-aged mega-ale, it contains 6lb of hops per barrel, thousands of pounds of grain, hundreds of pounds of Belgian candi syrup and its own yeast strain. It was three years in the making and is given four brews, when two is the norm, and conditioned for months in Kentucky bourbon barrels.

Magnificent Pagan Beast is the pride and joy of LCCB. A rare, limited release, showstopper of a beer, it ages a full year in barrel and is usually only produced bi-annually. It's only available to purchase at the brewery, and you need a pre-sale ticket to ensure the 750ml bottles are allocated fairly, but one sip of this extreme beer and the anticipation will be worth it. Pouring a dark brown, it oozes with flavour as chocolate, coffee, dark fruits, oak, vanilla and bourbon intertwine in perfect harmony. It's rich and viscous, but not cloying, and leaves with a pleasant, warming booziness.

The brewery itself is well worth a visit, and is set in 290 acres of rolling farmland in Goochland, Virginia. They grow their own hops, fruits, barley and herbs which go into brewing an amazing range of beers, from juicy IPAs to Russian Imperial Stouts. Founded in 2013, the brewery takes its name from the creek that runs through the property. A 'Lickinghole' is a pre-colonial term for a place where wildlife go to find water and Lickinghole Creek is such a place. It also reflects the brewery's ethos towards clean water for creatures, great and small, nature and people.

Despite being very rare, this beer warrants its place by being extraordinary.

Maui Brewing Co
Coconut Hiwa Porter

6% Porter 18 IBUs

Kihei, Hawaii

Maui Brewing Co was set up in 2005 by Garrett Marrero, when he was 26, with just one idea … to make local Hawaiian craft beer. After taking inspiration from his many trips to the island and realising that local beer wasn't actually made in Hawaii, he saw an opportunity, and after much borrowing of funds from family and girlfriend the idea of Maui Brewing Co was born. The response was incredible, and they soon moved to bigger premises. Now Maui is renowned all over

the States and exports to many countries overseas, but a focus on sustainability and use of authentic local ingredients remains at the heart of their operation.

Marrero comments: 'When we first released our Coconut Porter in 2006 it instantly won a medal at the World Beer Cup because there were no other coconut beers on the market at the time. After that we included the word "Hiwa" in the name, which means sacred, to set it apart.

'The idea behind Coconut Hiwa Porter was to take a beer style I loved, i.e., robust Porter, and use toasted coconut to round out the robust character. We toast coconut chips in the oven to a deep blond colour, rotating them for evenness, and use a special vessel called a "maxx lup" which contains a big sieve. We add the coconut, apply pressure with CO_2 to remove the oxygen and recirculate. The beer is steeped on the finished dried, toasted coconut and that's how we get all the oils and flavours out of the coconut and into the beer to give a mellow, subtle hint with a toasted, nutty sweetness.'

Coconut Hiwa Porter is a flagship beer for Maui and defines the brewery. It's a stunning beer and makes an equally stunning coconut ice cream float!

Nebraska Brewing Company
Mèlange á Trois

11.3% Belgian Strong Ale 31 IBUs

La Vista, Nebraska

Inhale a noseful of Mèlange á Trois Belgian-style Ale and you'd be forgiven for thinking it was wine and not beer.

That's because Paul Kavulak, owner of Nebraska, had developed a fondness for big, buttery Chardonnays in a previous life and wanted to create something truly unique. He decided the marriage between a Belgian Golden Blonde Ale and a big, bold Chardonnay could be a wonderful thing, and he wasn't wrong! Nebraska was one of the first American craft breweries to use Chardonnay barrels for the sake of the wine character, and even now barrels have to smell a certain way and truly embody the Chardonnay flavour. Multi award-winning Mèlange á Trois is considered a rare beer by the brewery because it can only be made when Kavulak and team can source the right barrels.

After spending six months in French oak Chardonnay barrels, the aroma packs a powerful punch with a combination of oak, wood, peach, honey and stone fruits coming from a malt bill of Pilsner and Caramel 40 hopped with Columbus, Chinook and Liberty. Further complexity from a peppery yeast character gives a long, sweet finish while oak tannins provide nuance and a dry, sweet, wine-like character. If a beer could be poised and elegant, Mèlange á Trois would take the title, hands down.

The name Mèlange á Trois is loosely based on French connotations. It's a blend of three – oak, wine and beer. As Kavulak says, 'Mèlange á Trois is incredibly special to us and proves that good beer can come from anywhere, not simply the already established craft beer regions.'

Nebraska produces innovative and creative craft beers and artisanal barrel-aged products. It was started in 2007 by homebrewer extraordinaire Paul Kavulak along with his wife, Kim, and is now a family-operated business.

New Holland Brewing Co
Dragon's Milk

11%   Bourbon Barrel-Aged Stout   30 IBUs

Holland, Michigan

Sumptuous, silky and incredibly moreish best describes Dragon's Milk, one of America's best-selling bourbon barrel-aged Stouts. Rumour has it that in medieval times the milk of the dragon was the reward for slaying it, and referred to the best liquid in the house. The brewers of New Holland decided it was an appropriate term for their bourbon barrel-aged Stout and the legend of Dragon's Milk Stout was born.

The brewery itself was started in 1997 by keen homebrewer and current CEO Brett Vanderkamp in an abandoned factory with his best friend, Jason Spaulding, when he was just 24 years old. It has grown to produce approx. 47,500 barrels a year and operates a brewery and distillery in one location and brewpub and restaurant in another. The city of Holland was first founded by Dutch immigrants and today the brewery's branding incorporates Dutch-inspired elements such as an orange windmill to reflect the Dutch national colour.

Their flagship beer, Dragon's Milk Stout, spends three months in bourbon barrels to give a wonderfully complex but harmonious blend of flavours. It pours a dense brown/black colour with a powerful punch of roasted malts giving aromas of chocolate, treacle, dried fruits and vanilla underpinned by a subtle bourbon note, while on the palate the beer is full, rich, creamy and thick with a woody, coconut note from the barrel-ageing and a long, smooth, warming aftertaste. More flavours intertwine and develop as the beer warms in the mouth leading to a satisfying but moreish finish. Balanced, nuanced and elegant, this beer is ideal for long, winter nights, and the perfect match for hearty, rich stews and decadent chocolate desserts or tiramisu. Dragon's Milk White is also available but that's another story.

North Coast Brewing Co
Old Rasputin

9%   Russian Imperial Stout   75 IBUs

Fort Bragg, California

A bold and beautiful, award-winning Russian Imperial Stout that's a classic example of its style best describes Old Rasputin. Rich, dark and complex, tasting Old Rasputin is like being embraced by an old friend you haven't seen for years. It's warming, smooth and creamy with lashings of bitter chocolate, coffee and molasses on the nose and a good balance between the roasted malts and hops on the palate, lingering well into the aftertaste like that old friend who doesn't want to leave.

Old Rasputin is produced in the tradition of 18th-century English brewers who supplied the court of Russia's Catherine the Great. The label is a drawing of Rasputin encircled by a phrase in Russian meaning 'a sincere friend is not born instantly'.

North Coast was established in 1988 by co-founder and brewmaster Mark Ruedrich in Mendocino County, sandwiched between a remote coastal range and the Pacific Ocean. It's a stunning, unique location that clearly helps inspire the brewers and brewing community of Fort Bragg. The brewery began life after Ruedrich spent time in England in his mid-20s and acquired a taste for good beer. After returning to the States he realised that in order to make quality beer he would have to do so himself. His first approach was to understand the classic beers of Europe and from there base North Coast beers on his interpretation of classic styles while being inspired by the beautiful location and the appreciative local community.

Luckily for beer lovers around the world, Old Rasputin is widely available in export markets, as well as the States, and produces 51,437 barrels per year at the last count. It's an ideal pairing with a hearty meat dish like steak, burger or a casserole.

Odell Brewing Co
90 Shilling Ale

5.3%　Amber Ale　32 IBUs

Fort Collins, Colorado

Odell Brewing was founded by keen homebrewer Doug Odell, his wife, Winnie, and sister, Corkie, in 1989 and became employee-owned in 2015. The original brewery was located in a 1915 grain elevator close to the current brewery in Fort Collins, and the first commercial release was Golden Ale, quickly followed by 90 Shilling, the brewery's top-selling, flagship beer. The brewery now has four venues in Colorado and brews approx. 128,000 barrels a year.

90 Shilling is a fine example of an Amber Ale, with a richness and depth of character that encourages a return to the beer again and again. It's burnished copper in colour with a caramel, toffee, biscuit aroma and a subtle candied-orange note. Brewed with British crystal and chocolate malts, 90 Shilling is hopped with Perle and Nugget to give a clean, refreshing and well-balanced beer with a smooth, light body and short, dry finish. The name 90 Shilling comes from the Scottish method of taxing beer with only the highest quality beers taxed at 90 shillings. It has won numerous awards across America and remains highly popular to this day.

A visit to Odell Brewing has long been on my bucket list and when I finally get there a much-hyped and highly crafted 90 Shilling will be the first beer I seek out. Odell beers have been available at UK beer festivals in the past, indeed Doug Odell himself has made many trips to the UK to meet beer lovers and pour his beer, becoming a bit of a legend in doing so. Unfortunately, Odell beers are unavailable in the UK currently. If they ever make it back to these shores, be sure to pick one up.

Oskar Blues
Dale's Pale Ale

6.5%   Pale Ale   65 IBUs

Lyons, Colorado

Dale's Pale Ale is an important beer in the history of American craft brewing because it was the first American craft beer to be launched in a can in 2002. It was a bold move back then by owner Dale Katechis when cans were considered inferior to bottles, but now Dale's Pale Ale is seen as something of a trailblazer that has helped change the perception of canned beer across America.

Jesse Kercheval, International Manager at Oskar Blues Brewery, explains how Dale's Pale Ale stays relevant to today's beer drinker: 'Dale's' hop profile has always targeted fresh citrus and pine with a good amount of bitterness, but the hops used to get there have naturally evolved over time. We originally leaned heavily on Centennial hops, but over the years we have moved more and more to Comet, which has been a cleaner hop for us. Agricultural products like hops and malts change from season to season, so we have made adjustments to how we use the raw materials to create our vision of the beer.

'Dale's originally had a higher sweetness but over the years we have lowered the terminal gravity to achieve harmony between the sweetness and bitterness, and to give better drinkability. We simplified the malt bill by removing most of the specialty malts, retaining a lighter Munich malt and the very special Simpson's Premium English Caramalt to retain that wonderful malty flavour and balance.'

Crack open a can and those lovely malty aromatics burst forth, followed by a huge citrus and resiny pine hop character. Take a sip and you'll be rewarded with an up-front hoppy bitterness, full body and a smooth mouthfeel. The interplay between malt and hops gives perfect balance and lip-smacking crispness to this well-crafted beer which leaves with a long, dry finish.

Port City Brewing Co
Porter

7.2%   Porter   45 IBUs

Alexandria, Virginia

For a classic American Porter that's more robust than a British version, Port City's acclaimed Porter ticks all the boxes. Port City has perfected brewing world-class, award-winning beers that are true to style and vary from traditional European beers to American craft staples. The brewery's mission is to be a reliable and innovative brewer of delicious, well-balanced beers that celebrate their raw ingredients. It was founded in 2011 by Bill and Karen Butcher, and a few years later (in 2015) went on to win Small Brewery of the Year at the Great American Beer Festival.

Its award-winning robust Porter is a classic American-style Porter with an amped-up but deceptive ABV of 7.2%. An all-pervading aroma of coffee, molasses, cacao and bittersweet chocolate laced with dried fruit assail the senses, followed by an enticing roasty, toasty caramel, chocolate malt note and a waft of vintage marmalade from the Magnum and Fuggles hop combo. There's a lot to like about this beer – the complex, rich, roasty flavours meld together in the mouth to give a sumptuous, smooth, silky, full-bodied feel and a long-lasting, bittersweet finish. The alcohol content is well hidden, making it refreshing and moreish at the same time, and an incredible depth of flavour reveals chocolate, bitter, and bright, fruity notes that merge together in perfect harmony to provide balance and nuance.

Port City Porter makes a wonderful accompaniment to many different food dishes and is versatile enough to complement meat-based stews, casseroles, meatballs or burgers, sweet dishes such as tiramisu or chocolate gateau, or cheeses such as Manchego, Gruyère or extra mature Cheddar. Port City Porter occasionally makes it over to the UK and is well worth seeking out when it does.

Rogue Ales
Dead Guy Ale

6.8%   Maibock   40 IBUs

Newport, Oregon

Rogue Dead Guy Ale was the beer that started my American craft beer journey back in the mid-2000s. It was unlike anything I had ever tasted before. Sweet and malty, but with a subtle floral bitterness, it completely blew me away.

Dead Guy Ale is brewed in the style of a German Maibock using Rogue's proprietary 'Pacman' yeast and has a robust malt profile and a sweetness balanced by the use of bittering hops. It was first brewed in 1990 to celebrate the Mayan Day of the Dead, and quickly gained popularity to become Rogue's flagship beer. It is gratefully dedicated by the brewery 'to the Rogue in each of us!' The foreboding looking skeleton that adorns the packaging is so iconic that the name of the beer, Dead Guy Ale, only appears in small print on the back of the can.

Crack open a can and you'll be rewarded with a blast of sweet caramel, nutty, bread crust aroma that's perfectly balanced by a spicy, floral hop character from Perle and Sterling hops. Full and satisfying to drink with a clean, gently bitter finish, Dead Guy Ale has a lovely, malt-forward sweetness and a well-integrated but subtle hoppy flavour.

Rogue Ales was founded by Jack Joyce in Ashland, Oregon, in 1988, and shortly afterwards moved to its current location in Newport. It grows its own hops on its own farms in nearby Independence, as well as botanicals, fruit and vegetables. Rogue also has its own cooperage making barrels out of Oregon and American oak, and distills a range of spirits. The brewery uses a 100-barrel system to brew 88,000 barrels a year which are distributed in all 50 states and also in 54 countries.

Sierra Nevada
Pale Ale

5.6%   Pale Ale   38 IBUs

Chico, California

Sierra Nevada is one of America's pioneering craft breweries and helped ignite the American craft beer movement that we now see playing out across the globe.

The brewery was started by Ken Grossman in the student town of Chico, California, in 1980 on a hand-built brewhouse made from recycled dairy equipment. He was a passionate homebrewer with a vision to develop full-flavoured beers with character and complexity as an alternative to mass-produced light lager. He soon perfected his first beer, the iconic Pale Ale, made exclusively with the recently discovered Cascade hop, and the rest, as they say, is history.

From humble beginnings to the present day, Sierra Nevada now produces approximately two million barrels annually. Pale Ale remains its flagship beer, made the same way it always has been – with American two-row pale malted barley, 100% Cascade hops and a top fermenting ale yeast strain which is then bottle conditioned. The result is a powerful punch of citrus, orange and pine flavours with a smooth, rounded mouthfeel and a harmonious balance between citrus bitterness and caramel malt sweetness.

But how has such a beer withstood the test of time? Steve Grossman, brewery ambassador for Sierra Nevada and brother of Ken, explains: 'Being the archetype for the style, as well as helping to establish the craft beer revolution, has certainly been a notable contributing factor. The high quality and consistency in taste has been extremely important as well. Perhaps the most plausible explanation is that its flavour profile speaks to casual drinkers and beer connoisseurs alike. The marriage of citrusy Cascade hops and subtle caramelised malt in a very well-balanced, eminently drinkable beer has almost universal appeal and has proven to be a winning combination throughout the years.'

Springdale Beer Co
Brig Mocha Stout

6.8%   Stout   9 IBUs

Framingham, Massachusetts

Brig Mocha Stout is a beer for the dedicated mocha coffee lover in all of us. It's sweet, roasty and creamy with a velvety texture that comprises a delicious package of chocolate, coffee and roasted malt in one big hit. Brig Mocha Stout contains locally sourced, Brazilian cold-brew coffee, cacao nibs, oats and lactose to balance the acidity that comes from the roasted malts, as well as natural acidity from coffee and cacao nibs. It provides a natural bridge between the elements of roast and sweet. The beer pours a dense, dark brown colour with an assertive aroma of chocolate and coffee, but hidden underneath you'll find dark muscovado sugar, tobacco and even a savoury soy sauce note. On the palate the beer is full, smooth and velvety in texture with a short, sweet finish that's undeniably chocolatey.

I like to pair this beer with a fiery chilli or a powerful curry because the smooth, luscious, sweet taste is a good antidote to the heat of the spices and will balance the strong, hot flavours. It would go just as well with a chocolate or coffee-based dessert.

But what of the name, Brig? It derives from brigadeiro, a Brazilian chocolate and coffee treat that resembles a truffle and comes from the local, Brazilian-influenced neighbourhood. When the beer was being developed, a name that was difficult to say, difficult to spell and therefore difficult to sell was not a good start so it became shortened to Brig.

Springdale Beer Co was launched in 2016 as a creative offshoot of Jack's Abby Craft Lagers and is renowned for exploring the boundaries of fermentation and flavour. Its brewers like nothing better than to push the limits of flavour when crafting their latest brew, and this beer is a flavoursome treat for any Stout lover.

Stone
Stone IPA

6.9%   IPA   71 IBUs

Escondido, California

Stone Brewing was founded by Greg Koch and Steve Wagner in 1996 and is now the ninth largest craft brewery in America with two brewing facilities, one in Escondido, California, and another in Richmond, Virginia. Their beers are available in all 50 states and more than 40 countries worldwide.

Stone IPA is a classic West Coast IPA that was first brewed in 1997 to celebrate Stone Brewing's first year anniversary and remains an iconic American craft beer to this day. According to Stone, the key ingredient is making the same beer at a consistent high quality every time they brew it.

The original recipe used crystal and 2-row malts, Magnum and Chinook hops for bittering, with Centennial and a touch of Chinook in the dry hopping. A few years ago, however, the recipe was updated, and along with Centennial it's now augmented with Azacca, Vic Secret, Ella and Calypso to add a more citrusy, tropical aroma to the beer. Stone uses the slurry method for dry hopping to bring out the tropical, pine and floral aromas. At the end of fermentation they dry hop in a separate small tank (i.e., add hops, then beer, mix, then pump back to the fermenter). They recirculate the fermenter a few times over a couple of days to ensure thorough mixing and then chill the tank. At the time of the update, many American craft brewers were using Cascade, and Stone's use of Centennial helped set their IPA apart.

This is a beer that appeals to the hopheads among us. It's more bitter on the palate than some IPAs, but the citrus, tropical, cedar and pine aroma of the hops express themselves eloquently and the beer is beautifully balanced with a long, dry finish.

Toppling Goliath
King Sue

7.8%   Double IPA   100 IBUs

Decorah, Iowa

A Double IPA with a hefty 100 IBUs conjures up visions of intense bitterness and a long aftertaste, but not so this luscious DIPA. King Sue is a juicy, moreish, drinkable hazy DIPA that's incredibly well crafted. Mike Saboe, executive brewmaster, explains how: 'Hiding the bitterness begins with understanding what contributing factors play a role in perceived bitterness beyond calculable IBUs. From there, it's a matter of building and enhancing the constituents which allow us to counteract said bitterness in an intentionally balanced way. It's not so much an absolute value that is of importance, but rather the balance able to be achieved through alterations in sweetness, acidity, and salinity.'

That balance is all important. Crack open a can and even before pouring a huge waft of juicy hop flavour is immediately evident. A hazy, light orange in colour with great carbonation, the beer's visual appeal and lush aroma is highly enticing. You'll find a juicy, sweet aroma from the mango, pineapple, orange and grapefruit notes due exclusively to the use of the Citra hop. On the palate, the beer tastes smooth, juicy and well-rounded with a touch of bittersweet dankness on the finish. Despite being hop-forward it's beautifully balanced by a solid malt backbone and just the right amount of bitterness that builds into the finish to give a dry, lasting aftertaste that leaves you craving another sip.

This is a beer for the hopheads among us, particularly if you're a Citra hop fan. It has garnered a string of accolades from media and beer review sites in America and it's easy to see why.

Clark and Barbara Lewey founded Toppling Goliath in 2009 and it quickly became world-renowned for its IPAs and barrel-aged Stouts. They distribute to 30 US states, producing approximately 43,000 barrels of 40-plus beers that rotate throughout the year.

Two Roots Brewing Co
Enough Said

0.5% Helles

San Diego, California

Any beer that's won two gold medals in three years at the Great American Beer Festival is worthy of attention, in my opinion. Enough Said is a Helles lager that calls itself 'Near Beer' and contains only 0.5% ABV, 80 calories, and is rich in Vitamin B12. Firmly rooted in the German Helles tradition, Enough Said is made with Pilsner malt and Hallertau hops to give a clean, refreshing 'near beer'.

It looks the part, too, with a clear, golden colour and a thick, frothy head of foam. Aromas of dough, flour, straw and fresh-cut grass, with a lemony/lime citrus zing assail the senses while on the palate the beer is remarkably well-balanced for a low-/no-alcohol offering and could easily fool the unsuspecting into thinking it was alcoholic. Yes, the mouthfeel is a little thin, but that's to be expected in a low-/no-alcohol beer and the lack of bitterness means it doesn't linger on the palate, nor does it detract from the beer's drinkability.

Two Roots' secret is to use the best possible ingredients combined with over half a century of brewing expertise to craft the brew in the first place. The brewing team uses state-of-the-art vacumn distillation technology to remove the alcohol and the calories leaving a beer with an award-winning aroma, mouthfeel and taste. It's ideal for those pursuing a healthier lifestyle, drivers, pregnant women or those who want to look like they're drinking beer when they're not.

Two Roots launched its non-alcoholic craft beer range in 2019 to take advantage of America's small but growing non-alcoholic beer category. They have also won acclaim for their IPAs, and though the range is unavailable in the UK currently, it's one to watch out for.

The Virginia Beer Co
Elbow Patches

6.2%   Stout   26 IBUs

Williamsburg, Virginia

Sometimes a beer comes along that's so classically on style that it is an absolute pleasure to drink. Such is the case with this Oatmeal Stout from the Virginia Beer Co (VBC). Elbow Patches is one of the brewery's four flagship beers and they also brew a constantly changing mix of creative and experimental small-batch beers.

Elbow Patches itself is a lusciously rich, roasty, creamy, chocolate hit of a Stout. You'll find notes of coffee, dried fruit, cocoa and milk chocolate wrapped up in a silky, smooth, roasty package with just the faintest hint of bitterness on the back end. The beer is hopped with Northern Brewer and contains a malt bill of 2-row, chocolate malt, crystal light, flaked oats, roasted barley and victory malt which contributes to the roasty taste and smooth mouthfeel. It's vegan friendly and oh-so easy to drink.

The brewery, in the form of a taproom and beer garden, was started in 2016 by two college friends and homebrewing lovers, Chris Smith and Robby Willey, who shared a passion for philanthropy, adventure and beer. Their brewery focuses on 'beer people purpose' and is a force for the good in the local community. They use their taproom as a gathering space to support the causes they believe in and actively give back to their local Williamsburg community.

Robby Willey, co-founder of VBC, comments: 'Our goal is to make our community, our state and our world better by focusing on the positive role a small business such as ours can play locally. We believe that people like to understand the soul of a brewery just as much as they like to enjoy the beer.'

Hear, hear! I'll drink to that!

Warped Wing
Baltic Porter

11.5%   Baltic Porter   35 IBUs

Dayton, Ohio

Warped Wing Baltic is no ordinary Baltic Porter because it is aged for two years in rye whisky barrels, giving an extraordinary complexity to this deeply intriguing beer.

Baltic Porters are generally cold-fermented and use a lager yeast, but Warped Wing's version is higher in alcohol than normal, partly due to the barrel-ageing process and partly because the brewery simply wanted to make it that way.

Warped Wing Baltic Porter is a treasure trove of flavours, with chocolate, coffee, treacle, whisky and dried fruit aromas that give a caramel, vanilla sweetness on the palate and a full-bodied, rich, warming mouthfeel. The clean finish is unexpected but unmistakably lager-esque.

Brewmaster John Haggerty explains: 'Yeast management for this beer is critical. We have to ensure the vitality is correct and that we're pitching enough yeast due to the magnitude of the beer and the alcohol content. The water treatment is important too because we're using so many roasted malts like European chocolate malt to create the colour and these will naturally acidify the mash. We buffer that by adding calcium carbonate to our water and giving the beer plenty of time for fermentation to work through to terminal density and for the barrel to do its job.'

Warped Wing Brewing Co started in 2014 and was inspired by Ohio's rich history of innovation and invention. The name pays homage to the famous invention by Dayton's favourite sons, the Wright brothers, called 'wing-warping', a system designed for lateral roll control of a fixed-wing aircraft. The brewery is built on that same spirit of invention, along with a few original 'warped' interpretations of beer styles.

Baltic Porter only comes out once a year in January. Unfortunately, it's not widely available, so trust me when I say it's incredible!

Roger Protz

My voyage of discovery began on a warm summer's day in a Munich beer garden. I ordered a beer and was handed a lager known locally as Helles that was a delightful and refreshing mix of rich malt and hop flavours. A few miles from Munich, I sampled the Dunkel beer from the Kaltenberg castle brewery run by Prince Luitpold. Here was another revelation – dark lager packed with rich chocolate, coffee and roasted grain notes. I also came across wheat beer, a Bavarian speciality and a member of the ale family, offering heady tastes of rich grain, banana and bubblegum.

As my voyage continued I found fine beer in such unlikely outposts as France and Italy while Belgium offered a cornucopia of astonishment with Trappist ales, sour red, spiced wheat and the ancient mysteries of spontaneous fermentation. Across the Atlantic, the United States was witnessing an amazing revolution, with thousands of new breweries bringing choice to drinkers desperate to break free from the icy grip of thin, lacklustre quasi-lagers, while in my home country, hundreds of new, small breweries were also bringing greater choice to drinkers and were adding genuine IPAs, Porters and Stouts to traditional Milds and Bitters.

Choosing some 33 beers to reflect the best in the world is an unenviable task. I have attempted to offer a blend of old and new. I include icons of their styles such as Cooper's, De Koninck, Duvel, Jever, Paulaner, Schneider and Timothy Taylor, and have added to the mix new beers that bring challenging interpretations of both old and new beers.

Join the ship and enjoy the voyage!

Achouffe
Houblon Chouffe Dobbelen

9% IPA Tripel 55 IBUs

Achouffe, Belgium

The brewery in the densely wooded Ardennes region of French-speaking Wallonia has grown from humble beginnings to one of Belgium's leading beer-makers, now part of the major Duvel Moortgat group. Chris Bauweraerts and Pierre Gobron began brewing in 1982 using a drum from a washing machine and boiling vats that had started life in a laundry. They brewed in Pierre's kitchen and then moved to a barn on a farm in the village of Achouffe.

The area is rich in folklore based on the activities of mythical gnomes who live in the woods. Sales of the beers took off when bottle labels and dispense equipment featured a jolly gnome with a red cap and sacks of barley and hops on his back. In 1986 Chris and Pierre moved again to a modern brewhouse with a visitor centre and bistro that draws 10,000 people a year from the Netherlands and France as well as Belgium. In 2006 the brewery was bought by Duvel Moortgat who export the beers to the US and French-speaking Canada. Chris is a now a roving ambassador for the company.

The IPA has quite a mouthful of a name: Houblon is the French for hop, Dobbelen indicates a strong beer while Tripel means three hops are used. The beer is brewed with pale Pilsner malt and the hops are Amarillo and Tomahawk from the US and Czech Saaz. At first it had 62 bitterness units but this proved too much for many drinkers and the IBUs have been scaled back to 55.

The beer has a spicy, peppery and floral bouquet, with biscuit malt and elderflowers on the palate balanced by spicy hops and orange fruit. The finish is bitter, dry, hoppy and malty with a continuing orange fruit note.

Adnams
Ghost Ship

4.5%   Pale Ale   40 IBUs

Southwold, Suffolk

Ghost Ship is a beer that haunts Adnams – in the least frightening way. The family brewery, dating from 1872, has for many years been best known for its flagship Southwold Bitter and stronger Broadside. But in 2010 head brewer Fergus Fitzgerald was inspired by the stories of shipwrecks and ghostly happenings in around the coastal town to celebrate the grisly history with a beer for Halloween called Ghost Ship. It created such a stir that it was brought back in 2011 and has not only become a regular beer but also is now Adnams' best-selling brand.

Adnams may be 150 years old but it's the model of a high-tech modern brewery. The plant can produce lager as well as ale and is eco-friendly. Steam is captured and recycled, energy costs have been slashed and rainwater is recovered from the roof of a warehouse and used to clean vehicles.

Ghost Ship falls into the category of Pale Ale, but it's unusual in having some colour in its cheeks as Fergus blends in rye crystal malt and caramalt along with pale malt. The main hop is the American Citra along with fellow American Chinook and New Zealand Motueka. There's a further addition of Citra in the fermenter: modern craft brewers are not shy of adding hops to both mash tuns and fermenters to extract maximum aroma and bitterness.

The beer has a superb aroma of citrus fruit, spicy hops and lightly toasted grain with a tantalising hint of violets. Tart fruit, hop resins and a malt biscuit note dominate the palate followed by a complex finish that's dry and bittersweet, with grapefruit and lemon to the fore, balanced by biscuit malt and tangy hops.

Alaskan Brewing Co
Smoked Porter

5.5%   Porter   45 IBUs

Juneau, Alaska

It's a fascinating thought that a beer made close to the Arctic Circle may give us a glimpse of what the original Porters of the 18th century brewed in faraway London may have tasted like. The Alaskan beer also has a powerful link to the smoked beers of Bamberg in Germany: the German connection underscores the fact that many Germans launched breweries in the region during the 19th century to quench the thirsts of miners searching for gold in the Klondike. All those breweries closed when the Gold Rush ended and was followed by Prohibition in the 1920s.

Brewing in the state was rekindled in 1986 when Marcy and Geoff Larson launched their company in Juneau, the state capital. Geoff had been a keen homebrewer and wanted to revive old beer styles as well modern beers. His first beer, Amber, was based on the German Alt style (Alt means old and is a top-fermented beer that pre-dates the lager revolution of the 19th century).

It was the Larsons' Porter that put them firmly on the world beer map. Smoked Porter has won more awards at the Great American Beer Festival than any other beer. It's an annual vintage, released in November, and its signature is smoked malt. The Larsons hired space in a local fish smokehouse where they laid dark malt on a rack with heat from below created by alder wood.

Smoked Porter is brewed with pale, black, chocolate and crystal malts and is hopped with Chinook and Willamette varieties that create 45 units of bitterness. It has a smoky and woody aroma and palate with spicy hops, dark grain, coffee and chocolate notes. Pure brewing water comes from the Juneau ice field. The finished beer is both warming and deeply refreshing.

Het Anker
Gouden Carolus Classic

8.5%   Belgian Ale   16 IBUs

Mechelen, Belgium

Gouden Carolus – Golden Charles – is named in honour of Emperor Charles V (1500–1558) who came from Mechelen and had beer from the city delivered to his court. The brewery started life in 1471 in a beguinage, a hospice where nuns were allowed to brew beer for the sick and dying. When the nuns left the hospice in 1865 the brewery was secularised and run by the Van Beedam family, who remain in charge today. They continued the religious connection by naming the brewery Het Anker, from St Paul's saying that hope is the anchor of the soul.

Gouden Carolus was launched in 1963 and quickly became a popular, award-winning beer, named Best Dark Ale in the World Beer Awards in 2012. It's produced in a brewery that's a mixture of old and new, with a mash tun, filter and copper that date from 1947, and conical fermenters added in 2004.

The beer is now called Gouden Carolus Classic as Het Anker has added two further beers to expand the range: Gouden Carolus Tripel (9%) and Gouden Carolus Hopsinjoor (8%), both Golden Ales. Classic is brewed with Pilsner, wheat, light and dark caramalts and roasted barley. The single hop is the Golding. Fermentation lasts for five days, and the beer is then filtered and rests in conditioning tanks to ripen. Fresh yeast and brewing sugar are added to encourage a second fermentation in bottle.

Classic has a ruby colour and an enticing aroma of port wine, chocolate and spicy hops. Raisin fruit builds in the mouth with chewy malt, chocolate and peppery hops. The finish has great length and is bittersweet with notes of liquorice, roasted grain, dark fruit, chocolate and bitter hops.

Baladin
Nazionale

6.5%   Italian Ale   31 IBUs

Piozzo, Italy

Teo Musso, founder of Baladin, is called the father of the Italian beer revolution. A country famous for its wine, and with a couple of industrial lagers, now has a thriving craft beer movement, with beer festivals packed with enthusiastic young people. The movement has been inspired by Teo, who, following a tour of Belgian breweries, opened a beer tent in Piozzo in 1996. A group of travelling French minstrels came to the tent and suggested he should call his tent Le Baladin, 'the storyteller', after their troupe. The small brewery quickly doubled in size and its success forced him to move to a bigger plant where he now produces 10,000hl a year.

Teo has spread out from rural Piedmont and opened a series of specialist beer bars in major cities including Rome and Turin. As well as draught, he produces a wide range of beers in elegant, club-shaped bottles that are sold in upmarket restaurants. He is challenging fellow Italians to treat beer as seriously as fine wine and to accompany beer with good food.

In a country short on barley and hops, he has planted both grain and hop plants in Apulia, Basilicate, Bisca and Piozzo. The hops include Italian versions of Cascade, Chinook, Comet and Magnum. They are used in generous amounts in Baladin's major brand, Nazionale, that's made entirely from home-grown ingredients. Spices and citrus zest are added to the beer that has a rich spicy and floral aroma with honeyed malt.

The palate is balanced between bittersweet fruit, spices, floral hops and a cracker biscuit malt note. The finish is long and lingering with spice notes balancing tart fruit and bitter hops.

Budějovicky Budvar
Budweiser Budvar Original

5%   Pale Lager   22 IBUs

České Budějovice, Czech Republic

Controversy surrounds one of the world's classic lager beers. Budvar is involved in endless court battles and trademark disputes with the brewers of American Budweiser, the world's biggest beer brand, owned by global giant AB InBev. AB InBev claims its beer is the original, but history is not on its side.

The South Bohemian town of Ceské Budějovice has been a major brewing centre for centuries, and under the town's old German name of Budweis, the beers were generically known as Budweiser. The royal court brewery was based in Budweis, enabling its products to be called 'the beer of kings'.

In the 19th century, German speakers in Budweis launched the Budweiser Burgerbrau, or Citizens' Brewery, and it exported its beer widely using the Budweiser name. In 1875 two German emigrants called Anheuser and Busch opened a brewery in St Louis, Missouri, and they called one of their products Budweiser with the tag 'the King of Beers', which may sound familiar.

Twenty years later, Czech speakers in Budweis founded the Budějovicky Pivovar, known popularly as Budvar. When the Czechs attempted to export their beer to the United States, sparks flew and litigation involving the two brands has rumbled on ever since.

The two beers could not be more different. The American version lists rice before barley malt on the label and has low bitterness units of around 10. The entire brewing regime lasts for 20 days, whereas Budvar is lagered for 90 days and is brewed with Moravian malt, Žatec hops and pure, soft water. It has a rich vanilla and floral hops aroma. Toasted malt and spicy hops dominate the palate followed by a quenching finish with juicy malt, spicy hops and a touch of lemon fruit.

Burton Bridge
Empire Pale Ale

7.5%   IPA   50 IBUs

Burton-upon-Trent, Staffordshire

The world is awash with IPAs, but for a taste of the true original you have to sample a version from the town that redefined beer in the 19th century. The first beers for the India trade may have been brewed in London, but they reached their apogee in Burton due to the mineral-rich water that brought out the full flavours of malt and hops.

Geoff Mumford and Bruce Wilkinson are steeped in Burton brewing. They worked for the giant Ind Coope brewery in the town before they opened their own plant in 1982 behind the Burton Bridge Inn. They brew a wide range of beers, but their Empire Pale Ale stands out from the crowd as it's only available in bottle and is packaged with live yeast. It has won many awards, including Best Bottle-Conditioned Beer in a competition staged by *The Guardian* newspaper in 1997.

The method of production is designed to replicate a sea journey to India in the 19th century. Following primary fermentation, the beer is conditioned for six months in cask and then has an addition of Styrian Goldings hops. The main hop used during the first stage of brewing is the English Challenger. Pale malt and invert sugar are used in the mash tun and copper: no darker grains are involved.

There's a pronounced orange fruit note from the hops and house yeast on aroma and palate. The fruitiness is balanced by biscuit malt and spicy hop resins, with a long and lingering finish that balances juicy malt, tart fruit and bitter hops.

The label stresses the imperial nature of the beer with an army officer in full dress uniform flanked by Union Flags.

Carlow Brewing Company
O'Hara's Irish Stout

4.3%   Stout   36 IBUs

Bagenalstown, Ireland

Carlow's flagship beer is proof there is more to Irish Stout than ubiquitous brands brewed in Dublin and Cork. Carlow has been at the forefront of the Irish brewing revival since it was founded in 1996 by Seamus and Eamon O'Hara.

Their fortunes were boosted when the Stout won a gold medal in the prestigious International Brewing Awards in 2000. Increased sales worldwide enabled the O'Haras to move to a custom-built new plant in Bagenalstown in County Carlow, the family birthplace. A €1 million investment in 2005 led to a big expansion at the brewery and the O'Haras now export 60% of their production to avoid the grip of the two Irish giants, Guinness and Murphy/Heineken.

The Canadian-built kit is based on a mash tun, lauter tun and brew kettle system. All the Carlow beers have an exceptionally long three-hour mash to enable the conversion from starch to fermentable malt. The sweet wort is then filtered in the lauter. The hard local water lies on a bed of limestone and is ideal for brewing Stout, Seamus O'Hara says. He uses Irish ale malt but imports specialist malts from Yorkshire. The Irish climate is too damp to grow hops and Seamus buys them from England, the Czech Republic and the US.

For O'Hara's Stout pale malt is complemented by roasted barley, caramalt and chocolate malt and is hopped with English Fuggles. It has a creamy malt aroma with hints of chocolate, espresso coffee and spicy hop notes. Roasted grain, coffee and liquorice dominate the palate, followed by a long finish with creamy malt, roast and gentle spicy hops to the fore.

A stronger version is called Leann Folláin (6%), meaning 'Wholesome Stout'. It's aged for three months prior to packaging and has pronounced chocolate, coffee and dark fruit notes.

Castelain
Ch'ti Blonde

6.4%   Bière de Garde

Bénifontaine, France

The Nord-Pas de Calais region of France, comprising Artois, Flanders and Picardy, shares a beer style with neighbouring Belgium that's known as Saison in Belgian Wallonia and Bière de Garde in France. The name means 'keeping beer', meaning it's aged for several weeks before being released for sale.

Castelain is one of the leading makers of the style and its Ch'ti trademark comes from Picardian dialect meaning 'It suits you'. The beers certainly suited generations of miners in the region who wanted a rich and refreshing drink after hours digging for black gold.

The brewery started life on a farm in the 1920s and was bought by the Castelain family in 1966. In the 1970s, as the mines closed, Yves Castelain reached out to younger drinkers with a new beer, Ch'ti Blonde, that's aged for two months. It was well received and Blonde has spawned other versions, including Ambrée and an organic Jade.

Castelain has attractive copper vessels visible from the road, ironically called Rue Pasteur as Nicolas Castelain, the son of Yves and now in charge of brewing, makes the point that his beers are not pasteurised. A wood carving of Saint Arnold, the patron saint of brewers, guards the entrance to the brewhouse.

Blonde is brewed with pure water from an on-site well. Four malts are used: pale, Munich, caramalt and torrefied. The hops are Flemish and German Hallertau varieties, used for aroma rather than extreme bitterness. The beer is fermented with a lager culture but at a warm temperature. After cold conditioning, the beer has a rich biscuit, perfumy hop and citrus fruit aroma, with fruit and hops dominating the palate. The finish is bittersweet with tart fruit, juicy malt and spicy hops.

Chiltern
Bodgers Barley Wine

8.5% Barley Wine 32 IBUs

Terrick, nr Aylesbury, Buckinghamshire

The Jenkinson family celebrated its tenth anniversary in brewing in 1990 with a Barley Wine that also restored the good name of the bodger. Today it means someone, usually in the building trade, who cuts corners to produce a shoddy job. But centuries ago, in rural areas such as the Chiltern Hills, a bodger was a craftsman who made wooden chairs and fences.

The Jenkinsons went on to celebrate 40 years of brewing in 2020 and can claim to run the oldest brewery in Buckinghamshire. Their Barley Wine helps revive a tradition of making strong beers that dates from the 18th century when England was regularly at war with France. Patriots, especially among the aristocracy, refused to drink imported French wine and consumed instead beers that rivalled wine in strength. The beers were brewed in the autumn from fresh malts and hops from the harvest then aged for a year before they were ready to be drunk.

Bodgers is brewed with Maris Otter pale malt, considered the finest English malting barley, and hopped with three English varieties: Challenger, Fuggles and Goldings. Following fermentation, the beer is conditioned for a month and is then filtered and re-seeded with fresh yeast. Bottles are then held at the brewery for a month before they are released.

The gold-coloured beer has a zesty aroma of orange fruit, honeyed malt and peppery hops, with more ripe fruit and tart hops dominating the palate. The finish is long and bittersweet with continuing notes of ripe malt, tangy fruit and peppery hops. Every year a batch of beer is aged in whisky casks and is made available to customers in Chiltern's pub, the King's Head in Aylesbury.

Cigar City Brewing
Maduro Brown Ale

5.5%   Brown Ale   25 IBUs

Tampa, Florida

It's a long way from Florida to north-east England but Joey Redner, founder of Cigar City Brewing, and his brewmaster, Wayne Wambles, have done their research. When they wanted to revive a Tampa traditional beer style they looked to Newcastle-upon-Tyne as well as their home city for inspiration.

There's a strong link between the two cities as industrial workers in both places wanted a refreshing beer that would restore lost energy after long hours of labour – which meant rolling cigars

in Tampa. It's called Cigar City as it was the centre of the cigar trade for many years. Tobacco was imported from Cuba and many Cubans followed to hand-roll the finished article.

The Florida Brewery Company was founded in 1896 and it brewed ale as well as lager. It was followed by the Ybor City Brewery – Ybor is a district of Tampa – and it produced Brown Ale, Porter and wheat beer. Both breweries eventually closed and Redner and Wambles set out to restore Tampa's brewing tradition in 2008 with their first beer, Maduro Brown Ale. The brewery has a 15-barrel plant with a taproom and visitor shop where regular beer and food events are held.

Brown Ale is brewed with pale, crystal and chocolate malts, special roast, flaked oats and Victory – the last named is a toasted malt.
The hops are Northern Brewer and Willamette. The beer has a fine claret colour and a pronounced chocolate note on the aroma, with roasted grain, a hint of vanilla, freshly baked bread and floral hops. The palate is clean and quenching, with dark grain and chocolate balanced by bitter hops. Toasted grain, vanilla and chocolate notes and spicy hops combine in the long and refreshing finish.

Coopers
Sparkling Ale

5.8%   Pale Ale   30 IBUs

Adelaide, Australia

Coopers has gone from joke to national icon. When the likes of Foster's and XXXX were in their pomp, nobody, it was claimed, wanted to drink an ale, especially one that was cloudy in the glass. Then along came a new generation of drinkers concerned about beer quality and the need to use the finest ingredients. Sales of Coopers took off and Sparkling Ale is now revered throughout Australia and in export markets.

The brewery dates from the 1860s. Thomas Cooper came from Yorkshire and worked as a shoemaker. When his wife became sick, Thomas made a homebrew that cured her, and friends were so impressed with his beer that he went into business as a brewer. Today, the brewery is run by Tim and Glenn Cooper, the sixth generation of a business that makes homebrew kits as well as draught and packaged beers.

Sparkling Ale is their leading brand and is both bottled and keg conditioned with live yeast. The beer is neither filtered nor pasteurised and has a slight haze in the glass: when a rival Adelaide brewery launched a similar beer it used the slogan 'Another cloud on the horizon'.

The Cooper's version is brewed with pale and crystal malts with around 18% cane sugar. The vigorous house yeast converts the sugar into alcohol, avoiding cloying sweetness. The gold/amber beer is intensely fruity with apple and banana dominating. The Pride of Ringwood hops contribute a peppery note to the aroma and a fine underpinning of bitterness through the palate and finish. Citrus fruit makes an appearance in the long finish with juicy malt and spicy hops. Following primary fermentation, the beer is filtered and a fresh dosage of sugary wort is added to encourage secondary fermentation.

Duvel Moortgat
Duvel Tripel Hop

9.5%　　Golden Ale　　30 IBUs

Breendonck, Belgium

A sign in Flemish outside the Duvel Moortgat brewery says 'Ssh … Duvel is ripening'. This strong, infinitely complex and superbly aromatic beer is conditioned, refermented and matured by a long, slow and pains-taking process. The beer, pronounced 'Doovul', means devil: according to a legend, a friend of the owners declared 'This is a devil of a beer' when it was first produced. It's now such an acclaimed international brand that the company, originally Moortgat, is now known as Duvel Moortgat.

The brewery dates from 1871 and has always been a specialist ale producer. Between the two world wars of the 21st century, the brewery asked a famous brewing scientist, Jean De Clerck, at Leuven University to study the yeast in a bottle of imported McEwan's Scotch, which was then a popular beer in Belgium. De Clerck isolated the best strains of the yeast which were then used to launch Duvel. It remained a dark beer until the 1970s when De Clerck analysed the yeast culture again and reformulated it to make a golden ale.

The beer is brewed with Belgian and French barleys and is hopped with Czech Saaz and Styrian Goldings. The beer enjoys three fermentations in the brewery and finally the bottle and emerges with its celebrated Poire William aroma and palate balanced by toasted malt and spicy hops.

Duvel is 8.5% but in 2017 the brewery produced several new versions brewed with different hops. It then invited consumers to vote for their favourite. This turned out to be one with the American Citra hop, which adds an additional aroma and flavour of tart citrus fruit as well as a beefed-up alcoholic strength.

Elland
1872 Porter

6.5% Porter 39 IBUs

Elland, West Yorkshire

Elland Brewery can't stop winning prizes for its Porter. It won the Supreme Champion Beer of Britain award in 2013 and has garnered CAMRA's Champion Winter Beer three times in 2010, 2013 and 2015, and also picked up a gold in the International Brewing Awards in 2004. To add to the impressive collection, it also won a gold medal from SIBA, the Society of Independent Brewers, in 2011. As a result, it's the most decorated beer in this category in Britain.

The name stems from the fact that the beer is based on an authentic recipe from 1872 and stresses the brewery's links with the town near Halifax. Elland Brewery was founded in 2022 and now has a capacity of 50 barrels a week. As well as supplying pubs in the region it has a taproom on site.

The recipe was given to the brewery by historian Dr John Harrison, who had made a special study of 19th century beer styles, IPA along with Porter and Stout. As well as malted grain, the original recipe used invert sugar, which has been retained by Elland.

Porter is brewed with Maris Otter pale malt, along with amber, brown and chocolate grains and – as befits the style – is hopped with two English varieties, Northdown and Target. It has a rich aroma of coffee and bitter chocolate with a delicious port wine note and peppery hops. Coffee, chocolate, roasted grain, dark fruit and bitter hops build in the mouth while the long, dry and bitter finish is balanced by dark fruit and continuing notes of coffee, chocolate and port wine. The beer is available in cask and bottle-conditioned formats.

Fuller, Smith & Turner
Fuller's Vintage Ale

8.5%   **Strong Ale**   IBUs vary

London, England

Fuller's Vintage Ale is the claret of the beer world, awaited each year with all the anticipation of wine lovers looking forward to the latest vintage from Bordeaux. The beer was introduced in 1997 by Fuller's head brewer Reg Drury and continued by his successors, John Keeling and Georgina Young. The aim is to produce a strong bottle-conditioned beer every September using different varieties of malts and hops.

Fuller's house yeast adds a rich, orange fruit note but there are subtle and even profound differences between one vintage and the next. The beer will improve over time, which means tasting notes for young or mature beer will be radically different.

Vintage Ale is based on Fuller's Golden Pride Barley Wine, a pasteurised bottled beer. Vintage comes from the same mash but is conditioned in the brewery for a month at the end of fermentation and re-seeded with fresh yeast. Some 50,000 bottles are produced every year, individually numbered in an attractive claret box. Over the years such barley varieties as Golden Promise, Optic and Maris Otter have been used with a range of English hops, including Challenger, Goldings, Northdown and Target.

The 2020 vintage marked a departure by using dark roasted crystal malt along with pale. The hops were two new English varieties, Godiva and Jester. The copper-red beer has a heady aroma of caramel, raisin fruit, plums, blood oranges and spicy hops with orange marmalade on the palate along with tart hops, roasted grain and bitter chocolate. The long, bittersweet finish has creamy malt, tangy fruit and peppery hops.

There were fears that when Fuller's sold the brewery to Asahi in 2019 the Japanese giant might phase out short-run beers, but Vintage Ale has continued to be brewed.

Interbrau/Meantime
Thomas Hardy's Ale

11.7%　Barley Wine　75 IBUs

Padua, Italy/London, England

The story of this internationally acclaimed strong ale is as dramatic as one of the novels of the writer who inspired it. It was first brewed by Eldridge Pope in Dorchester, which produced it as a one-off brew for a festival in the town in 1968 to celebrate Hardy's writing on the 40th anniversary of his death.

The beer aroused such interest that it became an annual vintage and was bought by beer lovers intrigued to learn that it would continue to improve like a fine wine for 25 years. When Eldridge Pope closed in 2000 the beer was brewed for a couple of years by O'Hanlon's Brewery in Devon, but it was discontinued as it took too long to brew.

The brand was bought by an American importer, George Saxon, who sold it to Sandro and Michele Vecchiato who run the Interbrau beer wholesale company in Padua. If Italy seems an odd place to own a famous English Barley Wine, the Vecchiato brothers gave it authenticity by brewing it at Meantime in London. The brewery called on the expertise of veteran brewer Derek Prentice who had worked at two famous London breweries, Young's and Fuller's.

Fittingly, floor-malted Maris Otter from the West Country is used, with brewing sugar to help achieve the high level of alcohol. The hops are Fuggles and Goldings that create 75 IBUs. The beer's ruby colour comes from caramelisation of the malt sugars during the long boil in the copper.

It's a stunningly complex beer. There are notes of fresh leather and tobacco with hints of spicy hops and candied fruit on aroma and palate while the long finish has liquorice, leather and sherry notes with bitter hops.

Jever
Pilsener

4.9%   Pilsener   44 IBUs

Friesland, Germany

The old moated town of Jever – pronounced Yay-ver – and its brewery are in German Friesland, a region with a group of islands divided among Germany, Denmark and the Netherlands. The islands, which once formed an independent buffer state, were the setting for the first modern spy novel, Erskine Childer's *The Riddle of the Sands*.

Drinkers in the region like their beers bitter and Jever Pilsener fits the bill with 44 units of bitterness. The brewery was founded in 1848 and soft water is drawn from a well that helps give the beer its rounded, malt character balanced by hops.

The brewery had a difficult time during World War Two when it was threatened with bombing and was starved of raw materials. Following the war it was so short of malt and hops that it could supply only a few local outlets, but it recovered and was soon able to distribute the beer nationally. Its popularity has led to Jever being the subject of a series of takeovers, first by Bavaria St Pauli of Hamburg in 1922, then the national brewery Brau und Brunnen in 1994, and since 2005 it has been owned by the giant Radeberger group, best known for Dr Oetker pizzas.

But Jever has refused to reduce the quality of its Pilsener or to soften its distinctive bitterness. It's brewed with pale malt and hopped with Hallertau and Tettnang varieties from Bavaria. It has a herbal, grassy and resinous aroma balanced by toasted malt and a hint of honey sweetness. Bitter hops burst on the tongue, while the finish has an iron-like intensity with only a small walk-on part for malt. It's a shatteringly bitter beer, but full-tasting and rewarding.

Kaltenberg
König Ludwig Dunkel

5.1%   Dunkel   26 IBUs

Geltendorf, Germany

His Royal Highness Crown Prince Luitpold of Kaltenberg may seem an unlikely brewer but he has almost single-handedly restored a major Bavarian brewing style. Dunkel, or dark lager, was a style that had all but disappeared as pale lagers dominated the market.

The Bavarian royal family lost power at the end of World War One, but Prince Luitpold had a castle to maintain and he decided to turn the small family brewery into a commercial venture in 1976. The castle dates from the 13th century and was redesigned in mock-Gothic style in the 1840s.

When Prince Luitpold took charge he decided to turn the local speciality, Dunkel, into the main brand and restore it to its rightful position as a proud Bavarian style. It's named in honour of King Ludwig, one of the prince's ancestors. At first the small brewery could produce just 25,000hl a year, but that has expanded to 100,000hl.

The prince uses Bavarian pale, dark and roasted malts and he hops the beer three times with Hersbrucker and Tettnang varieties from the Hallertau. The mash is a long, triple decoction system and following the copper boil the beer has a primary fermentation in small, conical vessels followed by a long ripening in steel tanks.

To avoid sweetness, Prince Luitpold attenuates or brews out the beer so that 80% of the malt sugars turn to alcohol. He also adds lactic acid bacteria to further counteract sweetness. The beer that emerges from this complex method of production is chestnut coloured with a pronounced roasted malt, coffee, figs and floral hops aroma. Dark grain and fruit flavours dominate the palate followed by a finish full of vine fruits, coffee and gentle hops.

De Koninck
Bolleke

5.2%   Belgian Pale Ale   23 IBUs

Antwerp, Belgium

De Koninck means 'the king' and it's without question the beer monarch in Antwerp. Blow-ups of the special glass – the Bolleke (the name means goblet in Flemish) – used to serve the beer hang in many bars and there is no need to mention the brewery when ordering a beer: just ask for a Bolleke.

The brewery dates from 1833 and was run by the De Koninck family who went into partnership with the Van Bogaert family following World War One. Bolleke was first brewed in 1952 and was inspired by English Pale Ales that were popular in Belgium at the time (Belgians were grateful to Britain for its support during both world wars). A modern brewhouse was installed in the 1990s and was designed to expand production but not to diminish the quality of the product.

Bolleke is brewed with pale Pilsner malt and darker Vienna malt with no brewing sugars. The only hop used is the Czech Saaz, added three times during the copper boil to extract maximum aroma and bitterness. The beer, which is filtered but not pasteurised in draught form, has a dense, rocky head of foam followed by an entrancing aroma of biscuit malt, hop resins and a spicy cinnamon note: the spice comes from the house yeast. Juicy malt, tangy hops, spice and citrus fruit dance on the tongue while the lingering finish becomes finally dry but is preceded by toasted malt, spice and tart fruit.

Brasserie Lepers
L'Angélus Blonde

7%   **Bière de Garde**   20 IBUs

La Chapelle-d'Armentières, France

One of the best known Bières de Garde – or 'keeping beers' – stresses the powerful link between farming and brewing in rural France. The brewery was opened by the Lepers family in 1905, using farm buildings that had once been cattle byres. A member of the fifth generation of the family, Bertrand, married Yvette who came from a small farm at Flers. They put the brewery on the map in the 1990s with the success of a golden beer called l'Angélus, which underscored the agricultural connection by using the famous Millais painting 'The Gleaners' on the label, which shows farm workers gathering in the harvest. The painting is revered in the region for highlighting the prosperity farming has brought to it.

The success of the beer led to Bertrand's son, also Bertrand, moving to a bigger plant at La Chapelle. It's now run by his son, Charles, and the plant has become a major visitor attraction, with open fermenters and mash tuns enabling the brewing process to be seen at close hand.

L'Angélus Blonde is brewed with pale malt and 30% buckwheat. The hops are Flemish varieties along with Czech Saaz. It's bronze coloured and has a rich, orange aroma backed by spicy hops, with more tart fruit in the mouth and a long bittersweet finish. The pronounced orange fruit character makes this the Grand Marnier of the beer world.

L'Angélus Triple (8%, 18 IBUs) is essentially the same beer with the addition of oats and coriander, and it has a big, spicy and herbal note alongside citrus fruit and hops.

Paulaner
Salvator Doppelbock

7.9% Doppelbock   21 IBUs

Munich, Germany

Paulaner is the classic Munich Bock beer, the benchmark of the style. The beer is so famous that other breweries have used similar names to Salvator for their interpretations of Bock. The brewery was founded in 1634 by monks who were followers of St Francis of Paula in Calabria, Italy. The monks built their monastery on a hill on the outskirts of Munich and added a small brewery where they could store (or lager) their beer in deep, cold cellars.

One of their beers was brewed for the Lent period and was known as 'liquid bread' as it helped sustain the populace during fasting. It was called Salvator, which means Holy Father or Saviour. The beer was sold commercially from the late 18th century to help raise funds for the upkeep of the monastery. When the monastery was secularised a century later, the new owner, Franz-Xavier Zacheri, promoted Salvator with such vigour that other Munich brewers launched beers with the same name. Zacheri took them to court in 1894 and the result led to his competitors dropping Salvator but renaming their beers with such endings as Triumphator and Kulminator.

Every year, three weeks before Easter, a cask of Salvator is tapped by the mayor of Munich in the brewery's beer garden. Drinking Doppelbock is known as the *Frühlingskur* or spring cure.

Paulaner is brewed with pale and Munich malts and hopped with Herkules and Hallertau Tradition varieties from the Hallertau region north of Munich, and is lagered for at least three months. It is russet brown in colour with a rich, malt loaf aroma, a yeasty/bready palate and a complex finish with sultana fruit, ripe malt and floral hops.

Porterhouse Brew Co
XXXX Full-on Stout

5%   Stout   50 IBUs

Dublin, Ireland

Porterhouse led the revival of independent brewing in Ireland when two cousins, Oliver Hart and Liam LaHart, opened a brewpub in the Temple Bar area of Dublin in 1996. In a city (and island) dominated by one giant brand, drinkers in need of choice beat a path to Temple Bar to relish the cousins' interpretations of Porter, Stout and Strong Ale.

Much to the annoyance of their noisy neighbour in St James's Gate, Porterhouse stunned the beer world in 1998 by winning the title of the World's Best Stout with its Porter in the International Brewing Awards. Success forced Oliver and Liam to move to bigger premises in 2000, and they expanded further with two more pubs in Dublin and one in Covent Garden, London.

They followed this with two bars in Manhattan in New York City, one of which, Fraunce's Tavern, is where George Washington said farewell to his troops at the end of the War of Independence. Oliver Hughes died suddenly in 2016 but Liam has continued to expand the business with an even bigger brewing plant in Glasnevin to keep pace with demand.

XXXX Full-on Stout is brewed in the Irish tradition of blending some unmalted roasted barley with pale malt, flaked barley and black malt. The hops are East Kent Goldings, Galena and Nugget. The beer has a rich aroma of roasted grain, liquorice, molasses and peppery hops. Dark malt, liquorice, espresso coffee and spicy hops fill the mouth, followed by a long finish dominated by creamy and dark grain, strong coffee, molasses and fruity and peppery hops.

Porterhouse has joined forces with the Dingle whiskey distillery to produce an oak-aged Imperial Stout, Around the Clock (12%).

Rodenbach
Grand Cru

6%   **Sour Red**   14–18 IBUs

Roeselare, Belgium

The West Flanders region is famous for a style known as Sour Red, of which Rodenbach is far and away the biggest producer. The brewery was founded in 1820 by the Rodenbach family who had come from Germany and threw themselves into the cultural and political life of the Low Countries, including the struggle for an independent Belgium.

In the1870s Eugene Rodenbach toured England to study brewing techniques and he returned determined to make the oak-aged beers he found across the North Sea. Frustratingly, no records exist of which breweries he visited. But whatever the inspiration, Rodenbach built a reputation for beers aged in 294 oak tuns, some of which are 150 years old. A large proportion of the workforce is made up of coopers who maintain the oak vessels and regularly scrape the inside of the vessels to maintain the correct balance of caramel and tannins in the wood. During the rest in wood – for as long as two years – natural bacteria add a sour and lactic quality to the beer.

The regular beers are Classic, Grand Cru and Alexander, with an annual Vintage. Grand Cru is the stand-out beer, brewed with water from an on-site well, pale and darker Vienna malts and a small amount of maize. Belgian hops from Poperinge create 14–18 IBUs. It's a blend of two-thirds beer aged for as long as two years in oak and one third young beer. It has oak, tannic, sour and fruity notes on aroma and palate, with a long, fruity, oak and tannic finish.

Rodenbach was bought by the large Belgian ale brewer Palm in 2016, which in turn was acquired by the even bigger Dutch brewer Bavaria, and to date the quality of the beers remains high.

Rudgate
Ruby Mild

4.4%   Mild   32 IBUs

Tockwith, North Yorkshire

Rudgate is proof that Mild Ale is popular and doesn't have to be low in alcohol. It underscored its popularity by winning the top gold medal in the Champion Beer of Britain competition in 2009.

Craig Lee founded the brewery in 1992 with a 15-barrel kit on a disused World War Two airfield that had housed Halifax bombers. Craig chose the site in order to benefit from the supply of fine water and also the brewery's proximity to a major road, the Rudgate. The road was built by the Romans and used by the Vikings when they invaded the area and built Jorvik, which became the city of York.

Craig and his team have doubled the size of the plant and supply some 350 outlets in the region with their beers. The range pays homage to the history of the area with such beers as Jorvik Blonde, Viking, Battleaxe and Valkyrie.

The Mild is not only strong by modern standards but also high in bitterness, with 32 IBUs. It's brewed in the Yorkshire tradition with whole hops and open fermenters. The recipe is complex, with Pearl pale malt augmented by pale and dark chocolate malts, brown malt, crystal malt and roasted barley. Challenger hops are used in the copper for bitterness with a late addition of Bobek from Slovenia for aroma.

The beer has a rich aroma of roasted grain, creamy chocolate, burnt fruit and spicy hop resins. Chocolate, fruit and roast flavours build in the mouth but the hops add a firm, pine-like balance. The long and lingering finish is bittersweet with a delicious creamy and wholemeal biscuit character, with further notes of chocolate, dark fruit and tangy hops. Rudgate also brews a Vanilla Mild.

G. Schneider & Sohn
Schneider Weisse

5.4%   Weisse   14 IBUs

Kelheim, Germany

Schneider has played a key role in the history of wheat beer brewing. In 1850 the Bavarian royal family, which had monopolised brewing of the beer style for centuries, licensed a Munich brewer called Georg Schneider to produce the beer for commercial scale. He brewed first in the famous Hofbräuhaus – the Royal Court Brewhouse – and later moved to the Tal or Dale, near the city centre.

Schneider was sufficiently successful to need a second brewery, and he bought a site in Kelheim in the heart of the Hallertau hop-growing region. The brewery in the Tal was destroyed by Allied bombing in World War Two, but a tavern selling Schneider beer stands on the spot.

The Kelheim brewery uses open fermenters, a rare sight in Germany where the fear of wild yeast infection keeps most vessels enclosed. Malts for the main Weisse beer are blended in the ratio of 60% wheat and 40% barley. Some Vienna and darker malts are added to give Weisse its bronze/copper colour. Hallertau Tradition and Herkules hops are used in pellet form.

In the fermenting hall the atmosphere is ripe with fruity aromas as the yeast goes to work on the malt sugars. Fermentation lasts for between three and five days, after which the beer is bottled at a warm temperature. Yeast and some unfermented wort are added and the beer is matured for a week. This produces a lively carbonation as secondary fermentation begins; it then has 14 days of cold conditioning.

The beer that finally emerges from this lengthy process has a pronounced banana, cloves and nutmeg aroma with a tart, spicy and slightly acidic flavour. The quenching finish has creamy malt, spices, fruit and gentle hop notes.

Shepherd Neame
India Pale Ale

4.5%   **IPA**   40 IBUs

Faversham, Kent

Shepherd Neame is Britain's oldest brewery, dating from 1698, and it stands in the heart of the Kentish hop fields. In its early years it brewed the beers of the time, Porter, Stout and Old Ale, but it was aware of developments in brewing in other parts of the country and in 1870 it launched its own interpretation of IPA.

It has recreated the beer using the original recipe that came to light in 2012 when the company's archivist, John Owen, found some ancient brewer's ledgers in a dusty corner of the cellars. When he sat down with master brewer Stewart Main they were intrigued to find that recipes from the 19th century had been written in code. The reason was that a rival brewer, Rigdens, stood across the road and Shepherd Neame was worried that a disgruntled employee might cross the street and divulge the secrets of the beers. Working with all the zeal of World War Two codebreakers, John and Stewart spent several months cracking the code and were able finally to produce a recipe for a true Victorian IPA.

It's brewed with pale and crystal malts and hopped with locally grown Fuggles and Goldings. The hops are added three times during the copper boil for maximum aroma and flavour.

The beer has a bright orange colour and has massive tart orange and lemon fruit on the aroma, along with spicy hop resins and cracker-like malt. Bittersweet fruit, juicy malt and bitter hops combine in the mouth while the long finish is dominated by bitter hops, citrus fruit and a solid underpinning of juicy malt.

The bottled version is a regular beer, the cask is a seasonal one.

St Austell
Proper Job

4.5%(cask); **5.5**%(bottle)   IPA   36 IBUs

St Austell, Cornwall

Proper Job, produced by one of Britain's oldest family brewers, is widely regarded as one of the finest of the new breed of IPAs. The beer was designed by head brewer Roger Ryman, who tragically died in his 50s in 2020. He fell in love with the fruity hops of the Yakima Valley in Washington State and went every year to the annual harvest to pick the best for his beer.

He combined the hops with England's finest malting barley, Maris Otter, which he encouraged farmers in Cornwall to grow exclusively for the brewery: the grain is called Cornish Gold in the region. The resulting beer so impressed judges in the Champion Beer of Britain competition that the bottle-conditioned version won the gold award in 2010 and 2011.

Following the mash, Chinook and Willamette hop pellets are added to the copper boil. The hopped wort then rests on a bed of Cascade, Chinook and Willamette whole hops. The finished beer is conditioned in the brewery for 10 to 14 days before being released to trade. For the bottled version, the beer is filtered and re-seeded with fresh yeast.

Proper Job is a Cornish term for a task well done and it recalls the role of the Cornwall Regiment that protected the British Residency in Lucknow during the Indian Mutiny of 1857. The beer has a powerful aroma of grapefruit, orange and mango with oatcake, malt and hops. Bittersweet fruit, biscuit malt and tangy hop resins dominate the palate while grapefruit comes to the fore in the long finish but is superbly balanced by biscuit malt and bitter hops.

St Bernardus
Tripel

8% **Abbey Ale** 25 IBUs

Watou, Belgium

Many commercial abbey beers have little connection to genuine monastic beers where monks are in charge. But Sint Bernardus has a long association with the Trappist ales produced by the neighbouring Sint Sixtus monastery at Westvleteren. For more than 40 years St Bernardus brewed identical beers to those at the abbey as a result of an agreement signed in 1946 that allowed the brewery to make beers for commercial sale but based on the monks' recipes and labelled St Sixtus. The Westvleteren yeast culture was shared with St Bernardus to help achieve authenticity.

The monks, who belong to one of the most reclusive Trappist monasteries in Belgium, preferred to brew beer strictly for their own consumption and wanted no association with the outside commercial world. But in 1992, when the contract came up for renewal, the monks' attitude had changed. They had seen the success enjoyed by other Trappist beers and decided to sell their beers on a restricted commercial basis.

St Bernardus was allowed to continue to use the original recipes, but it had to change the name of their beers from St Sixtus to St Bernardus. Westvleteren also asked St Bernardus to remove the image of a monk from their labels: this has not been done but the labels do carry the tagline 'Abbey Ales'.

What is not in dispute is the quality of the commercial beers. Tripel is brewed with pale malt, pale candy sugar and Northern Brewer hops. It has a hazy gold colour and a herbal and spicy hops aroma with cookie-like malt and apricot fruit. There's rich fruit on the palate with creamy malt and bitter hops while hop resins dominate the finish with ripe fruit, creamy malt and tangy, spicy hops.

Stewart Brewing
Stewart's 80/-

4.4%   Shilling Ale   30 IBUs

Edinburgh, Scotland

Steve and Jo Stewart have restored both pride and tradition to Scottish brewing by recreating old styles, including the 'Shilling Ales' of Victorian times when beer was invoiced according to strength, ranging from 60 to 80 shilling (60–80/-), followed by a strong ale known as Wee Heavy.

Steve worked for the British brewer Bass in Britain and the United States. It was while he was in North America that he came across Harpoon beers in Boston and was fired with enthusiasm to launch his own brewery. He opened in 2004 and his wife, Jo, added her professional marketing skills to help create a successful business.

They moved to new, custom-built plant in 2013 that includes a Craft Beer Kitchen. This is an 80-litre mini brewery where homebrewers can improve their skills with help from the brewing team. It's also used by students on the world-famous brewing and distilling course at Heriot Watt University in Edinburgh.

In the main brewery the wide range of beers includes 80/-, a style of beer similar to English Bitter that's known as Heavy in Scotland. As hops don't flourish in Scotland's cold climate, Heavies tend to be less bitter and more malt-driven than English Bitters.

Stewart 80/- is brewed with pale, dark crystal, wheat, oats and chocolate malts with a touch of roasted barley. The hops are Challenger, Bobek and Lubelski. The auburn-coloured beer has a big malt and dried fruit aroma with a gentle hint of hops. Floral hops build on the palate, but rich biscuit malt, dark fruit and a hint of chocolate dominate, while the finish is long and fruity with a wholemeal biscuit character, with continuing hints of chocolate and light hop bitterness.

Timothy Taylor's
Landlord

4.3%   Pale Ale   38 IBUs

Keighley, West Yorkshire

Landlord is a legend. It has won CAMRA's Champion Beer of Britain top award four times – more than any other beer – and the Brewing Industry International Awards Supreme Champion accolade. The family-owned brewery, founded in 1858 in an old mill town in the heart of Brontë Country on the edge of the Yorkshire moors, brews 70,000 barrels a year of which 80% is made up of Landlord.

It was initially produced in cask form in the 1960s. At first it was a regional beer sold in Taylor's own pubs and working men's clubs, but is now a national brand. To keep up with demand, some £8 million has been spent over the past 20 years expanding the brewery with additional fermenters, but the plant remains firmly traditional, with conventional mash tuns, coppers and some older open fermenters.

The unique character and flavour of Landlord comes from the malt and hops. Golden Promise barley, grown in the Borders region of Scotland and mainly used by whisky distillers, provides the malt. The brewers feel it gives a distinctive juicy character to the beer. Whole flower hops are Fuggles, Goldings and Whitbread Goldings Variety, with Styrian Goldings from Slovenia. The intense hop character of the beer is achieved by circulating the beer following the copper boil over a deep bed of Styrians. Brewing 'liquor', also crucial to the flavour, comes from a spring on site that's fed with water from the moors filtered through layers of limestone and black rock.

The beer has a superb aroma of sappy malt, spicy hops and tart citrus fruit. Tangy fruit, juicy malt and bitter hops pack the mouth while the finish is beautifully balanced between biscuit malt, lemon fruit and bitter hops.

Traquair House
House Ale

7.2%   Wee Heavy   35 IBUs

Innerleithen, Scottish Borders

This is a beer steeped in Scottish history. It's brewed at Scotland's oldest inhabited house, built as a royal hunting lodge in 1107. Mary Queen of Scots stayed there, and Bonnie Prince Charlie called at the house to raise support for his doomed attempt to win back the throne for the Stuart cause. The house is owned by the Maxwell Stuarts, a branch of the Stuart clan.

The brewhouse dates from the 18th century and it was installed to make beer for the family and staff. It's based in a stone building alongside the Quair, a tributary of the River Tweed that marks the boundary between Scotland and England. The brewery had lain idle for more than 100 years when Peter Maxwell Stuart, the 20th Laird, or Lord, of Traquair, decided to resume brewing in 1965. A recipe was devised for a strong Barley Wine, known as Wee Heavy in Scotland.

The brewing kit is made up of a wooden mash tun, an underback that receives the malt extract after the mash, a copper, and cooling trays. When the hopped wort has cooled it's pumped to the Tun Room where it's mixed with yeast in large oak vessels known as rounds. Following primary fermentation, the beer is conditioned for four to six weeks before bottling. Water, yeast and malt – pale with a touch of black – come from Scotland with East Kent Goldings hops from England.

Brewery and house are now run by Peter's daughter, Catherine, and she produces 1,000hl of beer a year. House Ale has a rich, vinous aroma and palate with notes of oak, vanilla, caramel and peppery hops. The finish is long and warming with notes of sweet sherry, oak, vanilla and spicy hops.

Unibroue
Maudite

8%   Abbey-style Dubbel   22 IBUs

Montréal, Canada

Unibroue has played a pivotal role in challenging the grip of global brewers in Canada. It has not only brought choice to drinkers but has also proved that beer can be full flavoured and memorable.

Many people in the Francophone region of Canada came from Flanders and Normandy, and brought with them a beer rather than a wine culture. This is reflected in the beer range at Unibroue, founded in 1990 by André Dion and Serge Racine. They received financial support from rock star Robert Charlebois, which enabled them to move to new premises in Chambly with bigger brewing equipment. The company was sold to Sapporo of Japan in 2000 and there are no reports of any diminution in product quality.

The beers, which are bottled conditioned and unfiltered on draught, draw their inspiration from Belgium with Wit, or wheat, beers and double and triple Abbey-style ales. They have eye-catching labels that reflect French Canadian history. Maudite, for example, means 'death' in French and celebrates a legend that tells how a group of French-speaking lumberjacks signed a pact with the devil that would allow them to fly their canoe home. But the devil reneged on the deal and led them to their death.

Maudite is described as an 'Abbey-style Dubbel' but it differs with the use of coriander and other aromatics. American and European hops are used sparingly to give full expression to the herbs and spices and pale and Munich malts. The beer has a deep red/gold colour and a tempting aroma of spices and nutty malt, with coriander and orange zest building in the mouth. The complex finish has nutty and juicy malt and a dry and herbal finale. The beer enjoys three fermentations and the bottled version will improve for eight years.

Westmalle
Tripel

9.5%   Trappist Ale   35–38 IBUs

Malle, Belgium

Westmalle Tripel is a sumptuous beer, revered as one of the finest Trappist ales and one that has given a definition – Tripel – to strong Belgian beers. The abbey was founded by monks who escaped from France during the revolution and were invited by the Bishop of Antwerp to establish a religious community in his diocese. In 1794 a farmer donated land to the monks, who were joined by other Trappists, and they set to work to build an abbey, which was completed in 1804.

A brewery was added in 1836 and was expanded over the following years. It was replaced in 1934 by a new brewhouse with Art Deco design. Classic copper vessels are set on tiled floors and the brew kettle is fired by direct flame, a method that gives a toasted malt and butterscotch character to the beers as some of the malt sugars are caramelised during the boil with hops.

Westmalle is the second biggest of the Belgian Trappist breweries, producing more than 100,000hl a year. Tripel can be found widely on draught as well as in bottle. The monks coined the terms Dubbel and Tripel for their two main beers, an indication not so much of strength but that Dubbel is a dark beer while Tripel is pale.

Tripel is brewed with pale Pilsner malt and Tettnanger, Saaz and Styrian Goldings hops. It's orange coloured with a floral hop aroma and orange/citrus fruit. The palate is fruity with spicy hop notes followed by a long finish with warming alcohol, hop resins and a hint of herbs.

Joe Stange

When someone recommends a great pizzeria, be sure to ask *why* the pizza is great. If the response is, 'I don't know, it's just good,' then you don't necessarily need to slide it to the top of your must-eat list.

A critic is anyone who can tell the difference between what's good and what they like, or even what's great and what they love. We easily lose sight of this difference in everyday discourse, social media rants, pub chat, and so on. A sentimental favourite becomes 'the best'. Something that's not for you becomes 'garbage,' even if other people dig it. We get lazy.

So, listen: these are *not* my 31 favourite beers in the world. These are 31 of the beers I felt most strongly should be in a book called *World's Greatest Beers*.

In recent years I've become more interested in the specifics of what makes these beers tick – how are they made, and why does that make them so delicious? If you can identify a beer style or even a hop variety you like, based on some beers that you've loved, then you can also identify a brewing technique that tends to produce beers you really enjoy. I've tried to include some of that context here without getting too bogged down in technical language. I hope it's useful.

In the end, despite my disclaimer above, I reckon there is a hell of a lot of overlap between this list and whatever would be my favourites, if forced to choose. I have a lot of love for these beers, and I don't bother to hide it. But I also know *why* I love them. Maybe that's useful too.

3 Fonteinen
Oude Geuze

6%   Gueuze

Beersel, Belgium

There has been a 3 Fonteinen café in Beersel since the late 19th century, and, like many Pajottenland cafés back then, it bought, blended, and served Lambic. Gaston Debelder left the family farm and bought the village café and blendery in 1953, two years after the birth of his older son, Armand (below). By the time Armand had taken over from his father as head blender, not quite three decades later, Lambic was out of fashion. It was in even deeper trouble when, in 1998, Armand Debelder installed a brewhouse – Belgium's first new Lambic brewery since before the Second World War – taking his craft beyond blending.

What possessed him? Was it keen vision or plain old stubbornness, rooted in love for a traditional product that deserves protection? Whatever it was, Debelder only grew in stature as blender, brewer, and one of Belgium's most outspoken ambassadors for Lambic and Gueuze. That voice – which sadly left us in 2022 after a long battle with cancer – deserves a lot of credit for helping to stoke wider global interest in these acidic, complex drinks. Now they're enjoying a renaissance, and the range of Gueuzes from 3 Fonteinen are among the finest available, even as a young team handpicked by the late master blender carries his vision forward.

Gueuze is the pinnacle of the blender's art. Oude Geuze is a blend of Lambics matured on oak through one, two, and three summers, and typically includes Lambic from the Boon and Lindemans breweries as well as their own. Redolent of white wine, musty cellar floor, and barnwood – aromas created by wild *Brettanomyces* yeast – expect a balanced acidity that pushes a burst of sharp grapefruit-lemon, before it all splinters into total dryness on lively, Champagne-like carbonation, leaving you with a sense of wonder for what just happened and a strong compulsion to go back into the glass and find out.

Alpine Beer Company
Nelson

7% IPA

Alpine, California

The world knows about West Coast IPA, but it could be forgiven for not realizing that the style fractures further into any number of subdivisions based on local geography and character. So, there is an argument for something called San Diego-style IPA, known for combining firm bitterness and minimalist malt structure with extravagant hop aroma and flavour. These may be the West Coastiest of West Coast IPAs.

Among the breweries known for such beers – including Green Flash, Pizza Port, and Stone – one that often draws superlatives from fellow brewers across the country is Alpine, founded in 2002 by Pat McIlheney after a few years of first having the beers brewed at nearby AleSmith. Well loved by its peers, winning multiple Great American Beer Festival medals, the brewery merged with larger Green Flash in 2014, though it maintains its taproom in Alpine, California, in the foothills of the Cuyamanca Mountains, about 30 miles east of San Diego.

For most of its history, the Alpine brand has stayed in its wheelhouse: clean, firm, beautifully constructed IPA that gets the most out of whatever hops happen to be in them, such as Duet, whose citrus-and-conifer character comes from the harmony of Amarillo and Simcoe. Unequivocally, these beers are polished, grown-up throwbacks to the days before IPAs grew softer, sweeter, and orange-juicier.

The Alpine beer most beloved by IPA aficionados is probably Nelson, one of the earliest beers to take full advantage of the Nelson Sauvin hop variety from New Zealand. Golden-orange in colour with a natural hop-driven haze, the nose offers notes of bright berries, grapefruit, limes, white wine, and cedar. The flavour is bitter, but balanced by restrained sweetness, getting some creamy heft and added earthiness from rye malt. Yet it never feels heavy; it's as brisk as a walk down Ocean Beach, best accompanied by a frisbee-catching dog, fish tacos, and more Nelson.

Au Baron
Cuvée des Jonquilles

7% Bière de Garde

Gussignies, France

From the back of the Au Baron brewpub in the French village of Gussignies, you can literally throw a rock and hit Belgium in the neighbour's backyard. However, the brewery's connections with Belgium run deeper. The Bailleux family that runs Au Baron has Wallonian Saison-brewing pedigree.

Roger Bailleux was a descendant of brewers, and his work as a pro took him to breweries in Hainaut, Northern France, and the Belgian Congo. The 20th-century trend of merciless rationalisation and consolidation followed him along the way, shuttering plant after plant. However, even in his later years, he remembered the flavour and technique behind the Saisons of his youth. He also had some heirloom yeast, and he advised his son, Alain, on how to assemble the brewery they added to the family restaurant in 1989. Their first beer, based on Roger's memories of those older Saisons, was ruby-amber Saison Saint-Médard – maltier than the modern standard, getting some moderate spice character from that yeast.

Today, Roger's grandson, Xavier, runs the brewery, a full partner with that peculiar house yeast they fondly describe as 'the princess'. She is finicky – she needs a warm-ish temperature range, just enough sugar, and room to breathe in the fermenter. Yet, when kept happy, she produces some of the most delicate, old-fashioned farmhouse-style ales anywhere in the world.

Cuvée des Jonquilles is the brewery's most popular beer. It's also the most elegant. Labelled as a Bière de Garde in the French tradition, it nonetheless has a lean, dry profile nearer to classic Belgian Saisons. Its pale base comes only from Pilsner malt, grown nearby, and its herbal hops also hail from the region. The nose is distinctly floral with soft, yeasty spice; on the palate, the light sweetness carries some grain and black pepper before rolling through moderate bitterness into a dry finish. It's a quenching beer and a champion with mild cheeses, drinking too lightly and easily for its strength.

Beerfarm
India Pale Lager

5.2% India Pale Lager

Metricup, Western Australia

With craft lager in the ascendance, the word 'crisp' gets used and abused to the point of meaninglessness. It's a false god: not all great lagers are crisp – there's much to be said for body and malty oomph. However, that firmness yet lightness of structure can be a beautiful thing when employed by great brewers with intention. Beerfarm IPL is *crisp*, neatly balanced, effortless to drink – and yet full of flavour.

But what's a Beerfarm? As it happens, it's a brewery in Metricup, Western Australia, in the continent's far southwest. Its emphasis on sustainability runs from solar panels to the herd of Angus cattle roaming the grounds and eating spent grains. Beerfarm produces a wide range, but its wheelhouse is in the kind of hop-forward yet highly drinkable beers – Pale Ales, lighter IPAs, and lagers – that really hit the spot when the weather gets truly hot.

So, what's an India Pale Lager? Simply put, it's an IPA fermented like a lager. Sounds great, but very few deliver on the promise of combining the best of these two traditions. Beerfarm's IPL does it simply by being lighter and more lager-like; its grist includes rice, for lighter body and – yes – *crisper*, drier finish. There are no caramel malts to weigh it down, and its ABV is more in the Pilsner zone than the 7-ish% of many IPAs. Its aroma hops also straddle both realms, combining tropical Mosaic with spicy Saaz – thus becoming something greater than the sum of its parts.

The nose is mellow but pleasant, suggesting lemonade and pine needles. On the sip, bitterness intertwines with lemon peel and quickly washes into a clean, dry finish. The burst of hop flavour doesn't interfere with drinking – it's elegant and refreshing. As Beerfarm says, their IPL is 'the beer the brewers make for their own selfish pleasure'. Nice of them to let others enjoy it.

Blaugies
Saison d'Epeautre

6% Saison

Dour, Belgium

That uncorked bottle; that grainy whiff over the glass; that ample, sturdy foam that will outlive us all; those peppery yeast notes that play perfectly into the earthy malt and spicy hop flavours; that utterly dry finish – you can almost *see* the grains they're growing out back; you can *taste* the brewery's centuries of history.

None of those things are true, though. The Blaugies brewery is not on a working farm, and the ex-schoolteacher couple who founded the brewery – Marie-Noelle Pourtois and Pierre-Alex Carlier – did so in 1988. Yet it's a credit to their recipe, their process, and their yeast that the beer tastes as delicious and old-fashioned as it does.

This is definitely Saison country – deepest Hainaut, southwest of Mons, just a few minutes' walk from the French border. There are plenty of farms nearby, but here the family is more occupied with making beer and welcoming visitors to their tavern, Le Fourquet.

Blaugies also brews a special strong ale called La Moneuse, and a Saison-ish fruit beer called Darbyste, fermented with fig juice. More recently they developed a hop-forward Saison called Vermontoise, in collaboration with Shaun Hill of Vermont's Hill Farmstead brewery – a one-off that's been so popular they just keep brewing it.

However, the beer that gets old-school Belgophiles to stand up on chairs and deliver moist-eyed soliloquies is Saison d'Epeautre, the modern classic that gets lemony, earthy edges from the use of spelt wheat in the grist. 'Our goal was always to brew Saison,' Carlier says. 'We decided to brew a Saison with malt and spelt. The first batch was very good. We did some little changes, and the second one was fantastic. And we never changed it.'

Maybe it's only been around a few decades, but we can hope it'll stay the same for a few more centuries at least.

Břevnovský Klášterní Pivovar
Benedict 12°

5%   Pale Lager

Prague, Czech Republic

An easy tram ride west of central Prague, the Břevnov Monastery Brewery has a claim to being one of the world's oldest, founded by St Adalbert in 993. Brewing here ceased from 1889 until starting anew in 2011, but even Bavaria's venerable Weihenstephaner brewery (since 1040, according to one document) has had its occasional stoppages for wars and fires.

Maybe it's best not to put *too* much stock into triple-digit founding dates. There's no need, when what matters most is what's in the glass today – and these are some of Czech Republic's finest beers. They include a tmavé pivo (dark lager), an 'imperial lager' of about 8.5% ABV, and even an IPA. However, the star is the klasická světlá dvanáctka – that is, the classic 12° pale lager, better known as Benedict 12°.

Czech Republic is awash in flavourful, addictive pale lagers, but the Benedict 12° has its own strut. Its hop aroma and flavour are distinctive. Classic Czech Saaz hops lean spicy and herbal, but here the nose is dialed up a notch to add sweet, grassy, floral notes that resemble chamomile or woodruff. This unusual flavour comes from a unique heirloom Saaz variety – old-vine hops, essentially. The classic Czech decoction mash helps to produce a soft, malty sweetness that gives that hop flavour a boost, yet is more than balanced by firm bitterness. Then it all vanishes into a typically clean, dry finish that leaves you wanting more.

Today's Břevnov brewery is squeezed inside the Benedictine monastery's former stables. The grounds feature serene walking paths, a comfortable hotel, Baroque architecture, and an on-site tavern that serves the Benedict beers alongside heaping, rustic Czech dishes.

Cantillon
Vigneronne

6.5% Lambic

Brussels, Belgium

It was a fateful decision. In 1978, with Lambic struggling to exist and widely overlooked by locals as an anachronism, Jean-Pierre Van Roy decided to open up the family brewery – established in 1900 – as a museum.

How many would-be brewers came to Brussels, walked through those doors, saw the antique machinery, and absorbed the story – not just the technique, but the passion for old ways of making beer, and the stubborn determination to avoid dumbing down their product? That kind of thing is contagious. These days, it's common for brewers to cite Cantillon as an important influence. Among enthusiasts, it's one of the most famous breweries in the world.

Jean-Pierre's son, Jean, is at the helm now, and Jean's son, Florian, works at the brewery too. None of them went to Lambic school to learn this. They grew up here, tasting the first wort in the morning, smelling the sweet steam coming off the coolship and the sour, vinous notes of the filled oak barrels. This place, through which tens of thousands of tourists have now walked, is their home and where they learned their craft.

On Jean's watch, the brewery has been dabbling more in the flavours of wine. Experiments that may become mainstays include Drogone, a liquid education in what happens when barrel-aged wine-grape pomace steeps in old Lambic for a while. However, one of the long-running grape-infused beauties from Cantillon is Vigneronne, produced since 1987.

The Lambic that goes into Vigneronne has matured for two summers in its barrels. Then the sweet white grapes – Viognier or Muscat –arrive in October, just before Lambic-brewing season. These grapes are unusually high in sugar, which mellows and softens the beer's acidity, though the beer remains quite dry. You can taste that lovely, juicy character, right there in harmony with the sharp, musty-grapefruit flavour of the Lambic. It's a beer that can be picked apart and savoured for hours, or decades.

Firestone Walker
Pivo Pils

5.3%   Pilsner

Paso Robles, California

This is a brewers' beer, and not just because Firestone Walker brewmaster Matt Brynildson formed and honed it with a few of his favourites in mind. It's also because many professional brewers in North America and beyond speak of Pivo in hushed tones of reverence, possibly spiced with profanity – or is that just envy?

Lager is enjoying a renaissance at American craft breweries, even if IPA is still their bread and butter. When brewers are making the beers they really want to drink, and can communicate that honestly to their customers, a funny thing happens. Often, the customers want to try it too. Then you've got them. A great lager is addictive – a repeat exercise in the disappointment of an empty glass. They'll come back for more.

And Pivo Pils is a great lager. Brynildson and his team are known as highest-level hop wizards, but that kind of acumen doesn't only work well for IPAs. It works beautifully in a great Pilsner, especially one like Pivo, directly inspired by the modern, Italian dry-hopped Pilsner tradition – more specifically by Birrifcicio Italiano's Tipopils.

Asked to describe Italian-style Pilsners, Brynildson describes them as 'sessionable, dry, balanced lager beers with an enhanced European-hop expression.' For Pivo, he gets that expression from German Saphir hops that he selects himself, and which tend to smell of lemon and lemongrass in the glass. Lots of hops go in late in the boil, so there is plenty of hop flavour to fill out that lean Pilsner body and ample, structured bitterness.

Pivo's availability and distribution wax and wane, but it's most often found these days on draught in savvier beer bars in the United States. If you see this brewer's favourite anywhere, then you're lucky – and you order it. Then we'll see if you want to order anything else.

Gutmann
Hefeweizen

5.2% Hefeweizen

Titting, Germany

It is one of the most alluring sights in all of food and drink: that tall, curvy half-litre weizen glass, filled with hazy yet luminescent yellow-orange liquid, capped by creamy foam. It's especially beautiful to a thirsty person, and particularly on a warm, sunny day. That's the power of a proper Weissbier, and one of the best comes from a town called Titting.

World-classics from the likes of Schneider and Weihenstephaner are better known, but German aficionados have other names they're quick to recommend. The one from Gutmann is virtually always near the top of that list.

The brewery has been here since 1707, founded by nobles – the building itself was a 16th-century moated castle. The Gutmanns bought it in 1855 and started brewing wheat beer just before the First World War. Today, on the watch of sixth-generation brewer Michael Gutmann, Weissbier is more than 90% of what they make.

It's stubbornly traditional, a product of interlocking ingredients and process steps fine-tuned over the years to produce a flavourful, aromatic Weissbier. That means working directly with farmers to choose the right wheat and barley; it means malting their own grains to their own specs in their own malthouse, highly unusual today; it means an elaborate, multi-step mash that includes decoctions to get the most from that malt; it means an expressive house yeast culture; it means fermenting in shallow, open vats where the beer can breathe, and lively kräusen forms those spiky, marshmallow peaks; it means conditioning in the bottle with fresh yeast, so that the beer is very much alive and evolving until it goes into your glass.

Putting your nose over that foam, expect bright banana with more subtle clove-spice; on the sip, there is a full mouthfeel and light sweetness balanced by a slight edge of citrus-like acidity and drying finish. Or, having been seduced, you can skip the analysis, quench the thirst, and get on with the conversation.

Birrificio Italiano
Tipopils

5.2% Italian-style Pilsner

Province of Como, Italy

The Germans know about dry hopping, and obviously have a word or two for it: kalthopfung is one; hopfenstopfen is another. However, it's not something they normally do to their lagers, even to their more bitter, hop-flavoured Pilsners.

Those hops go in the boil, not the fermenter.

However, in the mid-1990s in the very north of Italy – where German beer styles are as popular as wine – Agostino Ariolo wanted to brew his Pilsner a bit differently at his new brewpub, the first in the region. And it wasn't some American craft Pale Ale that inspired Ariolo to add some hops to his fermenting Pilsner – it was British ale. 'I took my idea from the English beer tradition, because they used to dry hop beer in the cask,' Arioli says. 'I saw this in England, and I just thought, "Wow, I could do that in my beers, because I love hops."'

The hops he adds to the tank are mainly of the Spalter Select variety and sometimes some Saphir, chosen by him from a farm in Germany's Tettnang growing region. They add an enticing lemon-zest aroma to an incredibly delicate beer, with a lean malt frame and smooth, balancing bitterness. The beer is unfiltered, showing a light haze and preserving its hop aroma.

That nose is alluring; the brewery's own marketing spiel (translated here from Italian) says it beautifully: 'She whispers stories of barley fields and hop gardens and hands us the quintessence of their perfumes intact.'

Somehow that beer is now a quarter-century old. It's inspired countless imitators in Italy and nurtured a strong cult following among brewers and beer enthusiasts abroad – which goes a long way to explaining how it inspired a new style of Pilsner that they call 'Italian style' (which has nothing to do with Peroni).

How do Italians say 'dry hopping' in Italian? Often, they just say it in English.

Keesmann
Herren Pils

4.6%   Pilsner

Bamberg, Germany

Visiting Bamberg for the beer can become a regular habit for certain sets of travellers and beer lovers. We can't seem to stay away from its easy walkability, hearty food, and plethora of excellent breweries making extraordinary beers. After repeat visits we compare notes, often changing our minds about which is our favourite beer in town. Is it the smoked beer from Schlenkerla or Spezial? Is it the Ungespundet from Mahrs? Eventually, though, most of us come around to Herren Pils.

Enthusiasts of German beer – and indeed, many brewers – often cite the Pilsner from Keesmann as one of the best beers in the country. Drink a fresh one in Bamberg and the allure is easy to understand. Its pronounced herbal hop flavour and aroma can stretch into notes of lime peel, with a marked bitterness and elegant thread of pure malt sweetness that gives that Noble hop flavour more depth. It's beautifully integrated, easily delicious, and totally addictive. There's a reason why this beer accounts for more than 90% of production, even if they also produce an outstanding pale Bock, a beautiful Helles, malty amber lager, and more.

Keesmann doesn't do a lot of export or marketing of itself to foreigners and tourists – it doesn't need to. It's usually packed with locals, there for crispy fried schnitzels, sausages, steaks, trout … and Pilsner. Lots and lots of fresh, bitter, herbal Pilsner.

The brewery has been here since 1867, when local butcher Georg Keesmann passed his master brewer's exam because he wanted to add some value to his meat shop and pub. It's directly across the street from another local brewing institution, Mahrs Bräu, but a healthy 2-km walk from Schlenkerla, the Dom, and the bustling tourist centre – all the better for working off all that schnitzel and Pilsner.

Knoblach
Lagerbier

5.3% Kellerbier

Schammelsdorf, Germany

Pedants who feel they need to differentiate and name various types of Franconian lager can do so to their heart's content. However, most of them will do what they've always done and simply call it 'lager'. Many villages here have their own brewery, after all, and that brewery usually specializes in one type of beer. So it is with the brewery in Schammelsdorf, about 9km east of Bamberg.

We could call the Knoblach Lagerbier a Kellerbier if we wanted, and we wouldn't be wrong. At the brewery's pub it's often served ungespundet, or un-bunged, a reference to a traditional way of serving lager where the lined, wooden cask (holzfass) is allowed to breathe a bit before the beer is poured into stoneware mugs via a spigot. It's fresh, but with less carbonation in solution, allowing more of the malt, hop, and even yeast flavours to come to the fore.

Knoblach Lagerbier has many hallmarks of typical Franconian Kellerbier – an orange-amber colour, light haze, a light kiss of caramelized malt, and an earthy, rustic flavour that can come from the yeast and the local water as well as the hops. However, what really sets this one apart is a firm smack of resinous bitterness – it's not even elegant, really, it's brusque and lingering, though the malt body goes a long way to help contain it. The appreciation pattern goes a bit like it does with smoked beer, with an inevitable and rapid progression from 'I'm not sure if I like this' to realizing that you've somehow killed three seidla while discussing the finer points of beer-style semantics.

The Lagerbier does get exported in modest amounts, but the experience at the pub in Schammelsdorf is worth the trek.

Kommunbrauhäuser of the Oberpfalz
Zoiglbier

5% typically   Zoiglbier

Oberpfalz, Germany

You won't find this one at your off-licence. They could import Zoiglbier, in theory, but they can't import the experience. That experience is like few things that still exist in our atomized, mediated lives. The Zoigl experience is a shared experience – from production to consumption.

It begins with the Kommunbrauhaus, a brewery that is literally shared by the brewers of the village – in each of five villages in the northern Oberpfalz region, just west of the Czech border. The two best-known Zoigl villages are Neuhaus and Windischeschenbach; they border each other, separated by a hill and a stream.

These communal breweries use traditional, wood-fired kettles. (The brewers even share the supply of logs.) The brewers each have their own recipe, but in practice they don't vary much – Munich malt contributes an orange, coppery hue, with pleasant malty sweetness balanced against easygoing bitterness; often, there is some intriguing, citrus-like character that seems yeast-driven. Unfiltered and softly carbonated, it is basically Zwickelbier or Kellerbier, but with more of a story.

The communal breweries have coolships, where freshly brewed wort cools overnight. The brewer returns in the morning with a truck to carry the wort home via dairy tank – the fermentation happens in their own cellars, usually at their own homes. Upstairs is where they host guests – but not all the time. The Zoigl brewers take turns opening their house-pubs, with a calendar for the year scheduled in advance.

When you arrive at the weekend's designated pub, you won't see folks sitting alone and looking at their phones. Instead, you'll be sharing tables and conversation, making new friends, drinking delicious lager, munching on crusty pretzels, and enjoying one of the world's last great communal experiences.

Kormoran
Imperium Prunum

10.5% Baltic Porter

Olzstyn, Poland

Poland is one of the world's great beer-drinking countries, up there in per capita volume with Czech Republic, Austria, and Germany, and likewise driven by lots of pale lager. However, the country's national treasure doesn't lend itself to drinking in volume, and that is Baltic Porter.

Briefly, Baltic Porter is a lagered offshoot of the strong Porters once exported from Britain to the Baltic region (and on to the imperial court in Russia). What's more relevant is what these beers are like today – rich, thick, smooth, and strong, often going upwards of 9% ABV. If US craft breweries once competed for how many bitterness points they could cram into their IPAs, Polish breweries have another low-key competition: how many degrees Plato of starting gravity? In other words: how rich, sweet, and dense is your wort before fermentation?

The Kormoran brewery is one of Poland's large independents, located in northern Poland, nearer to Kaliningrad than Warsaw. The brewery is best known for its Porter Warmiński, checking in at a hefty 21° Plato and 9% ABV. Like most Baltic Porters, it's a lager, and it matures a long time at cold temperatures – at least 21 weeks in this case, to produce a smoother, rounder beer. Thick and black, the beer has mellow sweetness and harmonious flavours of roast, chocolate, and even blackberries, with an alcoholic warmth that's felt in the belly and the head but not on the palate.

The Imperium Prunum, however, takes all that and climbs to another level. It's even heftier, its recipe getting 26° of malt-rich density and finishing at nearly 11% strength. Here's where it gets really fun: the beer matures on suską sechlońską – traditional smoke-dried plums, special to a small area in south-east Poland. These plums add vinous, dark-fruit flavours and a subtle yet comforting smoke character that could add more warmth on a winter night.

Live Oak
Grodziskie

3%   Grodziskie

Austin, Texas

The beer type known as Grodziskie, hailing from the town of Grodzisk Wielkopolski in western Poland, went fully extinct. At one time it was another link in the chain of interesting, top-fermented wheat beers stretching from Belgium to Prussia and beyond – think Lambic, Witbier, Berliner Weisse, Gose, and Lichtenhainer. Many others are lost to history – and the same nearly happened to Grodziskie.

Before the Second World War, Grodziskie was prospering, exported to 37 countries. However, the Communist government that followed often neglected local tastes and traditions. The beer became an obscure curiosity. A few years after Poland gained independence, the last brewery in Grodzisk closed, and Grodziskie disappeared with it.

However, Polish homebrewers kept it going, and writers would occasionally mention this fascinating old style that had disappeared, asking if someone might want to take a stab at reviving it. One of the first commercial breweries to answer that call (in 2014) was Live Oak, known for its dogged dedication to traditional Czech- and German-style lagers. Today, Grodziskie is one of their best-known beers, and a shining beacon of traditional weirdness that became commercially successful.

What makes it weird? For starters, the beer is made from 100% wheat malt – highly unusual, even in the world of wheat beers, where wheat rarely makes up more than half the grist (with the rest usually being barley malt). Another thing: the beer is very light, at about 3% ABV, and also quite bitter, typically getting an ample charge of Czech Saaz hops. The beer is also very smoky, since all that wheat malt is smoked – and it's not smoked with the milder, more common beechwood, but with more robust oak.

So the beer is light, dry, bitter, and smoky: in other words, it's challenging, an acquired taste. Yet the best tastes are all acquired, aren't they? It also works as a flavourful quencher, perfect for accompanying smoked Polish sausage – or a Texas barbecue.

Orval
Orval

6.9% Trappist Ale

Villers-Devant-Orval, Belgium

In Belgium's far southeast, the brewery at the Abbaye Notre Dame d'Orval produces about 78,000hl per year – of only one brand of beer. And, despite the beer's global fame, that is all the beer they want to squeeze out of the place.

That's made this unique Trappist Ale harder to find on store shelves, even in Belgium, as popularity has grown but production has not. The brewery's response is sensible: focus on hospitality. Don't worry so much about supermarkets, but get the beer into cafés that really know how to care for it – hence, there are now 420 establishments designated as Ambassadeurs d'Orval, including 28 in Britain and nine in the United States.

Freed from pressure to grow, the brewers stick to what they know. Current brewmaster Anne-Françoise Pypaert – the first woman to head up a Trappist brewery – came from the lab as an absolute expert in quality control and yeast-wrangling. Many give her credit for restoring Orval to a more old-fashioned, rustic character.

This beer is unique, practically a style unto itself. It's mostly pale malt, with just a small proportion of caramel malt to help provide an amber colour – though the beer is totally dry, fully attenuated by its mixed fermentation. The beer is also pleasantly bitter, and it gets a herbal-floral aroma boost from Slovenian and Alsatian hops in the maturation tanks. Famously, the beer undergoes secondary fermentation and conditions in the bottle with half-wild *Brettanomyces* yeast, leading to an evolution in the cellar – hoppier when it's young, funkier when it's aged.

This is why aficionados argue in good faith about how long to age a bottle of Orval, with some preferring fresh, or six months, or a year, or even a few years. It's a worthwhile experiment to buy several bottles and test it out for yourself, if you can find enough of them.

Oud Beersel
Oude Kriek

6% Kriek

Beersel, Belgium

After 120 years, the Oud Beersel brewery closed in 2002. Those were grim times for Lambic, when global interest had yet to stoke a renaissance. A young Lambic lover in Brussels, Gert Christiaens, heard an appeal for someone – anyone – to revive Oud Beersel and keep it going. That's just what he did, going on to nurture a successful blending business and produce some of Belgium's most underrated Lambic beers.

Despite being highly regarded among Lambic wonks, the beers of Oud Beersel have never attracted the same hype and reverence as those from Cantillon or 3 Fonteinen. There are a few reasons why, and all are unjust.

One is that Christiaens gets all his wort from Brouwerij Boon, so some see Oud Beersel as a kind of Boon offshoot. However, all that Lambic is brewed to Oud Beersel's own recipe, and Christiaens is now an experienced blender in his own right. Another reason may be that he is more of a serious artisan-entrepreneur than an ambassador, content to quietly hone his craft, not needing to inject all comers with contagious passion. Finally, the beers tend to be accessible and reasonably priced – a loveable trait, yet fools will assume a product is pedestrian if it doesn't involve an elaborate hunt and high price tag.

The good news: it means more beer for the rest of us – and this is excellent beer indeed. It perfectly balances austere Lambic character – dry, bitterish, with oaky accents and fine acidity – with a fat, juicy punch of cherries. The Oude Kriek really isn't sweet, but the volume of cherries involved – about 400g per litre of Lambic – are happy to convey that impression. Notes of amaretto-like almond, driven by the pits of the cherries, further add to the pleasant complexity.

Perennial Artisan Ales
Abraxas

13.5%   Barrel-Aged Stout

St Louis, Missouri

There is not really a special name for them – we just call them Imperial Stouts – but the measurable reality is that there is a bigger, thicker type of Stout emerging from trend-savvy small breweries in recent years. They're not necessarily dessert Stouts and not necessarily barrel-aged, though many are one or both of those things. What sets them apart is that brewers are pushing their starting gravities – that is, the sugary density of their worts – to extremes. That means packing their mash tuns as full as they can, boiling the wort for hours, and adding unfermentable dextrins and other sugars to make a thick, viscous product unlike any beers that have been made before.

These are incredibly rich, strong black drinks, not meant to be easily drinkable, but the best are beautifully balanced anyway. They're best suited for after-dinner sipping or sharing a bottle to blow your friends' minds. Many are designed specifically with months of whiskey-barrel ageing in mind. These are small batches for maximum flavour. They're expensive to make and expensive to buy.

Abraxas was one of the first Stouts like that to really catch on and inspire other brewers to take the leap. It started as one of former head brewer Cory King's homebrew recipes; the acclaim for Abraxas and others helped him to launch his Side Project brewery, where he now produces many huge, highly coveted barrel-aged Stouts of his own.

Abraxas is inspired by Mexican hot chocolate, steeped with cacao nibs, cinnamon, vanilla beans, and ancho chillies. Those chillies tingle the palate, folded in thick layers of chocolate and malt flavours with the heftiest body as their medium. It's indulgent, intriguing, and delicious. The barrel-aged version takes that complexity even further, most recently as a blend of Stouts aged 20–28 months in bourbon and rye whiskey barrels. The wood-spice, vanilla, and warmth of those barrels tends to dovetail perfectly with the Stout, which is plenty decadent enough to absorb it.

De Ranke
XX Bitter

6% Blond Ale

Dottignies, Belgium

Bitter beers never vanished from Belgium – consider Orval, Saison Dupont, and Westmalle Tripel. Yet those three legends were just about it for hop-forward Belgian beers when Nino Bacelle and Guido Devos founded De Ranke in 1996 – and all three were inspirations for them.

Westmalle and Orval were direct influences on their Tripel, Guldenberg, with bitterness similar to the former and dry hopping like the latter. Standing

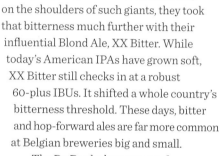

on the shoulders of such giants, they took that bitterness much further with their influential Blond Ale, XX Bitter. While today's American IPAs have grown soft, XX Bitter still checks in at a robust 60-plus IBUs. It shifted a whole country's bitterness threshold. These days, bitter and hop-forward ales are far more common at Belgian breweries big and small.

The De Ranke brewers are fussy about how they do it. The Hainaut village of Dottignies isn't far from some prime hop-growing areas, and De Ranke has been working with the same farm for years. The hops arrive as freshly harvested whole cones; De Ranke is one of the last breweries on Earth to insist on 100% whole-cone hops rather than the processed pellets that have become industry-standard. The whole cones are inefficient – they soak up a lot of wort – but to the De Ranke brewers, it's worth the cost. To them, no other form of hop can produce the same quality of aroma and bitterness.

Drinking fresh XX Bitter is the best way to understand what they mean. It really is bitter – yet it's a smooth kind of bitterness, with a big smack of spicy, herbal hop flavour, in balance with a modicum of residual malt sweetness and more subtle, yeast-driven fruit-and-spice notes. These are classical hops at heavy-metal volume, yet the beer drinks as easily as a sharp North German Pilsner.

It's one of the most important beers produced in Belgium in the past 40 years. It's also just delicious.

Schlenkerla (Heller-Bräu Trum)
Märzen

5.1%   Märzen

Bamberg, Germany

There is something about a whiff of smoke that goes right to our comfort centres, whether it's bacon or barbecue, or a Rauchbier or a campfire. To our inner cave-people, smoke means fire, and that means safety and food. Maybe that's why those who are at first put off by the smell of Rauchbier – and that's typically the reaction – soon find that it's not so bad after all. Then they find that they will need to order another, and another. And soon, they're planning a visit to Bamberg.

The Märzen is the flagship of the Heller-Bräu Trum brewery, better known as Schlenkerla, which is the name of its beers as well as its famous old pub in Bamberg's historic centre. The brewery itself is up the hill, where they malt their own barley with wood fires (hence the smoke), fed by beech logs they dried and seasoned themselves, before a double-decoction mash, fermentation with their house yeast, and cool lagering in the deep cellars that riddle the hill. You can brew your own smoked beer, but you can't brew Schlenkerla.

While they also produce a wonderful Helles, Weissbier, Bock, and oak-smoked Doppelbock, the Märzen is the beer most likely to be pouring via gravity from the barrels at the heart of the pub. It's widely exported in bottles, but drinking it fresh at the source from the barrels is a taste experience worthy of your bucket list: a surprising bitterness and soft mouthfeel join that intriguing, savoury smoke and moderately sweet, caramel-edged malt for one of the great drinks.

There at the Schlenkerla pub, you may end up drinking it in the Klause room, a former 14th-centruy Dominican monastery chapel. It's an impressive place to admire the mahogany beer with its sturdy foam and stripes of tan lace, smell that enticing woodsmoke, and take comfort in the fact that some great things just last.

Schneeeule
Marlene

3.5%   Berliner Weisse

Berlin, Germany

Once upon a time – 15 or 20 years ago – independent brewers looking for wider variety discovered Berliner Weisse. There was only one type left in Berlin at that point, and it was a sour, simple beer often mixed with sweet, colourful syrups. Widely copied, its method of 'kettle-souring' using *Lactobacillus* bacteria would become an important tool in the craft toolbox for adding wanted acidity – for example, in fruit beers. But what if they copied the wrong Berliner Weisse?

In 19th-century Berlin, Weissbier was by far the most popular drink. There were hundreds of breweries making it, and these weren't simple 'kettle-sours'. In fact, they were products of mixed fermentation, more like Belgian Lambic than today's sour-but-clean fruit beers. These fermentations typically involved *Saccharomyces* – brewer's yeast – *Lactobacillus* – the bacteria that produce lactic acid – and *Brettanomyces*, which over time can add signature notes such as leather, pineapples, flowers, strawberries, and more.

Fast-forward to the revivalists. Founder and brewer Ulrike Genz has made the most of her access to retired brewers, researchers, and old yeast strains to design and refine a beer that she believes tastes like authentic Berliner Weisse should. Her grist is half wheat malt, half Pilsner malt, with a careful dose of Noble hops to moderate the lactic-acid bacteria. She pitches that bacteria alongside her brewer's yeast, then adds the *Brett* after one week. She later packages it in squat, sturdy bottles that can handle Champagne-like effervescence. Variations include ingredients such as ginger, elderflower, roses, habañeros, or even dry hops – but Marlene is the elegant foundation.

Marlene is lemony, dry, softly tart, not sour – quenching, not puckering – and you can enjoy many, especially on a warm day. This is also a beer that evolves in the bottle; as the beer gets somewhat drier, the *Brett* adds new aromas and flavours, and we get to debate what age we like best. Meanwhile, we can hope that more brewers might choose to follow such an interesting example.

G. Schneider & Sohn
Aventinus

8.2%   Weizenbock

Kelheim, Germany

There are certain types of beer that have the power to convert those who think they don't like beer. A great Weizenbock is one of them – and there is arguably none greater than Aventinus.

The Schneider brewery refers to Aventinus as the first 'Weizendoppelbock', invented in 1907. The brewery gives credit for its invention to Mathilde Schneider. Women in Germany weren't supposed to be running breweries back then, but she did, somewhat covertly, for nearly two decades from her husband's death to her son's adulthood. Aventinus was a success. Until about three decades ago, when Schneider began to diversify its offerings, the brewery really only made two beers: Schneider Weisse and Aventinus. Today, Aventinus is a full 10% of the brewery's production.

If Weizenbock has so many fans, why don't more breweries make them? Probably because they are so difficult to brew really well. The process involves a lot of delicate, interlocking parts that all need to go just right to produce a beer that is not only delicious but also highly drinkable. Weizenbock requires an incredible attention to raw ingredients, an intricate mash regime, unusual yeast, and careful fermentation – traditionally involving open fermenters – to get a beer that is quite dry, balanced, and easygoing despite its strength. Then there is the refermentation in the package, so that the beer really isn't finished developing until you pour it in your glass.

Aventinus offers a great depth of familiar flavours – bananas foster, chocolate, caramel, clove – without any challenging bitterness that might turn some drinkers away. Instead, the beer gets its own sort of balance from a fluffy mouthfeel, lively carbonation, and a dryish finish. All of that makes the beer feel much lighter than its considerable strength, which also provides a cheering, crowd-pleasing effect. It is perilous.

Schönram
Schönramer Hell

5% Helles

Petting, Germany

I didn't want to include two beers from the same brewery. I'd rather spread the love. But in my heart, I'd know that while the beer listed next is (for me) the finest Pilsner in Germany – and in my top five beers on the planet – it would be a shame to omit my favourite Helles. And, by virtue of being a truly great Helles, this is also one of the most sublimely addictive beers, anywhere.

Germans are among the world's most voluminous beer drinkers – roughly 100l per person per year. Notably, Bavaria skews that average upward considerably. A major reason for that is the mere existence of Bavarian Helles, fine-tuned for more than 125 years to be the kind of undemanding beer that leaves you with a strong impression that you're going to need another one.

Imagine living in Germany's far southeastern corner, near the Bavarian Alps, where drivers from the Schönramer brewery will personally deliver crates of beautiful Hell straight to your house. If you're not home, just let the driver know where to find the key, and leave out some cash; they'll make change, carry the beer to your cellar, and take away your empties. After all, having Helles on hand is as important as bottled water and bread. It's a daily staple.

Schönramer exports a bit, but more than 90% of its beer is enjoyed within a 40-mile radius. More than three-quarters of its production is Hell. Brewmaster Eric Toft never has made radical changes to the recipe; instead, he has gently nudged it over the years, detail by tiny detail, into something drier, crisper, and *just* slightly more bitter than what you might find in Munich. Its floral hopping and brioche-like malt middle add interest without distracting, until you reach the familiar disappointment, again and again, of the empty glass – the mark of a truly great beer.

Schönram
Schönramer Pils

5%   Pilsner

Petting, Germany

If I'd been asked to choose five beers instead of 31, this beer would still be right here. That leaves me with the privilege of explaining why. Here is the short version: first, take brewmaster Eric Toft's almost maniacal pursuit of greater drinkability – the same bit-by-bit tinkering that he does with his Helles – so that you have all the same addictive qualities. Then, add lots of really beautiful hops.

Toft is American – born and raised in Wyoming – but let's not hold that against him. This is an experienced brewmaster at a German brewery who speaks excellent Bavarian dialect and owns several sets of lederhosen, not someone trying to turn Pilsner into American IPA. The hops are all Noble, all German, and this is a beer full of balance and class – and yet, might there be a certain not-very-German brashness in the 42 IBUs?

Pilsners are supposed to be hop-forward, and Schönramer embraces that idea. Hop varieties may shift a bit, depending on harvest – and Toft goes himself to a particular farm in Tettnang to select – but typically you're looking at ample yet smooth bittering additions, progressing on to big, floral and spicy ones later in the boil and whirlpool for a big aroma charge. The end result is a whole ride, an integrated experience: compelling floral hop nose; sweet, herbal hops on the palate given depth by some lightly honeyed malt flavour; a firm smack of bitterness and dry, clean finish; and a certainty that you will want to take the whole ride all over again, and again.

All those flavours come together beautifully, partly because the ingredients are of the highest quality and the process is exacting. But it's also because the beer is patiently fermented cool, lagered cool for at least six weeks, and never rushed at any phase. 'Time is a huge ingredient,' Toft says, 'and we make sure we take our time.'

Senne
Taras Boulba

4.5% Belgian Pale Ale

Brussels, Belgium

If you're a fan of this beer but have never had it near the source, you owe it to yourself to make the journey. Frankly, people ought to talk about drinking fresh Taras Boulba in Brussels the way they talk about Guinness in Dublin. Brewed since 2004, it's become a cult favourite among brewers who've made the pilgrimage to Belgium to visit the greats. In fact, it has become one of those greats.

It's no wonder that brewers love it. This always has been a brewers' beer – or, as brewmaster Yvan De Baets describes it, a 'selfish beer'. He and partner Bernard Leboucq first made it because they wanted something light, bitter, and quenching to drink after long days of brewing. It's inspired by De Baets' love of session-strength British cask ale, but also by his love of Noble hops, particularly German and Slovenian varieties.

The yeast plays a role, too. The brewers employ relatively wide, squat fermenters and give the fermentation space to breathe, encouraging the kinds of fruity esters that play beautifully with their chosen hops. Ultimately, these esters accentuate some lemony citrus-peel qualities in the hop aroma and flavour, alongside fresh herbs and mint. There is no tropical fruit punch here. These hops are all class, but Taras Boulba delivers them with intensity – like Goethe read by Jay-Z through a megaphone.

Likewise, the bitterness is unabashed – well north of 50 IBUs – but this is not a harsh bitterness, thanks to the choice of hops and how they are employed. Rather than coat your tongue in resin, it resets your palate after the quick hit of complex flavours, introducing an utterly dry finish.

Taras Boulba is wonderful from its elegant tulip glass – but possibly even better from half-litre mugs at the brewery's own taproom in Brussels, gulped while admiring the shining brewhouse and wide fermenters that recently produced it.

Tilquin
Oude Gueuze Tilquin à l'Ancienne

7%   Lambic

Rebecq, Belgium

Lambic producers enjoy an aura of mystery and often are happy to perpetuate it. Pierre Tilquin, however, speaks factually, bluntly, without any nonsense about how he blends his Gueuzes and steeps his fascinating fruit beers. He is detail-oriented, and his beers are the work of a sharp mind.

Tilquin worked at Cantillon and 3 Fonteinen, learning what he could from those masters before opening his own tiny blender in 2009 –the only Lambic blendery in French-speaking Wallonia. The beers were very good from the outset, but Tilquin's fine-tuning since then has made them consistently great.

In early 2022 his blendery became a fully fledged brewery, adding a small kit and coolship so that he can include some of his own Lambic in his Gueuze blends – though he will continue using components from Boon, Girardin, Lindemans, and Cantillon. His adventures in fruit Lambics have become increasingly interesting, including wine grapes of various origins, blueberries, blackcurrants, rhubarb, and quince.

One of the real delights of the range is the gleefully unorthodox draft version of his Gueuze. At 5.3% strength, it's a blend of one- and two-year-old Lambics diluted with weaker, young Lambic called

meerts, brewed at Boon especially for Tilquin. It's tart, quenching, and totally unpretentious. Knowing that hardcore traditionalists don't approve of kegged Gueuze only makes it taste better.

However, as with any serious Lambic blender or brewer – and Tilquin is a serious person – his Oude Gueuze is the standout of the range and his pride and joy. Expect a perfectly balanced lactic acidity, an ethereal juicy middle of lemon and grapefruit, a whiff of Riesling spilled on the cellar floor, and all of it finely splintered by lively, pinprick carbonation that accentuates the utter dryness of the finish. It's a shrewdly designed miracle.

Uerige
Alt

4.7% Altbier

Düsseldorf, Germany

There's nothing quite like a crawl around central Düsseldorf, hitting each of the old Altbier breweries whose names we dutifully commit to memory: Füchsen, Schlüssel, Schumacher, Uerige. This is how we learn that the classics at the first three are exercises in sublime balance, with easygoing malts and supple bitterness – delicious, but polite. The fourth is the edgy one.

Uerige Alt packs a decisively bitter punch (52 IBUs), accompanied by the earthy, spicy flavour of Spalter hops and some malt-driven toasted bread crust. Thus it may be wise to visit Uerige last, if you make the full tour around the Altstadt. It's easily the most characterful of the bunch, unfairly making the others seem more boring than they are.

The beers of Uerige – like all Altbier as well as the Kölsch of nearby Köln – are obergärige, which means top-fermented. Technically, if we decide such things based on the species of yeast, they are ales. Occasionally, a brewery will also label them as lagerbier – not because they get lager yeast, but because they are lagered cool for at least a few weeks before serving.

At Uerige and the other Altbier brewery pubs, the brewers rack the finished and naturally carbonated beer into spigoted casks, which then go upstairs to fill slender becher glasses in rapid fashion, with a sturdy cap of foam often poking from the top of the beautiful, copper-coloured beer. Waiters bring around glass after glass – fortunate, since yours always seems to be empty again.

Uerige exports a bit of Alt, but it doesn't travel all that well; time wears down those bitter edges and brings more malt to the fore – still tasty, but not the same. The best remedy for this is to export yourself to Düsseldorf, have a crawl around the Altstadt, and enjoy it freshly poured from those barrels just lugged up from the cellar.

Unertl Haag
Weißbier Original

4.9% Weissbier

Haag, Germany

The small market town of Haag in Oberbayern sits about 50km east of Munich. Its moated castle dates back to the 12th century, with an imposing tower that adorns Unertl's labels.

The brewery, however, is not so old. Alois Unertl II founded it in 1948, taking over the village brewery after the war. He was the son of Alois I, who, after working at Paulaner in Munich, founded the *other* Unertl brewery in nearby Mühldorf in 1929. The Mühldorfer Unertl is still there, run by the relations, and also specializes in excellent Weissbier.

However, the Weissbier from Unertl of Haag has an endearingly rustic character which, in my view, gives it a distinctive edge. Alois IV is brewmaster there today.

Much like the classic Schneider Weisse Original, Unertl's Original features a darker colour – the Germans say bernstein, for amber, but this is nearly brown – a throwback to the 19th century maintained by intention despite advances in malting and equipment. Unertl also employs an unusually high proportion of wheat – the minimum for German Weissbier is 50%, but here it goes up to 70. Typically that means a slower, gummier, more challenging mash, but clearly it's worth the trouble. Unertl also uses traditional open fermenters, harvesting that spiky, meringue-like kräusen daily to give the next fermentation a quick running start. The beers are bottle-conditioned with fresh yeast and unpasteurized.

The nose is full of fresh sourdough – a bready anchor for the yeast-driven banana, clove, and bubblegum. The mouthfeel is lively yet full – fluffy – while the flavour brings a welcome acidic tang that fits that sourdough impression perfectly while also nudging a zestier fruit flavour that suggests oranges or berries. This is no simple wheat beer, and you'll find yourself returning to the glass to see, again, what that was all about.

Wayfinder
Original Cold IPA

7% IPA

Portland, Oregon

For any who've grown bored with the sweet, heavy, hazy direction of IPA in recent years, here is your antidote: a crisp, 'wester than West Coast' IPA with bright clarity, actual bitterness, and bone-dry finish, yet still plenty of juicy hop flavour in the middle.

The Original part is accurate: Wayfinder brewmaster Kevin Davey developed what he calls 'cold IPA' in 2020, and it already has spawned hundreds of imitators in the US and farther afield. Before the beer took off, the brewery was better known for its beautiful lagers – often brewed with traditional decoction mashing, served on Czech-style side-pulls, and so on. With this beer, Davey's goal was to design a showcase of Pacific Northwest hops that had all the easy drinkability of a great lager.

Here's what makes it tick: the grist is like an adjunct lager or American malt liquor, with pale malt plus rice to help lighten the body. The fermentation gets a lager yeast strain that works cleanly at warmer, ale-like temperatures, so the hop flavour and aroma wind up centre-stage. Dry hopping also occurs warm, while the beer is carbonating naturally via kräusen and spunding – a German method that harnesses the CO_2 from fermentation, rather than injecting it externally. The beer ferments to dryness and is filtered for absolute clarity.

We don't need to know any of those details, of course, nor whatever it is that makes it a 'cold' IPA. ('Maybe I'm just trying to stick the image in your head of an ice-cold beer,' Davey says, 'but hoppy as f*ck.') The result is a delicious and physically attractive beer that captures the best of the West Coast style, but pushes its strengths further, packing a big hop punch – pine forest and candied-orange slices waft from the glass, finding shape in that firmly bitter flavour – yet drinking easily, dry and lean and clean, feeling much lighter than its strength and lighting up the conversation along the way.

Westvleteren
Westvleteren 12

10.2% Quadrupel

Vleteren, Belgium

Can there really be such a thing as the 'best beer in the world'? Sensible people would say no, but we can all be influenced by publicity and rarity. If this beer was expensive or hard to get, then it must have been worth the trouble.

The only place to buy it legally, with the blessing of the monks, is at the brewery itself and the affiliated café across the road. At the café you can sometimes grab a six-pack, but to get a case or two you need to call a designated number – at designated times, and you may have to hit redial repeatedly – to reserve a time slot a few weeks in advance. Grey-market bottles occasionally appear at some bars and shops at an extortionate price, yet people pay it.

No beer deserves all the hype that's been heaped on Westvleteren 12, but here's the thing: it really *is* a fantastic beer – certainly *one of* the best in the world – and there are reasons beyond hype that it is consistently ranked at or near the top on various sites that aggregate the scores of enthusiasts.

Notably, the Westvleteren 8 (at 8% ABV) and the Blond (5.8%) also are worthy of songs; the latter drinks like a great lager, with surprising bitterness and herbal hop presence.

The darker ales, and especially the 12, emit a heady mix of fermentation-driven dark-fruit character, a bit of caramel, a very light touch of roast, and a slightly more brusque bitterness than is found in most other Belgian dark ales. Like most Trappist ales, the 8 and 12 both get a fairly large dose of sugar in the kettle; this helps to lighten the beer's body while kicking up the ABV, so you get that special Belgian property of *digestibilité* in a strong ale. (Translation: it's dangerously easy to drink.)

Widawa
Porter Bałtycki Wędzony 24°

10.5% Baltic Porter

Chrząstawa Mała, Poland

Mark it on your calendars: the third Saturday in January is Baltic Porter Day, every year. If few outside Poland know about this special day, so what? It deserves wider observation – a collective moment to slow down and pay more attention to one of the world's seductive and interesting beer styles.

One of the most seductive and interesting examples of the style comes from a small brewpub east of Wrocław, in the southwest of the country. That's where Widawa founder and brewer Wojtek Frączyk squeezes the most from his modest kit to make this thick, rich, smooth, smoky Porter. As in the rest of Eastern Europe, the flavour of smoke is enduringly popular in Polish cooking, and its comforts work beautifully in their signature beer style.

To hit that gravity on his small brewhouse, Frączyk has worked out an elaborate double mash – packing his mash tun full of fresh malt, twice. The first time, the richest first runnings go into the kettle; the more moderate second runnings, however, take another tour through the next batch of fresh malt. The result is dense and sugar-efficient, if time-intensive. German Munich and smoked malts provide the base, while a range of roasted malts add darkness and depth.

Weighty on the palate, its body and residual sweetness is roundly balanced by that careful roast-bitterness and deepened by flavours of chocolate and darker fruit notes, like plums and dried berries. Bałtycki means Baltic, incidentally; wędzony means smoked, and 24° is the hefty starting gravity, before cool fermentation and long lagering polish it into a smooth, obsidian jewel.

Incidentally, we can thank beer writer Michael Jackson for the 'Baltic' designation, as he looked to differentiate them from the Porters he knew back home. Today's Polish craft brewers have adopted the word without complaint. Baltic Porter Day wouldn't be the same without it.

Index of
beer styles

AMBER ALE

Anderson Valley Boont *174*
Odell 90 Shilling Ale *192*
Mantle Dis-Mantle *32*
Stewart's 80/- *232*

BITTER

Acorn Barnsley Bitter *12*
Bathams Best Bitter *16*
De Ranke XX Bitter *256*
Five Points Best *147*
Fuller's ESB *28*
Harvey's Sussex Best Bitter *89*
Hook Norton Old Hooky *90*
Marble Manchester Bitter *63*

DARK LAGER

Ayinger Celebrator *46*
Hoppin' Frog Frogichlaus *184*
Kaltenberg König Ludwig Dunkel *221*
Notch Černé Pivo *127*
Rogue Dead Guy Ale *195*
Schneider Aventinus *259*

GOLDEN ALE

Dark Star Hophead *145*
Duvel Golden Ale *23*
Duvel Triple Hop *216*
Lost and Grounded Apophenia *31*
Senne Taras Boulba *262*

IPA

Achouffe Houblon Chouffe
    Dobbelen *204*
The Alchemist Focal Banger *76*
The Alchemist Heady Topper *108*
Allsopp's India Pale Ale *140*
Alpine Nelson *239*
Athletic Free Wave *175*
Avery Maharaja *109*
Bale Breaker Top Cutter *15*
Beak Parade IPA *47*
Beachwood 28 Haze Later *110*
Bend Fresh Hop *111*
Breakside Wanderlust *177*
Burton Bridge Empire Pale Ale *210*

Buxton Axe Edge *80*
Cigar City Jai Alai *179*
Cloudwater DIPA *81*
Devil's Peak King's Blockhouse *21*
Dogfish Head 90 Minute IPA *118*
Duration Remember When The Pub *22*
Elusive Oregon Trail *146*
Green Bench Sunshine City *88*
Molson Coors Worthington's White
    Shield *33*
Oakham Citra *158*
Other Half Green Everything *100*
Parish Ghost in the Machine *128*
Polly's Rosa *159*
Rockwell Velour Tracksuit *130*
Rooster's Baby-Faced Assassin *161*
Russian River Pliny the Elder *133*
Shepherd Neame India Pale Ale *229*
Sierra Nevada Celebration *69*
St Austell Proper Job *230*
Stone IPA *198*
Thornbridge Jaipur *39*
Toppling Goliath King Sue *199*
Tree House Julius *103*
Verdant Even Sharks Need Water *106*
Verdant Pulp *169*
Wayfinder Original Cold IPA *266*

MILD & BROWN ALE

Boxcar Dark Mild *48*
Cigar City Maduro Brown Ale *214*
Good Word Analog Life *120*
Rudgate Ruby Mild *227*
Tempest All the Leaves are Brown *164*

PALE ALE

3 Floyds Zombie Dust *172*
Adnams Ghost Ship *205*
Burnt Mill Pintle *144*
Carton Boat *115*
Coopers Sparkling Ale *215*
De Koninck Bolleke *222*
DEYA Steady Rolling Man *53*
Duration Bet the Farm *55*
Fyne Ales Jarl *86*
Little Creatures Pale Ale *30*
Oskar Blues Dale's Pale Ale *193*
Pressure Drop Pale Fire *101*

Ramsgate Gadds' Nº3 *160*
Sierra Nevada Pale Ale *196*
Stone & Wood Pacific Ale *38*
Timothy Taylor's Landlord *233*
Track Sonoma *72*
Wye Valley HPA *42*

PALE LAGER

Asahi Super Dry *13*
Augustiner Lagerbier Hell *45*
Baladin Nazionale *208*
Beerfarm India Pale Lager *241*
Bierstadt Lagerhaus The Slow Pour Pils *112*
Braybrooke Keller Lager *49*
Břevnovský klášterní Pivovar Benedict 12° *243*
Budweiser Budvar Original *209*
Chuckanut Maibock *116*
Cvikov Hvozd 11 *52*
Donzoko Big Foam *54*
East African Breweries Tusker Malt *24*
Firestone Walker Pivo Pils *245*
Früh Kölsch *25*
Fungtn Chaga Lager *26*
Heater Allen Pils *122*
Hofmeister Helles *153*
Birrificio Italiano Tipopils *247*
Jack's Abby Copper Legend *123*
Jever Pilsener *220*
Keesmann Herren Pils *248*
Knoblach Lagerbier *249*
Kutná Hora Zlatá 12° *61*
Lakefront Pumpkin Lager *124*
Lost and Grounded Keller Pils *93*
Mahrs Bräu aU *94*
Notch The Standard *98*
Paulaner Salvator Doppelbock *224*
Pilsner Urquell *65*
Rothaus Pils Tannenzäpfle *132*
Schönramer Hell *260*
Schönramer Pils *261*
Spaten Münchner Hell *37*
Tegernseer Hell *71*
Two Roots Enough Said *200*
Uerige Alt *264*
Únětické Pivo 12° *104*
Utopian Premium British Lager *168*
Utopian Rainbock *105*
Vinohradský Vinohradská 11 *73*
Zoiglbier of the Oberpfalz *250*

PORTER & STOUT

AleSmith Speedway Stout 173
Anspach & Hobday The Porter 141
Beak Pencil India Porter 142
Belching Beaver Viva La Beaver 176
Big Drop Galatactic Milk Stout 17
Brooklyn Black Ops 20
The Bruery Black Tuesday 178
Carlow O'Hara's Irish Stout 211
Denver Graham Cracker Porter 180
Deschutes Black Butte Porter 181
Ecliptic Capella Porter 119
Elland 1872 Porter 217
Fierce Very Big Moose 57
Firestone Walker Double Barrel
   Parabola 182
Five Points Railway Porter 84
Fremont The Rusty Nail 183
Fuller's London Porter 149
Goose Island Bourbon County Stout 87
Great Lakes Edmund Fitzgerald
   Porter 121
Guinness Foreign Extra Stout 27
Harvey's Imperial Extra Double
   Stout 151
Harviestoun Ola Dubh 152
Innis & Gunn Vanishing Point 154
The Kernel Export Stout 91
The Kernel Imperial Brown Stout
   1856 155
Kormoran Imperium Prunum 251
Left Hand Nitro Milk Stout 62
Maui Coconut Hiwa Porter 188
Mikkeller Beer Geek Brunch 95
Närke Kaggen Stormaktsporter 97
New Holland Dragon's Milk 190
North Coast Old Rasputin 191
Omnipollo × Dugges Anagram 99
Perennial Abraxas 255
Põhjala Öö 66
Port City Porter 194
Porterhouse XXXX Full-on Stout 225
Siren Broken Dream 162
Springdale Brig Mocha Stout 197
St Austell Black Square 163
Thornbridge Necessary Evil 165
Titanic Plum Porter Grand Reserve 166
UnBarred Stoutzilla 167
Virginia Beer Co Elbow Patches 201

Warped Wing Baltic Porter 202
Weathered Souls Black is
   Beautiful 137
The White Hag Black Pig 41
Widawa Porter Bałtycki Wędzony
   24° 268

SMOKED BEER

Alaskan Smoked Porter 206
Live Oak Grodziskie 252
Schlenkerkla Märzen 257
Yazoo Sue 138

SOUR/SPONTANEOUSLY FERMENTED

3 Fonteinen Oude Geuze 238
Alvinne Wild West 44
Blackberry Farm Classic 113
Blaugies Saison d'Epeautre 242
Bokke Zomersaison 18
Boon Black Label 78
Boon Oude Geuze 19
Boulevard Tank 7 114
Burning Sky Coolship 143
Burning Sky Petite Saison 79
Cantillon Fou'Foune 50
Cantillon Vigneronne 244
Fantôme Saison 56
Forest & Main Solaire 85
Hof ten Dormaal Zure Van Tildonk 58
Jester King Atrial Rubicite 185
Jolly Pumpkin Bam Bière 186
The Kernel Bière de Saison 60
Little Earth Project Hedgerow Blend
   157
Lost Abbey Red Poppy 125
Mills Brewing × Oliver's Cider Foxbic 96
New Belgium La Folie 64
New Glarus Raspberry Tart 126
St Mars of the Desert Jack D'Or 68
Oud Beersel Oude Kriek 254
Rodenbach Alexander 131
Rodenbach Grand Cru 226
Side Project Grisette 135
Tilquin Oude Gueuze à
   l'Ancienne 263
Verhaeghe Duchesse de
   Bourgogne 136
Wild Beer Co Modus Operandi 170

STRONG ALES

Au Baron Cuvée des Jonquilles 240
Baladin Xyauyù 14
Castelain Ch'ti Blonde 212
Chiltern Bodger's Barley Wine 213
Coniston N°9 Barley Wine 82
De Dolle Brouwers Arabier 83
Fuller's Golden Pride 148
Fuller's Vintage Ale 218
Greene King Strong Suffolk 150
Het Anker Gouden Carolus Classic 207
Interbrau/Meantime Thomas Hardy's
   Ale 219
J.W. Lees Harvest Ale 59
Lacons Audit Ale 156
Brasserie Lepers L'Angélus Blonde 223
Lickinghole Creek Magnificent Pagan
   Beast 187
Little Earth Project It's Life, Jim 92
Nebraska Mélange à Trois 189
Orkney Dark Island Reserve 34
Revolution Straight Jacket 129
Samuel Adams Utopias 134
Siren Maiden 102
SNAB Maelstrøm 36
Traquair House Ale 234

TRAPPIST AND ABBEY BEER

Chimay Blue 51
Kompel L'or Noir 29
Orval 253
Rochefort 10 35
St Bernardus Tripel 231
St Bernardus Abt 12 70
Unibroue Maudite 235
Verzet Rebel Local 40
Westmalle Tripel 236
Westvleteren 12 267

WHEAT BEER

Allagash White 77
Creature Comforts Athena 117
Gutmann Hefeweizen 246
Queer Brewing Flowers 67
Schneeeule Marlene 258
Schneider Weisse 228
Unertl Haag Weißbier Original 265
Weihenstephaner Hefeweissbier 74

CAMRA Books

Modern British Beer

MATTHEW CURTIS

FERMENT MAGAZINE BOOK OF THE YEAR 2021
Selected by Jaega Wise for BBC R4 The Food Programme Food & Drink books of 2021

This book is about why modern British beer is important. Over the course of the past two decades the British beer scene as we know it has changed, forever. Matthew Curtis gives a personal insight into the eclectic and exciting world of modern British beer from a choice of 86 influential brews; from how they taste, how their ingredients are sourced, to the engaging stories of the people behind the scenes working hard to bring exciting beer to drinkers all over Britain. This book is a fantastic starting point to explore British beer with an exciting location closer than you think.

RRP **£15.99**   ISBN 978-1-85249-370-7

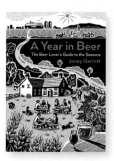

A Year in Beer

JONNY GARRETT

FORTNUM & MASON FOOD AND DRINK AWARDS 2022 WINNER

Chefs have been telling us to eat seasonally for decades, yet, when it comes to drink, we tend to reach for the same thing, whatever time of year. But beer is inextricably linked to the seasons, and thinking about it all seasonally opens the door to even greater beer experiences. *A Year in Beer* is an exploration of how our ingredients and tastes change with the seasons, and how Britain's rich brewing history still influences us today. Discover the best UK beer experiences, from summer beer festivals to the autumn hop and apple harvests – taking in the glory of the seasons that make them all possible.

RRP **£15.99**   ISBN 978-1-85249-372-1

United Kingdom of Beer

ADRIAN TIERNEY-JONES

There is a thirst for good beer on these islands, a thirst for beer that satisfies the soul, quenches the thirst and leaves the drinker glowing with satisfaction. Whatever avenue your desire takes you down, whatever the occasion, be assured that there is a beer for you and acclaimed beer writer Adrian Tierney-Jones will help you make the right choice with his selection of 250 of the very best beers in bottle and can from around these islands.

RRP **£17.99**   ISBN 978-1-85249-378-3

Beer Breaks

TIM WEBB

Renowned Beer writer Tim Webb invites you to explore and experience 32 of Europe's top beer destinations. Whether you want to share iced Imperial Stout on the Costa Brava, a hop-free rye beer from the Finnish lakes that tastes of cake, or some 17th century style lagers in a UNESCO World Heritage site, CAMRA's brand new guide to Europe's top beer cities is a must-have accessory for all globetrotting beer lovers.

RRP **£15.99**   ISBN 978-1-85249-364-6

Order these and other CAMRA Books from **shop.camra.org.uk**